WILLIE

The Life and Times of a
Rugby League Legend

by Mike Gardner

**The authorised biography of
Willie Horne**

Stand-off half and captain
Barrow RLFC, Lancashire,
England and Great Britain

1943 to 1959

Published by:
Mike and Lesley Gardner

Printed by:
Dixon Printing Co. Ltd., Kendal, Cumbria

© MIKE AND LESLEY GARDNER

ISBN 0 9523610 0 0

Publishing Advisors
Red Earth Publications

Front Cover Design
Simon Gray

Cover Paintings
Stuart Smith

Type Style
11/12 $\frac{1}{2}$ pt Palatino

First Printing June 1994
Reprinted November 1994

In memory of Alf Horne, a wonderful man who did so much to make this book possible.

Barrow skipper Willie Horne and his triumphant team celebrate their 1955 Challenge Cup final victory over Workington Town. Willie kicked six goals in the 21-12 scoreline equalling the record set by Len Bowkett for Huddersfield in 1933.

WILLIE HORNE

I was there, so many times, when Willie was the King,
Shared the strange elation, that only he could bring;
Travelled with the thousands, the hordes of blue and white,
Sang in praise of Barrow on many a famous night.

We stood and cried at Wembley, when Willie's boys won through,
He brought the cup to Barrow, and wasn't that a "do!"
Captain of Great Britain, a man without a peer,
And every knowing Aussie saying "That's the one we fear."

Those many famous battles, with the Ashes on the side,
I was there to savour, and share our Willie's pride;
And now those days are history, and fill the scrapbook's page,
Let's drink to a sporting gentleman, the greatest of his age.

CHARLES WILLIAMS

POET'S CORNER, North West Evening Mail, September 9, 1981

CONTENTS

	Introduction	7
	Foreword	10
1	A Star is Born	13
2	Pitch and Toss	19
3	You're Not Big Enough	25
4	Inside Left	33
5	Seconds Out	41
6	Unbeatable	47
7	Sign Here	53
8	Little Big Man	59
9	If the Cap Fits	79
10	Indomitable	87
11	Ashes to Ashes	93
12	Home and Abroad	117
13	Achilles Heel	125
14	Skipper	131
15	Against all Odds	153
16	An Idol of the Crowd	159
17	Gentle Giants	167
18	Up for the Cup	171
19	The Dressing Room	197
20	We Won the Cup	201
21	The Final Whistle	209
22	The Legend	231
23	The Tributes	237
24	The Shop	267
25	Bat and Ball	273
26	Home is the Hero	279
	Postscript	287
	Acknowledgements	291
	Appendix 1	293
	Appendix 2	298
	Appendix 3	302

INTRODUCTION

THE PHONE started ringing, rhythmic beeps echoing across 100 miles of invisible electronic wires. Suddenly I felt uneasy and nervous. It was inexplicable that I should feel like that. After all I used the phone perhaps ten times a day, trying to persuade men and women to reveal things they would prefer remain secret. As a journalist that was how I made my living, and to be honest, it was a part of the job I enjoyed, always had, chumming people, a bit of flannel. Usually I was relaxed on the telephone, at home, confident.

Yet here I was ready to put down the receiver prematurely when the ringing stopped and a "hello" rapped in my ear, a harsh, guttural Yorkshire voice. After a while you recognise the signs. An experienced reporter can tell you a lot from a three-second conversation – if they want to talk, if they're in a hurry, if they've got something to hide. The tone was courteous, neither friendly nor threatening. It was the sort of response I expected from someone familiar with the inconvenience of being pestered by nosey journalists.

Robert Gate is the Rugby League official historian. Robert will help you, I was told, he'll give you Willie Horne's playing statistics. Yes, I wanted to know how many games he played for Great Britain, the crowds, the tours, the cup finals – everything. But something else was worrying me. I was born in Barrow. I grew up with Willie Horne's name ringing in my ears. But the last time he pulled on a blue and white shirt was more than 35 years ago . . . when Harold Macmillan was Prime Minister, when you could buy a Sunbeam Rapier Saloon car for £695. How well known is Willie Horne outside the parochial confines of Furness, beyond Ulverston and Millom?

"Can you help me please, Mister Gate?" I asked. "I'm planning to write a book about a Barrow player from the Fifties called Willie Horne. Have you heard of him?"

"Heard of him?" he answered abruptly making me feel I was back at school asking irrelevant questions. "Willie Horne is a legend."

★ ★ ★

A week later a package arrived on my desk. It was full of Willie's golden career – big matches, reports of triumphs flashing before my eyes like calendar pages blowing in the wind. It was all here from the day Willie kicked 12 goals in a match against Cardiff to his sickening injury 12,000 miles from home when doctors said his career might be over with so much still left undone.

There were many questions unanswered by the lifeless figures, the fading memories of yesterday's news. He had a unique talent. I already knew that. He was an inspirational leader who got the best from those around him by example, by quiet encouragement. And for five wonderful years he was the best stand-off half in the world. There had to be more to Willie. This great game has produced many stars, yet most are forgotten, their dazzling skills burnt out like a trailing comet, remembered rarely by statisticians and nostalgic radio programmes.

Willie is from another era, a faraway time when 20,000 supporters crammed the Craven Park terraces shoulder to shoulder, wearing blue scarves and cloth caps, drinking halftime cups of coffee from striped thermos flasks.

On Saturday afternoons he led his players onto the field, fair hair sleeked back, head slightly bowed, face expressionless and deadly serious. Being a hero was something he had to live with, but you were left with the impression it didn't matter to him how many were watching or what was at stake. He played to win all right but defeat was preferable to betraying his ideals, of belting an opponent or trying to cheat. In more than 500 professional matches Willie was never sent off, booked or even spoken to by a finger-wagging referee.

All the top sides came to Barrow handicapped by their awareness of the difficulties awaiting them. You almost felt sorry for the visiting stand-off half, innocent, daunted and humiliated by such a public exposure of his frailties. Willie treated everyone the same, big or small. Many forwards limped off Craven Park black and blue, 18-stone men whose spirit was broken after being tackled by Willie as effectively as if they had run into a brick wall.

Furness has sired many sporting stars. England soccer internationals Emlyn Hughes and Gary Stevens were born here. We respect them; we are proud of their achievements. But we don't love them. Willie is known simply as *Our Willie*, the collective pronoun signalling the affection we all feel for him.

In Barrow, Willie Horne is worshipped with a sincerity normally reserved for yachtsmen who sail around the world single-handed or brave firemen who rescue crying babies from burning houses. He gave us something more permanent and important than an entertaining flair with an oval brown ball on a patch of grass every Saturday afternoon.

If my affection for Willie shines through every page, I make no apology. Anyone who has met him will know there would have been no other way to write this story. He asks nothing, yet he gives everything, a gentle, simple man who sees only good, never bad. He has a charm about him, a warmth, a friendship. To me he's like a saint, the sort of person you pray your daughter falls in love with.

Willie had a grim childhood in the dark years of the Great Depression. Yet when he achieved greatness on the rugby field he remained the same humble man, as proud of his trade as a turner as he was when he captained his country. And in 1955, with his best years behind him, he had one last piece of magic left for the Furness people who adored him. Barrow won the Challenge Cup in a glorious match at Wembley. Grown men cried, the town celebrated for two weeks. And Willie became immortal.

He was a prince among a host of superb stand-off halves, the best in an era that produced so many great stars. Willie earned his first international cap in March 1945 when he was 23. In the next nine years he played more than 50 representative games for Lancashire, England and Great Britain. But I have not mentioned them all. That would have been repetitive and boring. So as you flick through the pages of Willie's life you can be pretty sure his genius was used to help his county and country more or less permanently. His full playing statistics are reproduced at the back of the book.

I have tried to describe events in Willie's life in a way that will appeal to everyone, not just rugby league fanatics. But my determination to breathe life into heartless statistics did not overshadow my meticulous quest for accuracy. Everything described actually happened; all the people named are real, their descriptions authentic – from the policeman who predicted Willie would be an international when he was seven-years-old to Billy Little's harrowing life in a Cumberland coal mine.

In the following pages I reveal many things one might reasonably claim I could not possibly know. Such scepticism is natural. But please don't doubt me. You will discover what the Duke of Edinburgh said to Willie when he presented the Challenge Cup and there's much, much more. Like the time an Australian stand-off half shook Willie's hand and wished him well after Great Britain had won the Ashes on a blistering day at Brisbane almost 50 years ago. I know what happened because the people who were there told me.

I interviewed nearly 200 people and each one graciously opened his soul to a stranger to reveal a small piece of the puzzle that makes this shy man from a poor council estate so special, so loved.

I hope you enjoy this book, this personal tribute to Barrow's favourite son, a unique man with humility in his heart and magic in his fingers.

Willie Horne, this is your life.

FOREWORD

by Alex Murphy

WHEN I was a youngster growing up I watched Willie Horne play many times. Everyone knew him. He was one of the game's great footballing halfbacks.

Rugby League seemed to be in his blood and you could see all he wanted to do was play. Whenever Willie was on the field the game was never boring. He was an entertainer who was great for his side and great for the players who were fortunate enough to play with him.

I remember after I'd just turned professional, St Helens and Barrow met in the semi-final of the Challenge Cup at Swinton. I didn't play. I was only a kid. But I can clearly recall our coach Jim Sullivan telling the players in the dressing room how important it was to mark Willie Horne. The match ended in a 5-5 draw and we went on to win the replay 10-5 at Wigan.

That's the kind of attention Willie had 99 per cent of the time. In those days Barrow were an outstanding side who were also very entertaining. No one fancied a trip to Craven Park and every coach knew if they were to have any chance of winning, somehow Willie had to be stopped. Great players always attract attention and I'm certain Willie had plenty of big men after him. But like all class players he coped with that.

I played with Vince Karalius, one of the hardest loose forwards in the world and I know he won't have done Willie any favours. Willie was a matchwinner who had to be stopped, the sooner the better. If we lost it meant losing money, money that could have been needed to buy food. It wasn't like today when players get paid for nothing. Then we had to earn our money. No one liked losing and I'm afraid that meant watching stars like Willie. We did what was required.

It's not that any player wanted to do him harm, just that everyone respected what he could do both as an individual and for the team. I never expected any favours from anyone and I'm sure he didn't. Mind you I don't think anything we did had any effect on him. He was too good.

Great sides have great players. And Barrow had one of the best. Willie was the cornerstone of the team. Not exactly a one man band, the side had many excellent players such as second row Jack Grundy and scrum half Ted Toohey. Ted wasn't in the same footballing class as Willie but they made a great combination.

The modern game has no halfbacks to compare with Willie. No one playing today is as good. In the Fifties a number six beat his man up the middle and made a break.

Willie did that time and again and there on his shoulder would be the

Barrow centres Phil Jackson and Dennis Goodwin to finish off the move. And with deadly finishers like wingers Frank Castle and Jimmy Lewthwaite it shows what a tremendous side Barrow were. Willie was a team stand-off with the ability to be an individual as well. He could mix his game, a complete footballer who had a great pair of hands. He could also kick and he could tackle. Boy, could he tackle.

If he was 25-years-old today he would be priceless, the top money earner in the world. He didn't just do it here. He did it in Australia. It's like putting a price on a Penny Black.

Captains have to inspire other players. There are many different ways of doing that. Some roust people. That's the easy way. Willie had more than that. On the park he did everything and with his own example he was saying to his side: "Look, I've done it so now I'm expecting the same from you." It's a special skipper who can get the best out of his side without rocketing them. That was Willie. He had a kind of infection on the players around him.

He had a different temperament from me. He was a sportsman. His way was being Mister Nice Guy but that doesn't mean he didn't have a mischievous streak or that he was soft. Willie was a mild man off the field and for him to get a 17 stone prop forward to do what he wanted when the going got tough took special skills.

I've heard stories about people thinking he wasn't big enough at the start of his career. It makes me laugh. They said that about me too. You have to remember when Willie was 12 or 13 he would have been so much more advanced than the lads he played against, even if they were much older. And the big lads would not have liked a little squirt running them ragged. Then there would have been the jealousy. Willie got over all those barriers with his ability.

I don't believe in having regrets in life. But when I look back at my own career I sometimes think about how wonderful it would have been to have partnered Willie at half back. I'm sure we would have made a great combination. He was an outstanding footballer and I had the ability to do certain things. Together we would have caused a few problems. There are things in life you miss out on and that was one of mine. It would have been a privilege to play with Willie.

When anyone looks back at the history of this great game of ours and talks about stand-offs, Willie's name has to be up there at the top of the tree. He achieved many things but Barrow is an outpost of the game a long way from the heartlands of Lancashire and Yorkshire. Who knows what he'd have done if he had played at St Helens or Wigan? Life's all about ifs and buts. As it is, for me, I've never seen a better stand-off and I've watched, played and coached for a long, long time.

When Mike Gardner asked me to help with this book I agreed immediately. It's always a pleasure to write about great players. But Willie was more than just an outstanding rugby league player. He is a great man, a gentleman, one of the nicest you are ever likely to meet.

Willie was liked on the field for the things he could do with a ball but he was liked even more off it, by everyone he came in contact with. There are not many in rugby league who can say that.

The people of Barrow should be especially proud of this great man. Willie Horne is Barrow. I bet if they had ever sold him they would have had to shut the shipyard. I believe there's a street in Barrow named after him. To me that's not enough. They should name the town after him.

That's how much I think of Willie Horne the player, Willie Horne the captain but most of all Willie Horne the man.

ALEX MURPHY — scrum-half
St Helens, Warrington, Leigh, Lancashire,
England and Great Britain 1956 to 1975
Huddersfield RLFC first team coach

CHAPTER ONE

A STAR IS BORN

IN BARROW there are more than 10,000 men out of work existing on relief work or the poor law dole. Many families are only managing to find food through the Board of Guardians who at present pay 26 shillings (£1-30) subsistence a week for a man and wife with a further four shillings (20p) for each child. The callousness of the Ministry of Health is known to all. Assistance of any kind was refused emphatically. Means must be found for compelling the Government to shoulder the responsibility or else we must prepare ourselves for bankruptcy.

What little work being undertaken at the shipyard is nearing completion and no fresh contracts have been booked to absorb the labour. There are 4,000 workers employed at present and it is expected they will all be finished by the end of June. Of the shipbuilding berths 56 per cent are idle, 16 per cent are occupied by vessels on which work has been suspended or cancelled and the remaining 28 per cent only hold vessels upon which work is proceeding. Repairing is just as bad. In the last six months of 1921 the docks were empty for seven thousand dock days.

"The truth is," says a memorandum to the shipbuilding union, "if we let things go on as they are the industry will be left with barely a rivet to drive."

The outlook at Barrow is therefore, very gloomy.

NORTH WESTERN DAILY MAIL
Monday, January 23, 1922

ETHEL looked out of the bedroom window of her Norfolk Street home, one hand resting on her swollen tummy, wondering how long it would be before her baby was born. The midwife had said there were still four weeks to go, yet she could sense all was not well. Her baby felt restless kicking inside her and she had an overwhelming premonition it could be due any day. That was fine by her. This was her fifth baby and though childbirth held no painful fears, she was beginning to feel frustrated and weary. The effort of bringing up a family in a town sinking under the Depression was taking its toll.

It was January, 1922. Furness was in the middle of a cold, black winter. She could see the huge shipyard cranes dominating the Barrow skyline stretching out over row upon row of terraced houses, rooftops glistening white with the heavy frost, chimneys spewing out black clouds of smoke.

Ethel wiped her brow with a small handkerchief, her thoughts drifting back to a grim childhood on the streets of Middlesbrough. Her parents had died when she was barely eight and she had been sent to an orphanage in Shipley. Three years later she was working in the mills among the clattering machines, the air thick with white wisps of cotton. Even now hankies still brought on an unpleasant attack of melancholy.

High above number 38 there wasn't a cloud in the sky, leaving the moon an unrestricted path to illuminate the street below, footprints frozen in the iron-hard ground. Ethel could see other homes full of similar anxious families, their own light, like hers, piercing the twilight. She pulled the lace curtains across the window knowing they were too thin to keep out the draughts that crept in through the ill-fitting frame. It was more of a mental barrier against the dark, miserable world outside.

Four chimes drifted upstairs from an old clock on the mantlepiece startling her, a loud reminder that her husband Alfred would be home from the shipyard in a couple of hours. He'd be cold and hungry and she wanted to have a hot meal ready for him.

Ethel turned towards the kitchen, stopping on the way to check her family were safe and content.

"Is everyone all right?" she asked quietly.

"Yes thank you Mammy," answered Ada looking up from an exercise book, grateful for the intrusion into the mysteries of algebra. Ada was ten, going on 16. She revelled in the extra responsibility of being left in charge, an early taste of adulthood. Her mother would have been lost without her.

Ethel was a short, stocky woman with long, black hair falling over her shoulders halfway down her back. She had a cheerful face, bright intelligent eyes and though she was rather plain there was something about her that put strangers at ease. She was the kind of woman you liked the moment you met her. The children fed off her aura, her inner strength, her stoic acceptance of all fate threw her way. They felt she could cope with anything.

Six-year-old Alf was sitting on the threadbare rug in front of a healthy fire, staring into the flames dancing up the chimney, his cheeks bright red from the heat. Fires always fascinated Alf. They made him feel safe, secure. Close by, eight-year-old Doris kept toddler Florence occupied, patiently shaking an old spoon in front of her face so the light from the fire made it sparkle as if by magic. It took Ethel four steps to cross the eight-foot-square room along the faded lino, out into the kitchen, concrete floor cold as ice. How she hated it out here. She banged the door shut, shivering with the sudden drop in temperature, her breath clearly visible in the light cascading through the window. The pantry was almost empty but there were plenty of potatoes and yesterday she'd bought a rabbit from a poacher who regularly patrolled the streets selling skinny animals trapped in the Roanhead sandhills north of the town.

She began to feel guilty about her impatience to have the baby. After all at least her husband was in work that week. She peeled the potatoes with more enthusiasm. He'd be home soon.

★ ★ ★

Desperate, hungry men assembled on street corners, hands stuffed down empty pockets, lapels turned up as protection against the bitterly cold winds blasting in from the Irish Sea. The talk was of soup kitchens and pawn shops as the Furness economy buckled under the collective weight of the Great Depression and the worldwide collapse of the shipping market.

A few short years before, Barrow had been thriving. Families descended on the town from all parts of the country, boosting the population to more than 80,000. It seemed so long ago.

The meteoric rise from hamlet to boomtown had started in the middle of the 19th century with the exploitation of large deposits of haematite ore in the Furness peninsula. Mining was followed by the production of iron and steel; the first blast furnace was blown by Schneider and Hannay in 1859. Shipbuilding had come even earlier with William Ashburner's yard beginning production in 1847.

By the start of the First World War the iron and steel industry was declining as Vickers shipyard took a stranglehold on the workforce. At the height of the Great War, 31,000 workers were employed building battleships such as the Princess Royal and Renown, enormous vessels weighing more than 30,000 tons.

Barrow was the shipbuilding capital of the world. The yard made its presence felt in every corner of the community, a benevolent dynasty rewarding its loyal subjects with prosperity. It was a dangerous monopoly.

Shipbuilding was the first to feel the pain of unemployment as the winds of depression whipped around the world. The high price of coal and raw materials pressured company directors into slashing jobs to appease anxious shareholders whose personal wealth was rapidly deteriorating before their eyes.

Just one boat was launched in 1922, a hopper barge weighing 505 tons. Orders were cancelled as industrial unrest and empty slipways forced chairman Douglas Vickers to cut staff to 3,000 until the economy picked up.

Each morning barefooted, starving children waited outside the yard gates begging for food. Furness was sinking fast.

Further afield 1922 was just as eventful. Racists in the south of the United States launched the Ku Klux Klan, quickly gaining huge political power. Mussolini formed a fascist government in Italy while Irving Berlin wrote the immortal classic, April Showers.

Closer to home the North Western Evening Mail reflected the gloom, grey pages whispering grey news for grey people. An influenza epidemic raged through Glasgow, claiming 189 victims in one week in January. Back in Barrow, Masons fruit shop was selling Seville oranges for 9d (3p) a dozen under a jubilant heading proclaiming they were the cheapest for six years.

Barrow Trades Hostel boasted the cleanest rooms in England, available for 4/6 (22p) a week. And if you felt like a new suit Bamfords offered a wide selection from 38 shillings (£1-90). There were few takers in an age when many considered footwear a luxury. Town centre shops spent long days dusting down old stock and announcing outrageous price cuts in failed attempts to drum up business.

Among the bankruptcies and reports of sacked workers were sprinklings of aristocratic news of questionable interest to the working-class readers who could afford the penny cover price.

The engagement of Lord Louis Mountbatten and Miss Edwina Ashley was announced triumphantly, the second paragraph reporting that her personal wealth was in excess of £6 million. She was pretty, readers were told, and popular in society.

Meanwhile Central News was reporting that heavy snowfalls on the slopes near Geneva had provided ideal skiing conditions for visiting foreigners.

Back on the streets of Barrow, long queues of broken men formed outside the Town Hall for stale pieces of bread and lukewarm bowls of watery soup. The cost was 4d (1p) but it kept the discomfort of empty stomachs at bay for another few hours. Life was hard. And it was getting harder.

★ ★ ★

Alfred marched quickly out of Vickers' East Gate and headed for Norfolk Street, across the High Level Bridge, his quick, regimental steps making fresh prints in the recent snow. He was a man in a hurry. Ethel had warned him the baby was becoming impatient and he wanted to get home quickly. Not that he felt guilty about working that day's shift. They needed the money and anyway he couldn't risk jeopardising being asked in again the next time they wanted millers.

The Majestic Hotel's vacant rooms on the corner of Schneider Square were ghostly silent as he walked by. He slowed on the slight incline of Forshaw Street by the Tivoli Theatre where he and Ethel had spent so many happy Saturday nights holding hands, laughing, watching stars like Gracie Fields and the Vigaranto Trio. He couldn't remember the last time they had been there.

They had come to Furness eight years before, full of the hopes and dreams of a young family confident of a secure future. No regrets, no second thoughts. It was an exciting journey across the Pennines, an escape from the poverty, the black chimneys and the cobbled streets of Shipley. She'd fallen in love with him quickly, besotted by his broad shoulders and contagious laughter. The wedding was a year after they'd met. Twelve months later Ada was born.

He'd seen the advert in the local paper. **TURNERS WANTED. GOOD RATES OF PAY**. They didn't know much about Furness. Just that it was by the sea and a million miles from the satanic mills. The following week they were in Barrow searching for lodgings among thousands of immigrants eagerly swallowed by the shipyard. The town was bursting at the seams.

It all seemed so long ago he thought, his pace quickening down Dalton Road, empty shelves and boarded up shops stretching out before him.

Now he was in Abbey Road, dashing across the tree-lined avenue as a corporation tram clattered by, bell ringing, seats empty, the conductor staring blankly forward under his black, peaked cap.

Alfred called into an Ainslie Street bakery as he did most nights he was in work. Bread was cheaper just before closing time. The shop was in darkness, shutters down, a large hand-written sign nailed to the front door. **OWING TO THE INCLEMENT FINANCIAL POSITION WE REGRET TO SAY WE ARE CEASING BUSINESS**.

He marched on without giving the doomed shop a second thought. Bankrupt businesses were commonplace, a part of daily life. Besides, he had more important matters on his mind, like the birth of his new baby and the health of his wife.

Ada greeted him as he walked through the front door. "Mammy's gone to the hospital," she told him, surrounded by the other children sharing her eager anticipation.

Ethel had been taken to Risedale Maternity Home late that afternoon. The midwife feared complications and she wasn't prepared to take any chances.

Risedale had opened the year before. Patients paid 15 shillings (75p) for admission with a further charge of three shillings (15p) each extra day. They didn't usually stay very long. Families were means-tested but Alfred wasn't interested in money. All he could think about was Ethel and the baby. What if . . . ? He couldn't even think of life without her.

The home was just a couple of minutes away. It was a difficult birth, he was told, touch and go. For a while the little boy was in danger but he had pulled through, and, thank God, he was healthy and strong. They had prayed for a boy. His name would be William. In the 1920s boys were an insurance against the agony of growing old alone, without money, without dignity.

He could see his wife but she had been through hell and he mustn't wake her, the nurse said. Alfred sat by the bed, smiling with pride, stroking Ethel's dark hair, wondering what life had in store for their new son.

William Horne, later to be worshipped by thousands as the greatest rugby league player in the world, had made his entrance.

CHAPTER TWO

PITCH AND TOSS

NO ONE had much money in Chinatown. Families struggled just to put food on the table. We were luckier than most. Dad was a skilled tradesman who wasn't out of work as much as some of the other men on the estate. Mam worked miracles and somehow we never went hungry.

At Christmas we each got an apple or an orange and if we were lucky, a bag of nuts between us. Things like that didn't seem to matter then. The thing I remember most about growing up was how wonderful and loving our parents were. No one ever had a better mam and dad.

ALF HORNE – 1915-1993

IT HAD been threatening rain all afternoon. Banks of dark clouds hung over the Furness peninsula, forcing down the temperature and turning the summer's day into a chill reminder that autumn lay just around the corner. When the first drops fell on Roose Cricket Club it was no more than a gentle drizzle, a minor irritation to the players who carried on without leaving the field.

Ten-year-old Tommy Milmine looked up at the black sky above the crowd who shuffled in preparation, umbrellas flapping open. He came to Waver Meadow every Saturday. Roose were his team. The dangerous unpredictability of the pitch banished the side to permanent exile in Division Two of the North Lancashire League. But in truth they were as good as the top sides with wonderful attacking batsmen such as Herbert Coombs, a left-handed opener who had an entertaining penchant for blasting sixes into the grounds of St Perran's Church.

Within a few minutes rain began splashing down, forcing players to dash to the pavilion, soaking shirts clinging to their skins as thunder clapped across the Irish Sea. There would be no further play. Tommy joined the crowd squelching across the field to the exits and home to the terraced houses of North and South Row. Outside he turned right, along Roose Road, by the railway station and towards the town centre.

He was disappointed with the premature and inconclusive end to the match but it was still only 4 o'clock – plenty of time to meet his pals for a game of rugby. Within a few minutes he heard the high-pitched voices of excited children filtering across rows of gloomy houses.

Left into West Way, left again and he was by a field on the other side of a four-foot sandstone wall. Standing on his toes, he peered over the top. Tommy watched, surprised at the ferocity of the tackling and the skill of the tiny hands moving the ball from one side of the pitch to the other.

The field was about 50 yards square, half the size of a full pitch. It was covered with thick grass but there were no markings or posts. They were signalled by heaps of jumpers at either end. Rules were followed without question or argument. Knock-ons were freely accepted and no one moved offside, not on purpose.

There were 20 children, ten-a-side, each team having an equal number of big and small. Some were 14, young men about to start work, others were just seven or eight. Sometimes the bigger boys enjoyed the arrogant feeling of power as they pushed aside smaller children, who would pick themselves up, holding back the tears, ready for another go. It was a tough place to grow up.

Suddenly Tommy's silent vigil was broken by a booming voice.

"There's some good lads out there."

Tommy turned, startled. It was Nevile Lorain, the local policeman. He was a big man who dwarfed the little boy in front of him, a long black cape stretching below his knees as protection against the rain still falling relentlessly from the black sky. Everyone knew Nevile. And everyone knew he was a good man. He was an old-style bobby who didn't like red tape and filling in forms. If anyone went too far on his patch they got a clip around the ear.

"Who's that little lad on the right, the one with the blonde hair?" he asked, one hand leaning on the wall, the other propping up a rusty bike.

"That's Willie Horne, from Middle Square," answered Tommy obediently. "He's only seven."

"One day he'll play for England," Nevile announced in a matter-of-fact tone as he climbed on his bike and rode off through the deepening puddles.

★ ★ ★

Willie was four months old when the family moved across town. His mother and father were encouraged by the change as they walked the two miles from Norfolk Street to Roosegate, pushing a cart loaded with possessions. Ethel looked at the pans, the old settee and a few boxes of secondhand cutlery and plates, thinking momentarily how little they had to show for 12 years of married life. She wasn't worried. Her family were all she cared about, her family and Alfred. Now things were looking up; she was almost overwhelmed by optimism and positive thoughts of a happier, more secure future. They were making a fresh start.

Alfred pushed the cart effortlessly down Park Drive and left into Roose Road. Ethel walked in front holding Willie in her arms, Florence hanging onto her spare hand. Alfred knew only three things about Middle Square—the rent was cheaper, they would have hot and cold running water for the first time, and it was where all the boys played rugby.

★ ★ ★

The estate was known officially as Roosegate but locals called it Chinatown, a sarcastic reference to the questionable building standards of the prefabricated accommodation. There were 200 single-storey terraced houses, originally built during the First World War for billeted soldiers. Many were damp and they were all cramped and draughty. The rent was four shillings (20p) a week. Most tenants were in arrears.

To the south, rolling green fields, wild and uncultivated, stretched towards the shores of Cavendish Dock where flocks of hungry cormorants would sit like soldiers on parade watching the cold, motionless waters. In the distance, the church spire of St. Michael's looked down upon more rich countryside flanking a railway line, breaking the pastoral tranquillity of Rampside and across the bay to Roa Island.

Families walked the two miles on summer outings for a day by the seaside, when children would gaze towards Piel Island mesmerised by its ancient ruined castle, menacing and mysterious.

Number four was next to the end of a row of 28 identical houses, full of identical families with identical problems of poverty and long-term unemployment.

Behind the front door was a long, narrow corridor. To the left the bathroom, small, rectangular, claustrophobic. Beyond the corridor the living room and kitchen. It was ten feet square with a white sink protruding from the wall next to a small gas cooker. Opposite stood the fireplace that provided the family with hot water — when they could afford coal.

Outside there was a small patch of earth where they grew potatoes and cabbage, out of necessity rather than horticultural interest. Another door led to the bedrooms, separated by a thin plaster wall. Alf and Willie shared a bed in one while mam and dad slept with the three girls in the other.

It was a spartan existence, an uncertain life of hunger and unemployment. Chocolate sundaes and sirloin steaks were strange delicacies eaten in the affluent, detached homes of Infield Park and Hawcoat Lane. The Hornes, like everyone on Roosegate, existed on a repetitive diet of "tattie hash," – bowls of potatoes, corned beef and carrots.

Ethel baked every day, filling her family with slices of home-made bread and dollops of dripping. She helped make ends meet with weekend trips to Barton Street where she joined forces with Maggie Shaw making bottles of bee's wine, a tasty soda pop. They walked the streets of Roose selling the drink for a penny a time — a day's work yielded a profit of 1/6 (7p). Every little helped.

Alfred was luckier than most. He was a horizontal borer, a highly skilled turner who was one of the first to be asked to work and one of the last to be laid off. When he had a full week at the shipyard Alfred brought home extra bread to distribute among less fortunate neighbours, families where the father might not have worked for more than 12 months.

Sometimes Alfred would buy a couple of eggs for the children. They took turns to eat the yoke, Ada one day, Doris the next and so on through the family. Alfred was a decent man who was devoted to his wife and family. But he had an expensive affection for gambling, and a fondness for beer. Most Fridays he could be found at the Washington, a pub a mile along Roose Road. He finished the night at the Strawberry Hotel, to the north, on the outskirts of the town.

Ethel could have lived with that. It was her husband's obsession with pitch and toss that brought her family most hardship. It was a simple game. Two coins were flung in the air and men gambled on how they would fall; two heads, two tails or one of each.

Hundreds gathered each night at Cocken Tunnel, to the north of the iron and steelworks half a mile west of the Ormsgill estate, sheltered beneath an unsightly slagbank of rubble and granite produced by three generations of Furness miners. The game was strictly illegal. Competitors positioned lookouts making it difficult for police to catch the organisers who would disappear into the countryside dragging bags full of silver coins behind them. The next day they were back again.

Fridays were the busiest. It was pay day. You could lose a week's wage in ten minutes. Many did. Alfred stopped short of going home with nothing but sometimes he lost badly.

Back at 4 Middle Square, Ethel waited patiently. At least she knew where he was. If he made a small profit Alfred brought home bars of chocolate for the children before pecking Ethel on the cheek whispering promises that it was his last visit to the murky world beneath the slag bank. He always went back. Usually he lost. Then it would be a different husband and father who came home. He'd sit, hunched in his chair reading the newspaper, quietly, mournfully.

Ethel obediently accepted her husband's failings. They were matters they did not talk of. She loved him but her acquiescence stemmed more from a sense of duty and the Victorian values she had been taught in the orphanage at Shipley so many years before. Men went to work and it was a woman's place to obey, stay at home and meekly submit to her husband's dominance.

So she used the pawn shop.

On Mondays, when Alfred was in work, Ada walked to Risedale Road, carrying her father's best suit in a brown paper parcel. The shop was called Tooner and Dennisons. Today the building is a doctor's surgery but in the 1920s it played an equally important role in maintaining the health of the working-class families who lived in the area.

The manager gave Ada four shillings (20p) and a pink piece of paper with a number on it. Four days later, after Alfred had given Ethel the housekeeping, Ada returned to exchange the paper for the suit, this time for five shillings (25p). It was back in the wardrobe before her father could find out.

Slowly the economy picked up. And when Vickers won orders to build two 20,000-ton passenger liners, the Orama and Otranto, workers at last began to feel more secure, more confident.

In 1924 George was born. He was Ethel's seventh child though only six had survived. Bertha had died after suffering a fatal dose of pneumonia when she was a few days old. Alfred was a predictably proud father and though Ethel shared his joy, she made a private vow to be more careful in future. Contraception was a lock on the door and she wasn't getting any younger. Beneath relief at the baby's good health was a deep-rooted fear of the future. George was another mouth to feed, another child to take care of. Ethel had had enough.

Everywhere they went the children wore goloshers, black, cheap and practical. But on Sunday Ethel put on her best dress and the children wore black shoes shined so vigorously they could almost see their faces reflected in the glossy leather.

The family worshipped at Risedale Gospel Hall, close to Barrow Park. They sat at the back of the church singing hymns, thanking God for their humble lives, praying for Him to take care of them. Alfred never made that 20-minute walk. He was a Christian but he prayed privately, away from the elderly women, the long sermons and the old, tuneless organ. Churches made him nervous.

The Christian faith was the central part of their lives. Ethel insisted on that. Each night the children whispered private prayers. They were good kids who never got into trouble, perhaps they were too soft, too trusting.

Willie started school at Cambridge Street at the back of Friars Lane. Even at five-years-old it was obvious he was unlike other children. His academic work was good. In the classroom he was attentive and alert. But in the playground he stood out. Willie was a fast runner, quick enough to beat children much older, much bigger. He was a skilful soccer player, as good as anyone in the school, but rugby league was banned. The headmaster considered it too brutal and dangerous.

Demolition rumours began circulating Roosegate as families were rehoused, leaving empty streets, silent corners and ghostly, boarded-up buildings. The Hornes moved to number five Corporation Terrace, a mile west towards the town centre, a few doors away from the Riflemans Arms.

In June 1932 Willie left Cambridge Street for a long summer holiday before starting at Risedale Secondary Modern. He passed the rigorous test to qualify for the Grammar School, and prepared to join the middle-class sons of vicars, businessmen and shipyard managers, the men who ran the town.

Willie didn't much fancy Grammar School. After all, it wasn't meant for the likes of him, the son of a poor shipyard worker. As things worked out he needn't have worried.

Grammar School pupils were obliged to wear a special cap, special socks, a special tie and a special blazer – navy blue and decorated with gold braid, august and elitist.

One trip to McDowells tailors in Cavendish Street told Willie's mum what she already knew. They couldn't afford it. She would have to fork out more than 25 shillings (£1-25p) to buy the uniform. Sorry son, but you'll have to go to Risedale, she told him.

He was relieved. Willie had heard Risedale was a caring school run by patient, likeable teachers. But most of all he had heard about the school's rugby league team.

He could hardly wait.

CHAPTER THREE

YOU'RE NOT BIG ENOUGH

WILLIE was streets ahead of everyone else in the school, even when he was just 11-years-old in the first year. One or two of the older lads said he was too small to ever make the grade but that was a load of rubbish. He proved that every time he played.

There was a lad at Risedale called Jimmy Cawley who lived in Gloucester Street. He was a giant, perhaps four stones heavier than anyone else in the school. To be honest the rest of us were frightened of him on the rugby field. It took at least four of us to tackle him . . . except when Willie was in our side.

He brought him down on his own, every time, with a little flick of his hands. Willie did that time and time again. In fact, he made Jimmy, big as he was, look a bit of a fool, being tackled by someone so much smaller. In the 1930s there were a lot of good young rugby players in Barrow but Willie was the best, yet when you talked to him you would never have guessed he was special in any way. He was so modest and unassuming. Everyone who met him liked him right away. He was that sort of lad.

EDDIE WORRALL
Centre threequarter, Risedale and Barrow Boys, 1933 to 1936

IT WAS six o'clock in the morning when the alarm went off, its bell vibrating through the bedroom, an enthusiastic announcement that it was time for Alfred to get up, time to prepare for work.

He opened his eyes, turning to catch the button on the side of the clock, simultaneously swinging his feet from under the warm sheets and into his slippers positioned at the side of the bed. Shivering in the cold air, Alfred stumbled sleepily across the room, arm outstretched searching for the switch to light up the early morning darkness enveloping the house.

He shuffled across the corridor and into the bathroom where he gazed at himself through tired, bloodshot eyes. He was still half asleep. In the next room Willie was already awake, sitting up in bed, sheets pulled to his neck, listening to the familiar noises of water gushing through pipes, his father splashing around, shaving and cleaning his teeth.

Most mornings it woke him but today he'd already been awake for two hours, unable to sleep, his mind dancing with excitement and anticipation of what lay ahead on this special day.

Squinting, he could make out the shape of a chair leaning against the wall on the far side of the room, illuminated by a shaft of light piercing the gloom through the half-open door. Willie knew his brown tweed jacket had been carefully laid on the chair the night before on top of his grey trousers. Beneath, a pair of black shoes. They were his best clothes, the clothes he normally wore on Sundays when the family went to church.

To the side of the chair was a brown bag. He knew what was inside. But to put his mind at rest he closed his eyes making a careful, mental note of its contents as a final check to make sure nothing had been forgotten. There was a fresh bar of soap, a towel, a comb and a jar of wintergreen. And most important his rugby boots, polished like new, with fresh laces that had been meticulously threaded by his sisters the night before. Willie was going to St Helens for a Lancashire trial. It was the most important day of his life.

Soon everyone was up, Ethel in the middle of a human conveyor belt, frying eggs and pouring hot cups of tea. It was still dark outside when Alfred opened the front door, young Alf a respectful distance behind him.

"Just remember Willie," he said, flicking a shilling (5p) across the room. "Whatever happens today I want you to know how proud I am, how proud we all are."

"Thanks dad," said Willie catching the coin, embarrassed by his father's public show of emotion. Then they were gone, swallowed in the teeming mass of cyclists, each one dressed in black, pedalling frantically towards Michaelson Road and the shipyard that lay beyond its bridge.

Later, one by one, the family left the house, walking along Salthouse Road, empty and quiet now following the chaotic rush hour. George was the last to go leaving Ethel and Willie alone in the empty house, time slipping by slowly, painfully. Willie was restless and impatient.

"I'll wait at the front door," he said picking up the bag and kissing his mother on the cheek.

Outside he stared along the deserted street, concentrating, as though his gaze could somehow hasten the arrival of Ted Parke, the Risedale teacher who was driving Willie and two other boys to Knowsley Road for the trial. There wasn't a car in sight.

He could see the 19th century tower of St. George's church, a lonely sentinel guarding Cavendish Dock. Half a mile across the grey water stood the black buildings of the shipyard behind dozens of cranes rising up like rows of medieval gallows. In the church grounds large trees, elm and sycamore, bent back and forth, buffeted by the bitter wind blasting in from the north, gusts tearing tired, yellow leaves from bare branches on this cold, November day.

After 20 minutes Willie could make out the black shape of a car travelling towards him. He was almost as excited about the journey as he was about the match. In 1934 cars were so rare Furness children stopped in the street staring as the mechanical miracles chugged by. Many hungry youngsters thought the only people who could afford cars were the aristocracy; kings, dukes and lords, the privileged who lived in castles and stately homes, employing devoted servants, who wandered along ghostly corridors following their master's orders obediently.

"Hello Willie, are you OK?" Ted asked as he pulled up in his aging Austin Seven.

"Yes thanks, sir," answered Willie, clambering into the back seat holding the bag as a small girl might caress the fur on her favourite kitten.

Along Roose Road left into Friars Lane, Rating Lane and by Furness Abbey on the way to Dalton, the region's ancient capital where they picked up Jimmy Watson and Ernie Metcalfe at Tudor Square. They too had earned the chance to be selected for Lancashire, the chance to be among the finest young rugby league players in the county.

Jimmy and Ernie were 14. And they were big — very big. Willie was two years younger and though you would expect the age gap to produce significant physical differences he seemed so small, so innocent. Willie was still very much a child. Jimmy and Ernie would start work within a year. Already they had begun to try out the private pleasures of manhood. Many of their friends smoked and each morning they woke up and proudly stroked the speckled stubble that had sprouted on their faces overnight. Jimmy and Ernie were young men who had eagerly waved goodbye to childhood.

Three hours later Ted parked the car before leading the three youngsters along a long, straight corridor beneath the main stand at Knowsley Road. The home dressing room lay behind a wooden panelled door painted garishly red, an unmistakeable and tasteless proclamation of the colours worn by the Saints.

A handwritten sign was pinned halfway along the corridor. At the top it read "**PROBABLES**". Below, a list of names, positions and schools. Jimmy and Ernie disappeared behind the red door while Willie was ushered further down the corridor to the away dressing room, less imposing, less comfortable.

Another sign, another list of names, this time under the heading "**POSSIBLES**". Halfway down, alongside number six — William Horne, Risedale School, Barrow; stand-off half.

Ernie played at open side prop, a position where size and weight were fundamental necessities. Jimmy was centre threequarter but he could have moved into the pack with no loss of strength or power to the team. As members of the Probables all that was required from them to ensure selection for the forthcoming trip to Yorkshire were workmanlike and proficient performances.

For Willie it was going to be different. It needed something special if he was to force himself in the side. As stand-off half he already had plenty to think about. He was the link between the backs and the forwards. And he was expected to back up, create openings, kick and tackle with faultless efficiency.

A loose forward from Wigan was named captain of the Possibles. Five minutes into the game he abandoned his leadership duties, leaving the smallest boy on the field in centre stage, organising 12 strangers who followed his instructions without question.

Willie was everywhere, taking the ball at first receiver, sending out quick, accurate passes, left then right, directing his forwards through gaps, bringing the backs into the game frequently but with a speed and unpredictability that left the Probables' defence stretched, unable to cope with each threatening attack.

And in defence he ignored the relative safety away from the rucks and outside the two packs locked in battle in the centre of the field. He stood among big forwards tackling tenaciously, throwing the opposition to the ground with courage, skill and confidence.

At half-time the Possibles had scored two tries to none. The players stood in two huddles either side of the halfway line sucking oranges and drinking water.

"One, six and twelve change teams please," ordered a tall man holding a clipboard. The six boys swapped muddy, sweaty shirts before taking up positions among their new teams for the second half. Again Willie was creative, busy and influential, helping the Probables to regain the lead over a team who were now ineffective and leaderless without the quiet, sandy-haired boy from a Barrow council estate.

After the final whistle the players mingled, shaking hands, wishing each other well. All the boys could think about was the imminent team announcement. Had they made it?

Willie, Ernie and Jimmy showered and changed before waiting in the car while Ted attended the selection meeting. The Dalton lads had played with spirit and vigour. They felt they had done enough . . . and they said so. Willie was silent, distant. He knew in his heart he had performed well and, more importantly, he was confident he had outplayed his opposing stand-off half. All he could do now was wait.

Ted climbed into the car, expressionless.

"Well done Ernie and Jimmy," he said. "You're in. I'm sorry Willie. You didn't make it."

It was too much for him to take. Willie began sobbing, long tears running down his cheeks as Ted started the car, sitting erect and still, debating whether to reveal the full story of what had happened behind closed doors. With the car engine spluttering away in the background Ted turned and began talking quietly but with a certain confidence as if he knew he had made the right decision to be honest and open.

"They said you had a wonderful game Willie. But there were so many pushing for the other lad. Perhaps I didn't say enough. I think I let you down."

"You did your best, sir."

"One more thing Willie," Ted said as he put the car in gear and drove out of the car park. "They said you weren't big enough."

Willie stopped crying and looked back at the imposing sight of

Knowsley Road stadium slowly fading into the darkness, its red brick walls and corrugated roof lit by the yellow glimmer of street lights.

So I'm not big enough, he thought to himself. One day I'll be back. One day I'll show you.

★ ★ ★

Willie was a bright, articulate child, intelligent enough to have gone on to further education and qualify as a teacher or perhaps work in a bank. They were never acceptable options. At least not to Willie's dad. In pre-war England boys followed their fathers . . . if they were lucky enough to get a job. And anyway working-class families could not afford the luxury of young men not contributing to the weekly budget. Even at infant school most children knew where they would end up — in the shipyard, no matter how well they did in examinations. Boys' aspirations were limited to joining the morning army swarming to the lathes and workbenches of Vickers.

So Willie did his best. That was the way he been brought up. It was outside the classroom where he was so obviously different from everyone else. At Cambridge Street his natural co-ordination and speed of thought had made him stand out. And now older, stronger, faster, his unique gifts were if anything accelerated. Willie was way above the sporting standards of his classmates.

He was still small, yet in the playground he had a stubborn reluctance to accept his physical limitations. Willie joined in with the bigger boys refusing to yield an inch, never taking a backward step – like an angry guard dog snapping at the heels of an unwelcome intruder.

Willie didn't like getting beat. Not at anything. Not that he was a bad loser. He'd just worked out at an early age that it was more pleasant to win. So he wouldn't give up. Never.

The children at Risedale School were forced to play rugby league during the weekly sports sessions, a policy that was easy to understand considering the deputy head was Sid Lawton, chairman of the town's professional team. Apart from his love of the game he was always on the lookout for fresh talent to lure to Craven Park. Barrow had sired many internationals, stars such as Jack Woods and Bill Burgess who toured Australia with distinction.

Once, under pressure from school governors and parents, Mr Lawton allowed the children to play a soccer match. They lost 16-1. After that humiliation there was no chance of football being played at Risedale. Not as long as Sid Lawton was there.

Willie started at Risedale in September, 1933. Two weeks later he was in the school rugby team, despite being three years younger than the other boys. Games were held at Little Park, Roose, the former home of Barrow RL before the move to their town centre home at Craven Park in 1932.

The children from 1A made the mile walk every Friday, down Bridgegate Avenue, across the Red River, over the railway crossing, up a small hill to the Ship Inn where they changed.

Science teacher Harold Egan was in charge of the first year. Within a few minutes of watching 11-year-old Willie he realised he was witnessing a unique talent, a boy with special gifts. Willie had been schooled on the Bungalows pitch, among bigger opponents who were many years older, many stones heavier and many inches taller. Now against children of more comparable proportions he was virtually unstoppable. When he got the ball Willie skipped and sidestepped around his bewildered classmates with the ease of someone who was familiar with a more taxing challenge. Egan reported what he'd seen to Sid Lawton, who picked the school team. He was not convinced. The following Friday he went to Little Park to see for himself. Egan was excited with his discovery, walking up and down the touchline, pointing to the skinny child almost arrogantly as though he had discovered a rare Lowry painting in his uncle's loft. Willie was named as scrum-half for the school's next match. It was natural for him to play there. He could run. Quickly. And his passes from the scrum were so accurate he gave the stand-off half that extra second to accelerate, beat his marker and set up tries for enthusiastic threequarters.

That was the theory. In practice, no one could match Willie's creativity or pace. So Mr Lawton made him stand off half giving him more room to weave his magic. Before the end of the season Willie was appointed captain.

Two years running Risedale won the Daily Despatch tournament and the right to represent Furness and take on other schools. They travelled to Oldham and Leigh and though each time Risedale lost they did so with a courage and sportsmanship that brought great pride to this forgotten corner of Lancashire. It was an outstanding team. Centre threequarter Eddie Worrall and winger Eddie Babbs were the try scoring backs while front row forwards Sid Grey and Jimmy Cawley led a formidable pack. But Willie was the inspiration.

Alfred Barrow were their great rivals. They too had outstanding players such as scrum half Jack Postlethwaite and centre Jack Taylor who grew up to become the Barrow RL physiotherapist.

Willie's meteoric rise at Risedale was matched with an equally successful career for the town team. Alfred Barrow teacher Albert Parkinson helped run Barrow Boys. He was always fair, never showing favouritism to his own players. You had to earn the right to play for his team. After just one game Willie was again named captain.

The team played in the North of England Schools' tournament against sides from Wigan, Leigh, Warrington and Salford who beat Barrow in the semi-finals of the Lancashire Cup. Later that year Willie made his tearful trip to St Helens for the Lancashire trials. Despite the failure he came back with his confidence unaffected. His influential and distinguished performances for school and town continued. Already he was being talked about as a future professional, though more often than not his supporters mixed admiration with fears that he was too thin and too light to withstand the rigours of the big time. Everyone still thought he was too small.

Willie's life was a perpetual cycle of school and sport, classwork and rugby, with the odd game of cricket thrown in. Most nights he met Roland Goldsworthy, his best friend who lived at Kent Street. They spent hours on Marsh Hornets pitch practising kicking, honing skills destined to be a valuable part of a talent that would earn Willie a place on the 1946 Lions tour of Australia, ten years later. Now the pitch is gone, replaced by the homes of Cloisters Avenue and Urswick Green to the east of Friars Lane.

Willie stood at one end while Roley waited in an identical position 50 yards downfield. It was repetitive and tiring, kicking to each other over and again, attempting to bounce the ball infield before spinning unpredictably into touch. Willie had to be dragged away each night, unwilling to break off his determined quest for perfection.

At weekends too it was more rugby — after Willie had helped his mum with the housework. The games he had gatecrashed as a six-year-old at Chinatown had evolved into a more organised and accurate reflection of the real thing, except for the duration of the matches; sometimes as long as TEN HOURS.

They played at the Pulp Works soccer pitch, a mile east of Cavendish Dock. It was known as the Rifle Range, situated where the Roosecote Power Station is now, its grotesque silver tower, modern, ugly, in unnatural contrast to the soft countryside.

Selection was simple, an unwritten and respected law that you belonged to the Raglan Street team run by Henry Ogilvie or to the Bungalows side with Alf Horne in charge. They started around ten in the morning and continued until dark. Most stayed all day while others who lived near the pitch rushed home for a sandwich before returning to the fray eager to make up for lost time, the score long since forgotten and unimportant.

Even at night a handful of boys carried on, reluctant to abandon the marathon match. It got so dark they couldn't see a hand in front of their faces, the only light weak beams when the moon hesitantly poked its way through banks of dark clouds that seemed to hang over the pitch permanently.

These energetic weekend matches, full of simple, healthy fun, were repeated every year. Willie was still clinging to his childhood through weakening fingertips, not wanting to let go of a contented existence that seemed to him so perfect and fulfilling. He hadn't a care in the world.

In September, 1936, he went to the rifle range for the final time. Willie made his final tackle, threw his last pass, ending an imaginary link with adolescence. As he prepared for his last term at Risedale Willie was anxious and a little frightened, knowing within a year he would be at work. He would be a man.

It had been a spectacular summer, full of long, steamy days when the searing rays of a brutal sun burned his skin deep brown, the colour of stained mahogany. Now he was stronger. Willie was still thin but his narrow frame had filled out giving him a build similar to other boys of the same age.

But when he played rugby, no matter how well, there were still those who remained unconvinced Willie could survive in the frequently violent world of adult competition.

His schoolwork was accurate and imaginative, consistently putting Willie near the top of the class. He had a knack of surprising teachers. Some felt his preoccupation with sport precluded a sharp, inquisitive mind. It didn't really matter. As things worked out high marks were not important, not to any of the fourth form boys. Hitler was on the move and the British Government was slowly waking up to the menace of thugs in brown shirts forever marching, singing aggressive songs, paying homage to their glorious Fuhrer. Europe was heading for war. Vickers was booming and they needed young men. Fast.

The following spring, Willie's final term at Risedale, his class spent an idyllic week at St Bees School, 50 miles north along the Cumberland coast. Each day was a fresh adventure, a bewildering journey watching kittiwakes and guillemots glide across cliffs blackened with countless nests, the sky full of nervous birds scavenging, fighting for food to feed the begging throats of a thousand chicks. And the boys played soccer. Every day.

Rugby League were dirty words at St Bees. It was a middle-class school run by middle-class teachers who believed the sport was a brutal way of occupying the empty minds of miners who lived in squalor a few miles along the coast at the pit-infested town of Whitehaven.

Sometimes the headmaster visited Wigan to debate financial budgets or school reforms. He hated seeing starving children huddled together on street corners, hands held out, begging for food, desperation and hopelessness written on white, emaciated faces.

Back home, cocooned among the farmers, doctors and engineers in the privileged, isolated world of St Bees he rarely questioned the inequality of 1930s Britain. To him the working class didn't know any better. Why else would they live like that, he thought, as he shovelled coal on his fire momentarily thinking of the awful lives miners led to keep him warm in his detached house.

For most of the children it was the first time they had travelled beyond the parochial confines of the Furness peninsula. Apart from summer scramblings through the sandstone ruins of the town's 12th century abbey they lived narrow, repetitive lives among the tenement buildings of dour, grim council estates.

Willie returned to Corporation Terrace with more lasting memories than the other children, who rushed home to share their transient knowledge of wildlife with brothers and sisters to whom migratory birds were as mysterious as the dark side of the moon. Willie enjoyed the soccer matches so much he came back determined to give rugby a rest and try his luck with a local team.

His ambitions were destined to threaten his career. A year later he was lying in a hospital bed watching doctors who never spoke, staring at X-rays of his shattered leg, exchanging glances that said more than a thousand words.

It was a bad break. He might end up a cripple.

CHAPTER FOUR

INSIDE LEFT

VICKERS yard is a private city of noise and steel, a fevered fantasy in a surrealist nightmare. On the vast slipways the grinning near-skeletons of every type of war vessel, from cruisers to rat-like submarines . . . and above everything, the noise, the screams, groans, howls and agonies of labour.

UNBROKEN by Alastair Mair

WILLIE had always been fascinated by the shipyard workers who rushed past his bedroom window every weekday morning. There was something mysterious about the chaotic scramblings of the nameless men hurtling down Roose Road, some on clattering bicycles, some walking, each one carrying optimistic hopes and boxes of sandwiches from the council homes scattered across the area.

Sometimes the noise woke him early. Willie didn't care. He would sit on the end of his bed gazing out of the window wondering what problems lurked beneath the flat caps everyone wore. The men all looked the same . . . black coats over dark blue overalls, hobnailed boots scraping the ground, so many looking like his father.

It was 7am, Monday, September 5, 1937. Now he was one of them, among the chattering crowd, a strange new world, smoke drifting from curling pipes, everyone in a hurry, mumbling strange swear words he'd never heard before.

His father led the way, walking quickly, with purpose, long steps effortlessly eating up the ground. Willie struggled keeping up. Every 30 yards or so he was forced to break into a trot to regain ground, to keep in touch, pulled forward by an invisible link he was determined would not break.

Alfred was older now. Middle age had turned his hair white and his torso plump, a generous belly bursting over a tightened belt losing an ongoing battle to hold back the softening flesh.

It was the first day for hundreds of young men starting an apprenticeship at the shipyard. Many were upholding a tradition going back to great grandfathers who had built wooden sailing schooners that took iron ore from Furness to hungry Welsh ports to feed the insatiable empire.

The new starters stood out like dandelions on a cricket field, dozens of new boiler suits, creases straight as an arrow, carried by nervous legs below pale faces. The blue army surged past the Harbour Hotel, the Ship and Alfred Barrow School, the crowd swelling at the bottleneck as thousands of men squeezed onto Michaelson Road.

Every morning it was the same. Beneath the mournful gaze of Henry William Schneider's marble statue surrounded by grimy grass trampled by legions of workers searching for shortcuts beyond the thickening mass.

Men came from every part of Barrow . . . Hawcoat, Ormsgill, Hindpool, Abbotsmead and further afield – Dalton, Lindal, Askam and Ulverston. They were hardly moving now, toe to toe, arms outstretched touching the backs of strangers before at last Alfred and Willie squeezed through.

On the High Level bridge progress was still slow. Willie stopped worrying about losing his father and looked around, breathing in the unfamiliar atmosphere of a grown-up world. He felt out of place, an intruder. To the north, Devonshire Dock, three Argentinan destroyers, the Entre Rios, the Corrientes and the Buenos Aires dwarfed by a battleship, black numbers the size of a house painted on the side. To the south Buccleuch Dock and more warships.

Ten yards over the bridge Alfred turned, motioning Willie to follow him to the right and through the Engine Gate entrance, between tall iron railings, green paint peeling. Right again and they were standing in a huge imposing room full of shiny walnut furniture that stank of oil and stale tobacco.

On one wall was an enormous clock, the biggest Willie had seen, ticking so loud he could hear the tap of each clockwork movement despite noise from the workers still pouring through the gates a few yards behind them.

Ahead, framed photographs of ships, submarines and aircraft carriers, passenger liners and tankers, filling the wall so completely it was impossible to see the paper behind. Above, a brass sign etched with the words **BUILT AT BARROW — THE FINEST SHIPYARD IN THE WORLD**.

"Welcome to Vickers son," said a short man wearing a black uniform, silver buttons bursting for freedom down the front of a bulging chest. Willie looked into the face, into the blue eyes, above a large nose more violently red than the brightest post box. He wore a peaked hat that did not fit well, giving him a slightly comical appearance that put Willie in mind of a pantomime dame he had once seen at Her Majesty's Theatre in Albert Street the Christmas before.

"If you make half as good a tradesman as your dad you'll be OK," he said shaking Willie's hand so vigorously he thought for a moment of letting go. Then he remembered what his father had told him: "Shake hands hard son, like you mean it, like a man." So Willie held on tightly. The man let go, smiling, before turning to talk to another anxious youngster on his first day at work.

Willie and his father rejoined the crowd, thinning at last, moving along a wide road between sandstone buildings rising to a sky full of squawking seagulls buffeted by the wind. Willie thought about the handshake from the man in the uniform. He sensed a sincerity in that momentary grip and the way he smiled as though he was a distant uncle – someone you saw rarely but who you could trust, someone who would look out for you.

Ever deeper into the factory, Willie became hopelessly lost in the narrow alleys and roadways, trucks flashing by laden with steel cargoes, clanking under tarpaulin sheets.

Several minutes later they reached the Submarine Engine Shop. Inside Willie stopped, looking around, staring, unable to take in its monstrous size, the terrible noise and the countless number of men scurrying about.

He followed his father, passing long bays so enormous you could park a dozen cars between each one and still have room to spare. Deeper into the huge building they passed capstan setters, fitters, millers, drillers, everyone making a noise, hammers hammering, riveters riveting, lathes turning. And in the background, a crescendo of other noises, painful and ceaseless.

Alfred ushered Willie into the turners' bay, where they took off their coats and stood before a rumbling lathe as long as a saloon car.

For the next few days Willie learned the fundamentals of his new trade, listening, watching his father, baffled at first as Alfred's educated hands flicked over knobs and turned buttons methodically, making everything look so simple.

After four weeks they began the treadmill of shiftwork — alternating a week on days, a week on nights. Willie hated the long nights. He found it difficult to sleep during the day and he became almost paranoid about the dangers of falling asleep on the job.

Like everything else in his life, Willie learned his new skills quickly. It wasn't long before he was imitating his father's measured technique with an accuracy and dedication foremen had rarely seen from someone so young and inexperienced.

Two months after he started, Willie left his father's influence and began working on his own, producing countless engine valves for the sinister submarines that were sprouting like black weeds on nearby slipways – the Triumph, the Thistle, the Triad, the Truant and the Ursula.

At the end of each shift he was replaced by Tommy Davies, another apprentice introduced to the shipyard by his father. Jack Davies and Alfred met regularly at the Washington Hotel for a few pints of frothy beer to discuss the political turmoil in Eastern Europe and what might win the 3.30 at Wincanton. The evenings always finished the same, with a friendly comparison of their sons' progress on the lathes of the yard. They weren't bragging, or trying to outdo each other, just sharing a collective pride in Willie and Tommy's latest achievements.

Willie's best friend at Vickers was Alec Anderson who worked on the next lathe. They sat together at break time, supping tea, talking about sport, what was on the cinema and how they planned to spend what was left of their 7/6 (37p) weekly wage after mum had been paid for the housekeeping.

One night, when Willie was about to leave, a stranger tapped him on the shoulder.

"Hello Willie. I've heard you're a good rugby player," said Les Young, manager of the Sub Engine Shop football team. "How do you fancy playing soccer for us?"

"I'll have a go, sir," said Willie, his mind drifting back to St Bees school and its daily soccer matches.

"Good. We train Tuesdays and Thursdays at the Park. I'll see you there," said Les before waving goodbye and disappearing, swallowed by the claustrophobic exodus hurrying home.

The following week Willie was in the team, scoring goals. He enjoyed every minute. Rugby would have to wait, he thought, at least for now.

★ ★ ★

All through childhood Willie had been one of those lucky boys who could do anything. He had a mysterious aura of confidence about him. Not that he was conceited, arrogant or boastful. He was never like that, never could be. It was the things he did rather than the things he said.

Every school boasts one exceptional child with a flair for sport. Willie had more human gifts in his modest, friendly personality than merely being able to run faster than everybody else. He was a born leader, someone who instilled spirit and determination in those around him. With Willie in the team, whatever the sport, his friends felt they were capable of beating anyone. His effect was almost hypnotic.

After five minutes of Willie's first training session the committee and players of the Sub Engine Shop were nodding heads in harmonious admiration. They could see immediately how good he was and how good he might become — if he abandoned rugby.

Those familiar with his rugby league reputation had anticipated that Willie would be a valuable asset. A stand-off half needs many things to be successful. He must be fast, quick-thinking, creative and above all he must have courage, the capacity to dig deep when those around him are in danger of losing their spirit. Giving in was never an option to Willie. Like everyone he enjoyed the thrill of winning but his attitude to sport was simple . . . he tried his best — always.

Willie played inside-left. Today the position is loosely known as attacking midfield. He scored goals but he made more extensive contributions to the team than merely an opportunist with a flair for converting half-chances. His number 10 shirt was everywhere, covering, tackling, making space for others. He was a free spirit in a thrilling sport still three decades away from the stifling strait jacket imposed forever by Alf Ramsey's muscular World Cup heroes. Willie ran wherever he wanted, wherever he thought he could do his best for the team.

After half a dozen matches, Barrow AFC wanted him. A few weeks later Les Young received a letter from First Division Bolton Wanderers. They had heard a lot about a certain Willie Horne, it read. Would he come to Burnden Park for trials? Willie wasn't interested. He didn't want to leave his family.

Besides there was still rugby. Perhaps he'd go back to it. Eventually.

★ ★ ★

There was less than five minutes to go when it happened. Sub Engine Shop were three goals up. Sacred Heart hadn't exactly given up — at least not publicly. But there was a lethargic acceptance in the way their players ran, heads slightly bowed, and the way they failed to reach passes they would have expected to make 30 minutes before. It was too late for thrilling comebacks. They had lost. Everyone knew that. Except Bill Smith.

He was still competing with the same energetic enthusiasm he had when the match kicked off. Bill was ambitious. He also wanted to impress anyone still watching in the hope someone with influence at Barrow AFC might scribble his name down on a piece of paper. Who knows, he thought, there might be a trial, then perhaps a run-out for the reserves.

Bill's hero was Barrow centre-half Maurice Brown. He was tough, reliable, someone he looked up to and respected, someone he wanted to be like. Barrow were at the wrong end of the Third Division North and they had recently appointed former England international Fred Pentland as manager. Now the word was out. Pentland, who excelled with Blackburn Rovers, Stoke City and Queens Park Rangers, was on the look-out for local talent.

He had been in charge just four weeks when he signed Askam wing-half Jimmy Watson and centre-forward George Caine, a teenager from Beach Street Methodist with a prolific scoring record. Bill might be next.

Everyone can dream, and although he was a competent local player Bill realised the limit of his aspirations was likely to be the odd run-out at Holker Street, home of the town's professional club. To him that would be enough. Even at 16 he had the sense to know he had as much chance of playing for Manchester United as he had of walking on the Park lake.

Bill was tall, very tall. In fact, had he been born in Philadelphia or Pittsburg or Atlantic City, he might well have ended up a star basketball player. As it was his height was ideal for a soccer centre-half. Bill dominated Sacred Heart's penalty area, heading clear any aerial danger with the passionate intensity of someone who relished a physical challenge. And he tackled with a precision and power you would not expect from someone with such a slight frame.

The pass was no more than a hopeful poke into Sacred Heart's half of the field. Les Young sensed something bad was going to happen as he watched Bill and Willie run towards the ball. Bill was ten yards nearer but if Willie could get there first, the chance of a goal perhaps . . . CRASH!

The two youngsters lay on the pitch motionless for a moment as nearby players ran towards them. Bill was the first to get to his feet, shaking his head like a has-been boxer recovering from a knock-out. Willie lay motionless, surrounded by anxious faces above fading tracksuits, a wet sponge rubbing into his face.

"Are you OK, Willie?" asked the Sub Engine Shop trainer.

Slowly he opened his eyes, instinctively grabbing his right leg, and clenching his teeth with the sudden, horrible realisation of how badly he was hurt. Willie was not unfamiliar with the discomfort of sprained ankles, pulled muscles and twisted knees. He knew how they felt. Had them a thousand times. This was different. It hurt too damn much.

The referee blew the final whistle as Willie hobbled off, ashen-faced, dizzy and nauseous, not quite knowing where he was, motioning concerned inquiries away with a wave of his hand. He didn't like making a fuss. Shouldn't he go to the hospital his friends asked.

"Don't worry. I'll be fine in a few minutes," he said with a touch of defiance in his voice. He wasn't going anywhere. Except home.

"Do you want a lift on my bike?" asked George Troth, a friend who had been watching the match. "You can sit on the crossbar."

"Thanks, George," said Willie stuffing his boots into a bag and pulling on his trousers over a leg that was stiffening and swelling more with each passing minute.

Out of the gates and up the slight incline from Greengate Street to Park Drive they rode. Here George turned right, his tyres flat with the extra weight. Into Risedale Road, the gentle slope allowing the bike to gather speed as they free-wheeled beyond the Gospel Hall bringing Corporation Terrace ever nearer.

George had known Willie since they were small boys. He loved sport too. He was a champion sprinter, the fastest in the town it was said. A few years later he was playing on the wing for Bradford Northern before being transferred to Workington Town. And when he grew tired of the black eyes and broken teeth he became a professional sprinter.

"Thanks a lot," Willie said as George disappeared pedalling towards his Salthouse Road home.

Ethel's experienced eyes told her something she did not want to know. Her son was hurt. And it looked serious. The lump on Willie's leg, swollen the size of an apple, was surrounded by black, tender bruising.

"George, will you run to Church Street for Doctor Thompson?" she asked her youngest son who turned and left the house immediately not wasting time giving an answer.

Half an hour later the doctor came, riding an ancient BSA motor bike and sporting a long handlebar moustache, white and outrageous. He was not a young man. In fact he was born 20 years before the start of the Boer War. Doctor Thompson had seen it all before. And he knew all about sporting injuries. Or so he thought.

"It looks like bad bruising," he said. "How painful is it young man?"

"I can't lift my leg," said Willie before lapsing back into sombre silence as the doctor caressed the leg with deft and gentle movements.

"He'll be all right when the swelling goes down, Mrs Horne," Doctor Thompson said as he left the house slamming the front door behind him.

Willie went to bed, unconvinced by the doctor's confident diagnosis. All he had for the terrible pain were two aspirins and the prayers of a family united by a mutual belief that all was not well.

He tossed and turned for three agonising, sleepless nights before Ethel recalled the doctor. She was frustrated and not a little frightened by her son's lack of progress.

"I'm sure the leg is broken, doctor," she said, emphasising the word broken as someone afflicted with vertigo might speak of a high mountain.

The doctor looked at the throbbing, swollen leg and he knew instantly he had made a dreadful mistake. Willie needed orthopaedic help. And he needed it fast.

Ten minutes later an ambulance arrived, bell clanking violently, before returning to North Lonsdale Hospital carrying a solitary patient, a frightened young man who was beginning to wonder if the pain would ever go away.

His right fibula was broken. It was a clean break, they said, but a full recovery was not certain. Willie might be left with a permanent limp. As for sport — prognosis unknown.

The plaster cast was on for six weeks. When it was removed his right leg was half the size of his left, the muscles shrivelled and emaciated. The hospital gave him a walking stick and an appointment to return in a month. The rest, they said, would be up to him.

"Make sure Willie uses the walking stick for at least three weeks," the doctor warned his mother in a dominant, confident voice as a headmaster might order a daydreaming pupil to pay attention. Ethel was left in no doubt the time was not open for negotiation. Willie's thigh was thinner than a strong man's arm, too weak to support his body. It needed time to heal. That was nature's way, they'd said.

After five days Willie placed the stick under his bed, out of sight, using deliberate, calculating movements. To him it had been a symbolic link with the pain and uncertainty of the blackest two months of his young life. He was going to get better . . . without the stick. That was his way. There were too many unfulfilled dreams to accept being a cripple at 17.

Two weeks later he was walking briskly, without a limp. Another week and Willie started jogging every night at the Grammar School playing fields. He was going to be all right.

An amazing recovery, the doctors told Ethel as they eyed revealing X-rays. Perhaps you can try walking without your stick they said, announcing a further appointment would not be necessary.

September 1, 1939. Willie continued his determined efforts to regain full fitness as German tanks rumbled into Poland. The British Government announced compulsory military service for all men aged between 18 and 41. With the shipyard in full production most Furness workers were in reserved occupations.

Risedale Old Boys Rugby League Club met every Tuesday and Thursday for training sessions although the imminent season was unlikely to begin as the country prepared for war.

Soon Willie was training with the same eager dedication he had before the injury. There was no loss of speed or agility. The only visible proof of the injury was a small lump in the middle of his shin.

To sharpen reflexes and accelerate a complete recovery Willie joined his brother Alf, who gave boxing classes to the boys from Risedale School. He had always enjoyed training, keeping fit. It gave him an inner confidence, a warm sense of well-being, knowing he could run all day.

When the children grew tired of swinging ropes and boxing shadows, they secretly watched Willie rattling off 100 press-ups in less than two minutes, expending less energy than other mortals might take walking to the corner shop.

One November evening, a rather dangerous young man with ambition in his eyes and mayhem in his hands made an unexpected visit to their makeshift gymnasium.

Even now, 55 years on, those who witnessed what happened have not forgotten the night Willie Horne met Freddie Cotton. And they never will.

CHAPTER FIVE

SECONDS OUT

I NEVER saw the huge old Drill Hall so full to witness boxing, and the sport was thoroughly enjoyed. The event I was most anxious to see was the bout between Tom Worton and Fred Cotton. I have seen and greatly admired the ability of Worton, but had not previously witnessed Cotton in action.

I received a welcome surprise and after Cotton's display I predict a bright future for this talented Barrow boxer. As a matter of fact, Worton received something in the nature of a boxing lesson, try as hard as he could. Light as eiderdown on his feet, Cotton was in and out of distance very cleverly playing lefts and rights, interspersed with beautiful uppercuts, with lightning-like precision – hits that hurt.

He must have surprised other onlookers besides myself. He has I know, boxed many of the leading lights, and I am told that on December 17 he meets Jim Brady, the Empire champion. Good luck to Fred from all local boxing fans.

"PEGASUS"
North Western Evening Mail, December 5, 1938

THE walk gave him away. He moved with the arrogant swagger of a confident young man who knew what he was doing and knew he could do it well. Freddie Cotton was a professional boxer who relished the harsh, physical demands of a sport where danger and serious injury were never far away.

He was just 18, though you would never guess his violent occupation from his physical appearance. Freddie was more like a choirboy than a fighter. He was 5 feet 7 inches tall and weighed around nine stones. He fought as a featherweight, among other small men with the courage of a lion and the speed of a dancing firefly.

Fully-clothed he looked frail, weak and undernourished. Yet stripped off you could see he was unlike other boys. His legs were wiry, allowing all his weight to fill out a muscular upper body perfectly developed for professional boxing. He was a handsome man whose good looks revealed a lot about his ability to survive the rigours of a profession not known for the attractive features of its participants.

He was, as they say in the trade, a stylish boxer. He danced around the ring, dazzling and confusing opponents with his non-stop, nervous energy, a frustrating combination of speed and perpetual motion. He was difficult to hit, reacting swiftly to deflect incoming blows. Yet Freddie was no one-punch specialist. He was an intricate artist who won bouts by classic boxing and an accumulation of direct hits and wicked combinations that left opponents senseless before the referee stopped the fight – if they were lucky. Freddie was formidable and dangerous.

He was also brave. Freddie had been beaten and beaten badly but he always came forward ignoring the risks and the stinging pain pounding into his body and face. Boxers are like that, and he had more than his fair share of the special blend of courage unique to fighters, reminiscent of war films about British soldiers going over the top. Boxing is like no other spectacle on Earth, except perhaps the bullfight. Every Sunday afternoon, under the Spanish sun, shadows lengthen while brave men taunt enormous bulls with horns as thick as a strong man's arm, sharp as a surgeon's scalpel, their only defence a small piece of red cloth draped over a stick. Like the matador, the boxer must cheat serious injury or even death, his only allies are his speed and unbreakable spirit.

Now Freddie's career was beginning to burn out but he faced one last throw of the dice the following weekend at Port Talbot when he was taking on Dundee's Jim Brady, the British and Empire Bantamweight champion. Brady's best days were behind him but he still represented an awesome threat.

A year before there was talk of the big time, a chance to appear at London's Earl's Court where you could make more money in one night than a turner earned in a month, sweating over the lathes at the soulless shipyard on the other side of Michaelson Road bridge.

Promoter Sid Hulls watched Freddie destroy an opponent at The Rink on the Strand half a mile from Barrow Town Hall. It was more of an execution than a sporting contest. Four weeks later he was living in London, under the wing of a new mentor, confident he could harness Freddie's aggression and turn him into a champion.

It hadn't worked out. Freddie was homesick, fed up with daily sparring sessions against other determined boys who, like him, saw boxing as a painful escape from the monotony of life in pre-war Britain.

Now he was back, though recent defeats by nationally-ranked boxers Jackie Robertson and Kid Turner had reversed his rise to the top. Saturday could be his last chance or he faced a one-way ticket to anonymity, fighting in local halls for 15 shillings (75p) a time.

Freddie always struggled to find suitable sparring partners. Not that he wasn't popular. Outside the ring he had friends and admirers. And in common with most boxers, he never saw any reason to prove his manhood by adopting uncompromising stances or settling arguments with a punch to the face.

But once those gloves were on he underwent a transformation. Although all professional boxers need unlimited supplies of aggression, he seemed incapable or unwilling to recognise the less demanding challenge of a sparring session.

These workouts were essentially designed to improve timing and footwork before a big fight, the final preparation to sharpen reflexes. Punches were thrown but they were glancing blows, lacking power. Freddie, however, was unable to hold back. Not because he was nasty or a bully. That was just the way he was. Take it or leave it.

Many tough youngsters fancied their chances with him. They all failed. Hard Barrow kids such as Jimmy Shanks, Bill Anderson and Pat McCarten had donned gloves in foolhardy bravado. They didn't try a second time.

Now Freddie was looking around the gyms and halls of the town for a suitable sparring partner. The Brady fight was only a few days away. It wasn't going to be easy.

★ ★ ★

It was six years since Alf Horne had grown bored with the demands of a sport where success was measured by his ability to separate young men from their senses as quickly and flamboyantly as possible. It wasn't a question of morals. The working class had always boxed and probably always would.

Alf had learned the tricks of the noble art in Dalkeith Street Boxing School, now the 99 Club, guided by George McLaughlin and Tommy Robson. Alf was a natural fighter who had lost just one bout in a four-year career, a close points decision against Cumberland champion Billy Murdoch.

Now he was 23 and all he could remember were the long journeys to towns he had never heard of, to halls all looking the same. That and the cigar smoke and blood-stained towels wrapped around his face between rounds, the constant shouting, empty words that had long since lost all meaning.

Then there were the Sunday mornings after a tough fight, when he could hardly walk, his face swollen so badly that his own mother couldn't recognise him. He was glad to get out. Nevertheless when a teacher from Risedale School asked him to show some children how to defend themselves he was glad to help out.

They met every Wednesday night in the school hall. Willie went along to help. There were usually 20 children aged around 14 all eager to try out a sport with the added incentive of financial reward – if they were any good.

It happened on a winter's night. Johnny Martin had taken Freddie under his wing. He was something of a boxing expert who had quickly recognised the talent, courage and potential earning capacity that lay untapped in the swift hands and brave heart of his young friend. He led Freddie into the hall carrying a large bag, boxing glove laces scraping the floor through an open zip, the stench of liniment announcing their arrival.

The boys were in the middle of a set of press-ups, their young chests bouncing up and down in perfect unison, groans echoing around the hall.

"Hello Alf," said Johnny. "Will any of your lads give Freddie a couple of rounds. He's got a big fight with Jim Brady on Saturday?"

"I'll have a go," said Alf, always a soft touch for someone who wanted a favour. He knew Freddie well, knew he was ruthless, unforgiving. And he knew he wouldn't be holding back. Not that he was frightened. He never had been. But now his body was trained for less demanding pursuits such as stroking a boundary through extra cover on a pleasant summer's afternoon or halting the progress of a rampaging second-row forward.

The boxers stared across the makeshift ring, a coat at each corner, the perimeter defined by a row of children eager for an unrestricted view. Alf was looking serious and apprehensive. He had made a reckless, impulsive decision, one that he was beginning to regret. But it was too late to change his mind even if he had wanted to. And now the menace was less than 12 feet away wearing what Alf took to be a smile of hungry anticipation.

Freddie stood motionless as Johnny clapped his hands signalling the start of the first round, clicking his stopwatch simultaneously. Freddie stepped forward confidently, shaking his head, holding his hands high. They circled the ring, each throwing long jabs, testing reflexes and timing. Freddie hit the target first, a left hook thumping into the side of Alf's face who continued coming forward, refusing to give up ground.

But Freddie was too fast, too evasive, dancing, moving, all the time working quick combinations that had the boys wincing as they watched, enthralled. Alfred was neither elusive nor sharp. He had been away too long. But he had lost none of his bravery. Johnny clapped to end the round. Freddie stepped back casually but with impatience, thinking perhaps the break was an unnecessary intrusion, while Alf retreated to the sanctuary of his corner bearing the look of a tired child who had been kept up too long past his bedtime.

Round two was more of the same. Alf constantly bobbing, ducking, anything to evade the vicious leather driving into his face and body. His stamina was draining away. Then, without warning, he was down, clutching his side and gasping for breath.

"I'll be OK," he said. "Give me a minute."

He was clearly stunned. Before he could protest he was ushered away from the ring, no longer a player in the drama unfolding before a captivated audience.

In his place, Willie pulled on the gloves as Freddie patted Alf on the back before turning his attention to the new invader. Willie prepared himself, fists together, showing no sign of fear as Freddie moved forward, arms glistening with sweat.

A left flashed towards Willie's face, Freddie's arm straight as a piledriver, the punch grazing against his fair hair. Another cross whistled past Willie's ear as Freddie mounted an impressive attack. Lefts, rights, crosses, each time Willie dodging clear of the danger, a ghost Freddie could see but could not touch.

Freddie was becoming frustrated by his inability to hit Willie whose boldness was growing visibly. Then Willie mounted his own offensive. His punches were crude and unorthodox but Freddie was startled by their power and accuracy, as fatigue brought on defensive carelessness. Freddie looked unconcerned but his eyes betrayed self-belief draining like air from a burst balloon.

Round two and they were together again, Willie's limitless energy continuing to render Freddie's best moves harmless and ineffectual, his speed of movement keeping his head and body a fraction ahead of the lethal punches.

Willie's counter punching was crisp and sharp, dazzling Freddie as his head snapped back, draining his energy as he searched in vain for an answer. His legs had stopped working, his movements were suddenly weary like a drunk who's had one whisky too many. Then it was over.

"That's enough," Johnny shouted as he took Freddie by the arm between the children who parted obediently. Freddie followed meekly, without protest, stopping only to whisper to Willie through shaking lips, "Thanks, mate." It was as though he had been freed from the slavery of combat and reunited with his warm personality, safe from the monster within.

Freddie and Johnny headed back up Greengate Street, heads bowed, talking nervously. He lost his match with Jim Brady after ten gruelling, bloody rounds. He was never the same again. Perhaps that night in Risedale School his fighting spirit had been ripped from his soul.

Willie didn't box again. He had a more pressing appointment in the middle of a rugby pitch with a number six shirt flapping on his back. Privately he knew he could play. Now it was time to see how good he really was.

CHAPTER SIX

UNBEATABLE

BARROW were beaten by Wigan 22–4. That there was a weakness in the team was patent to the most inexperienced eye, but there were compensations. Let me pay tribute to the excellence of the Barrow tackling, and they had a lot to do, for Wigan were in possession of the ball quite 10 times out of 12. With an equal division of the ball I think the match would have been one of real thrills.

The game proved at least one thing for which the committee may be thankful. It brought to light the rare football ability as a stand-off half of W. Horne, a young local of distinct promise. His play revealed ability as well as a rare knowledge of the position he occupied.

NORTH WESTERN EVENING MAIL
Monday, December 14, 1942

RISEDALE Old Boys were a formidable team with an unsettling air of invincibility. They dominated amateur rugby league with style and confidence. They felt they could beat anyone.

In 1941 the average age of the side was only 20 and though youth and ambition were important qualities for success it went much deeper than that. They enjoyed rugby. Everyone. Players were friends, and not just on match days. There was a kindred spirit, a special bond linking them together in a collective, intimidating determination. When he pulled on that blue and white shirt each player did so with a fortitude that sent a warning signal to rivals. They were halfway to victory before a match had even started.

Over the following three years, six players joined professional rugby league clubs across the north of England . . . Barrow, Hull, Bradford Northern and Rochdale Hornets. Risedale Old Boys had remarkable players, from the impudent artistry of nine-stone scrum half Geoff Tweedle to the power and tireless work-rate of 16-stone prop forward Fred McMurray. They had it all.

And on top of everything else there was a wonderful stand-off half whose progress was being discreetly monitored by admiring Barrow RL directors. He could play all right, but was he big enough?

Willie was the captain. His unpredictable talent set him above his teammates. He was the natural choice. There was never any debate. It had to be Willie. Good as he was, there were other reasons for his appointment.

He demanded maximum effort from everyone. Willie was relentless in his pursuit of victory. Dropped passes and missed tackles were forgiven. There were never post-mortems about who'd done what and when. But if a forward went hiding among the threequarters or if a back kept disappearing to the blind side one time too many when they were defending . . . well, they were sent back into the middle with a black look and an accusing finger. Chances were the following week they would not be in the side. Everyone was treated the same. They all knew what was expected of them.

Yet no one grumbled. Risedale Old Boys were too successful for probing questions about the way the team was picked or if their style of play was too flamboyant and hazardous. The game plan couldn't have been simpler.

Forwards shared the work, toiling ceaselessly without complaint, each one taking his turn, tackling ferociously, carrying the ball into the opposing pack, driving on and on, always forward. Then, when Willie sensed the time was right, the backs threw the ball about with a refreshing disregard for the consequences of failure. They enjoyed living on the edge.

Alf Horne and Tommy Roberts ran the club. Alf was a creative and brave loose forward but he rarely played. He wanted youngsters in the side. Training was uncomplicated. It never changed – three laps of the Holbeck Park pitch at Roose, 20 minutes stretching, then out with the ball for a chaotic game of tig and pass. That was it. No tactics, no team talks, no planned moves. And the matches were equally spontaneous. Willie had no idea what he was going to do when he got the ball and he wasn't going to stifle creativity by shouting numbers or passwords. To him rugby was about instinct and imagination. There was no place in the Risedale team for robotic, predictable plans. Team talks didn't amount to much.

"Right lads," Alf would say as the 13 players huddled around him before the kick-off. "Support the man with the ball, move up quickly when you're defending and get Willie into the game as much as you can."

Alf was popular with everyone. He was bubbly, supportive, always laughing. Alf enjoyed being involved in the team. His enthusiasm rubbed off on those around him. Tommy was two years older and though he had never played rugby he loved the game with a sincerity players respected. He rarely spoke. Tommy, a yard crane driver, didn't go in for small talk. He left that to Alf. But when he had something to say, everyone listened. He made sense, and it was usually worth waiting for. Tommy had a gift for saying the right thing at the right time, never a word out of place. It could be a pat on the back, quiet encouragement or he might bring someone down to earth if he had played well and was in danger of becoming a bragger.

Money to run the club was raised by selling raffle tickets for 6d (2 p) each. Players were expected to sell 20 each week.

Willie was working 12-hour shifts helping Vickers produce warships at a rate never seen before in shipbuilding. Nineteen thousand men and women united in determined defiance of the insatiable Germans whose swastika was engulfing Europe like a ravenous spider.

Submarines, cargo ships, frigates and cruisers slipped into Walney channel quietly, without ceremony, before sailing to unknown destinations. Many were never seen again, as sailors paid the ultimate sacrifice.

Denmark, Norway, Holland, Belgium and Luxembourg were overrun like falling dominoes by the swarming Panzers, before France was occupied leaving Britain alone, brave and resolute.

Barrow had been luckier than most industrial towns. Apart from ineffective lone raids, the geography of Furness, on the west of the country, far away from German airfields, had left the town safe from the nightmare of bombing raids. On April 14, 1941, everything changed, including substantial parts of the Barrow skyline.

The Trevelyan Hotel in Dalkeith Street took a direct hit, whole rows of Abbey Road buildings were bombed – the Ritz cinema, a Baptist Church, a library, the swimming baths. That dreadful night started three weeks of air-raids, the wail of sirens dragging frightened Barrovians from their homes as bombs whistled down from black planes, high, invisible, terrifying.

Each night they came – Dorniers, Heinkels and Junkers, across the North Sea from occupied Norway. On May 10, parts of Abbey Road, Park Avenue and Hall Street were hit. Then silence. It was over.

Eighty-three people lost their lives, a further 330 were injured. More than 1,400 bombs had been dropped destroying hundreds of homes. Residents in Corporation Terrace were lucky; no injuries, no damage, apart from the odd blown-out window.

Many rugby league clubs played friendlies throughout the war. Barrow didn't bother. Supporters had to wait until 1942 before they saw a professional game. But the amateur league continued playing, albeit with a curtailed fixture list.

Risedale Old Boys' supremacy continued unabated. They won the league without losing, conceding only one try. They won the Lancashire Junior Cup, beating old adversaries Barrow Island in the final at Craven Park 8-0. Again their defence was superb. This time not a solitary point could be scored against them in three rounds. And to finish off the season they won the league final with a more comprehensive 40–0 destruction of Barrow Island. Risedale Old Boys were unbeatable.

The North Western Evening Mail employed a colourful, eloquent young writer who went under the byline "Paddy". His match reports give a graphic account of Willie's contribution to his side's embarrassing superiority:

RISEDALE OLD BOYS 38, STUDENTS' UNION 0

Tries: Horne (3), Troth (3), Turner and Benson.

Goals: Greaves (7)

Troth and Horne combined well. Horne, an adept at the sidestep had little difficulty in scoring his treble.

RISEDALE OLD BOYS 44, ENGINE SHOP 0
Tries: Horne (3), Peters (3), McMurray (2), Tweedle (2), Troth.
Goals: Greaves (7)

Horne opened the scoring with a clever try. He was always outstanding, repeatedly opening up play with kicks. Horne baffled the Engine Shop defence before transferring to Peters who crossed near the touchline.

RISEDALE OLD BOYS 8, BARROW ISLAND 0
Tries: Horne, Troth.
Goal: Greaves

Horne was prominent and the first thrill came when he broke away and raced to within ten yards of the line. Finding himself hemmed in he swung a long pass to his threequarters, but the whistle had gone for a forward pass. This did not deter Horne, however, and three minutes later he snapped the ball up and burst through himself near the posts to give Risedale a three points lead.

Naturally the tackling and spotting were deadly, but even so, some of the combined efforts were good to see. Horne gave his usual brilliant exhibition. His sidestepping and change of step were a treat to see, and the cut through which gave him his try left spectators and players bewildered.

The game was clean but robust, but had any incidents taken place I should have blamed those of the spectators who, from the security of the grandstand, took a delight in rousing tempers.

In pleasing contrast to these pitiful displays were the sporting tributes paid to their opponents by Willie Horne on the one side and Bill Rose on the other.

RISEDALE OLD BOYS 40, BARROW ISLAND 0
Tries: Tweedle (3), Turner (2), Peters, Troth, Fallowfield, Wilson and Benson.
Goals: Horne (3) and Greaves (2)

Both clubs fielded strong sides, and on paper it seemed it would be very close, but, due to the genius of Tweedle and Horne at half back for Risedale, Barrow Island were routed. Although Horne did not score a try himself he was instrumental in "making" most of the others.

★ ★ ★

Willie loved his family and he was fond of his job and workmates, but sport was what he liked doing best. He had been born with a great gift, a skill, a talent to achieve things no one else could, and quicker, by instinct. It was an uncertain time and he was happy to avoid disagreeable thoughts of what might happen if Germany invaded, if they lost the war, by immersing himself in keeping fit and maintaining Risedale's ascendancy.

A year earlier, in 1940, he had a fleeting flirtation with rugby union while the Barrow league was inactive as players joined the forces, inspired by Churchill's rousing speeches and black and white newsreels of German soldiers shooting civilians and burning down orphanages. Fellow turners John Gabriel, Bill Postlethwaite and Bill Rogers persuaded Willie to try the less demanding challenge of the 15-a-side game with weekend trips to Millom, an iron mining town five miles across Duddon Bay.

He enjoyed the extra space, the extra time, the cucumber sandwiches and halftime flasks of coffee. They travelled to St Bees, Kendal, Workington, all over Cumberland and everywhere they went middle-class men with groomed accents kept asking the name of the quiet fly half who made so many tries and tackled bulky, lumbering forwards without fuss, and with such energy and enthusiasm. At the end of the season he was back at Risedale Old Boys, active once again, winning matches. Nothing had changed. Towards the end of the season Willie broke his collar bone. It was painful and debilitating but before too long he was back, his skill and courage unaffected.

Back on the bloody battlefields of mainland Europe three million German soldiers invaded the Soviet Union, urged on by Hitler's arrogant boast that the war would be over by Christmas.

"We only have to kick the front door and the whole rotten edifice will come tumbling down," he told his generals as armoured spearheads moved eastward, pouring forward, the soil soaked in Russian blood. Seventeen days after the first onslaught, the Nazis had captured 300,000 prisoners and 2,500 tanks.

The Russians fought like tigers. Hitler's plans foundered as the first flakes of snow fell on his army and winter came, freezing the life out of exhausted soldiers who began retreating towards the Fatherland.

The United States joined the Allies after being forced into the war by Pearl Harbour. Immediately American industry accelerated its production of tanks, planes, guns and ships as the Germans buckled, their civilian spirit broken by merciless bombing raids.

In Furness everyone knew the war was won as life began slowly returning to normal. Joe McMurray, a shipyard coppersmith, and Billy Peters, who worked at the Corn Mills on Hindpool Road, were Willie's best friends. Most nights, when Willie wasn't training, they went to Risedale School to play badminton, table tennis and basketball. Monday was their favourite.

At 7.30pm Dora Parkinson gave dancing classes, patiently explaining the mystifying steps of the waltz and the foxtrot. The charge was a shilling (5p). Willie and his pals loved it. On Saturdays they headed for the Skating Rink on the Strand to stumble and trip their way through the evening, making friends and having a good time. Drink was banned. That didn't bother Willie. He was teetotal, and still is. Good music and good company were all he ever needed to enjoy a night out.

On Tuesday, December 8, 1942, Barrow RL announced a friendly fixture with Wigan at Craven Park the following Saturday. The next day Willie received a letter from secretary Edgar Senior. Would he like a trial? Before the war the club's regular number six had been Ieaun Lloyd, a fast, likeable Welshman with a match-winning habit of scoring long range tries. Ieaun had now joined the Artillery, and the word was that he wasn't coming back. Barrow needed a new stand-off half.

Ever since he had been a small boy watching the jinking runs of Charlie Carr at Little Park, Roose, Willie had dreamt that one day he might play for Barrow. And now he was making his debut against the stars from Central Park, including legendary full back Jim Sullivan. What could be better?

All the Hornes watched the match – mum, dad, brothers and sisters, the men shouting encouragement, the women sitting in silence, bewildered by what they saw, smiling with pride as their young brother dodged around large, muscular men.

More than 5,000 supporters watched Wigan bulldoze Barrow's forwards, who defended with fortitude and passion. Try as they might the home side could not overcome the absence of experienced men such as captain Alec Troop, Alf Marklew and Gordon Rawlings.

Willie, who was partnered at halfback by Wally Bowyer, was workmanlike, brave and lively, an encouraging debut considering his side's appalling lack of possession. Barrow lost but there was good reason for celebration after the club's first match for three years.

Willie was too modest to talk about his impressive trial. But he knew he had played well, and when his father told him Barrow would be in touch he dared hope it would prove an accurate prediction. But the days drifted by and there was no knock on the door or brown, official envelope inviting him for talks.

Would he ever play for Barrow again, he wondered as he prepared for Christmas, now less than a week away.

He didn't know it then but Willie would be spending Christmas Day away from his family, among strangers, playing for another team, 100 miles from Craven Park.

Oldham wanted him so badly he would be offered more money than he had ever dreamed of.

CHAPTER SEVEN

SIGN HERE

BRADFORD Northern beat Oldham 11–8 but there was much to celebrate in the display. The two Wigan forwards, Ken Gee, a mighty prop and a grand forager, and Joe Egan, a skilled hooker and calculating worker in the open, played as if for the honour of their own club. The half backs, Lamb and Horne, responded to the initiative of the forwards, and were definitely master of the opposition.

Horne, who had been working all night, played a wide-awake, eager game, enthusiastic to the end. He has good hands, tackles well, and beats a man or two in a tight corner with the easy style of a natural footballer.

OLDHAM EVENING CHRONICLE
Monday, January 18, 1943

THE room was smart, imposing, opulent even. As Barrow Rugby League Club secretary Edgar Senior prepared to call the meeting to order he felt an unexpected flush of pride as he glanced at the wealthy men chatting, half drunk glasses of port being raised beneath the ghostly, blue haze of cigar smoke. They all had money and influence. Now he was one of them. Not bad, he thought, for a joiner from Westgate Road, a modest row of terraced houses a drop kick from the railway station.

Mr Senior had earned the right to be considered an equal by the men before him. There had been no silver spoon in his mouth when he was born in 1883. He made a comfortable living by hard work and using his astute business brain. Everyone respected him. He was a short, plump man who weighed around 18 stones yet he was less than 5 feet 9 tall. You had the feeling Mr Senior suffered more than his fair share of mickey-taking at school. It never worried him. He was too friendly to fall out with anyone for very long, and if he did it was forgotten immediately. He was that sort of man. Straight and fair.

Behind them, grinning faces gazed down from mahogany walls, former players who had worn Barrow's blue shirt, frozen forever by pioneer photographers. Mr Senior stood and banged a small gavel on the walnut table as the chit-chat and clinking glasses subsided to a whisper, then finally, silence.

They had much to get through that December evening. The retreating German army had fuelled great optimism that was washing over Britain like a powerful tidal wave. It was time to prepare for a fresh start. Despair had been replaced by hope, fear by optimism.

First a financial report, long lists of numbers, the treasurer droning on and on about deficits, budgets and surfeits. The club, it seemed, was solvent. But we need to be prudent, warned the ageing treasurer staring over rimmed spectacles, below strands of receding hair, veins standing out on his white forehead like thick, blue pencils.

There was the leaking roof on Clive Street toilets followed by the latest news on Barrow players who were in the front line, brave soldiers and sailors. Some wouldn't be coming back, others were too old. It was time for rebuilding, time for signing local talent. Everyone agreed on that. Names were read out, names they all knew — Tweedle, too young; McMurray, too slow; familiar players, no surprises.

"What about young Horne?" asked Sid Lawton enthusiastically, as he had so many times before. "He's fast and he makes things happen. Look how well he did against Wigan last week." His voice lacked conviction, as though he sensed there were other, more influential doubters ready to outvote his proposal. Yes, he can play they said. But against the giants of the professional game, week in, week out . . . was he big enough? Would he be as effective? And could Horne take the knocks?

We'll carry on monitoring him, they decided. After all, where else could he go?

★ ★ ★

All day long Ethel had been grumpy and impatient. No idea why. She'd snapped and picked on her family without provocation since she had first opened her eyes that morning. Of course the weather didn't help – cold, damp and cheerless. And there was Christmas, just a few days away, her annual worry about making the holiday as special as possible for her loved ones. It had been easy when they were children expecting nothing more extravagant than an apple or an orange, a bag of nuts and a few pieces of chocolate. Now Ethel's family were grown up but she still took her maternal duties seriously enough to try her best to make sure everyone had a good time.

As soon as she heard the knock on the door Ethel knew the caller was bringing news she'd rather not hear. It was an uncanny gift that had never failed her, a sixth sense, an intuition. She didn't know how or why it worked, just that it was unerringly accurate. Now it was about to be proved right again.

Tommy Roberts, trainer of Risedale Old Boys, was escorted into the living room, talking quickly, breathlessly, his words gushing out as though he was revealing a vital secret and time was running short. It was unlike him, chatting like that. He was bashful, you see. But now he was in full flow, his shyness masked by unabated enthusiasm.

"Oldham want Willie to go for a trial," he said swivelling in mid-sentence away from Ethel's inquisitive eyes and on to Willie, sitting silent and noncommittal. "They've had you watched. Can you play against Leeds on Christmas Day?"

Oldham secretary Bert Summerscales was Tommy's uncle. Tommy had been sending regular reports to the Watersheddings on his young protege's progress. Barrow think he's not big enough he warned them. Yes, but can he play, they asked, undeterred by Craven Park's apparent lack of interest.

Alfred and Ethel felt like parents who were sending a son to a faraway battlefield. He was wanted. They felt pride in that. And, like a fresh-faced soldier with a head full of ideals and patriotic fire, they knew Willie would not let them down. He would play with courage and sportsmanship. That was the way they had brought him up. Again, like the soldier's well-wishing parents, they didn't want him to go, but they wouldn't stand in his way. Willie was a man who could make his own mind up.

So off they went, Willie and older brother Alf, on the 7.10am to Carnforth and on to Yorkshire, the carriages bursting with backslapping servicemen, hurrying home to enjoy a Christmas many had feared they might not live to see.

Both clubs had difficulty getting 13 men on the field. Oldham lost badly but the board considered that fulfilling the fixture at all was reason enough for celebration – that and the display of a mysterious young stand-off half strangely undaunted by the crowd, the pressure and the presence of so many seasoned professionals. This was how the local newspaper reported the match.

> *When Oldham arrived at Headingley there was a joint team selection pow-wow among the officials of both clubs, and Leeds spared a forward, Desborough, and a back, Murphy. Mr Summerscales found a soldier in the crowd who looked a likely lad and recommended himself as a former team-mate of Oliver Morris, the Welsh international out-half. The soldier turned out in the game and gave a good account of himself.*
>
> *Leeds were able to call on many of their stars and had Australian international Vic Hey and Croston in the middle, so that, taking all things into account, no further explanation is needed of the final score, showing Leeds 36 points, Oldham 5.*
>
> *There was one bright spot in Oldham's display. Horne played well enough at out-half to impress not only the experienced scouts but to cause Vic Hey to ask who he was. At the age of 20, Horne is a very promising player.*
>
> OLDHAM EVENING CHRONICLE
Monday, December 28, 1942

Willie and Alf were in a hurry after the match. They had a train to catch. "Thanks for turning up, Willie," said Mr Summerscales thrusting a ten shilling (50p) note into his hand. "We'll be in touch."

Back home, Willie's family were still awake, keen to hear the story of his brush with the big time. Ethel asked the right questions, feigning enthusiasm. But deep down, beneath the handshakes and the talking, they were not happy parents. They did not want their son to sign for Oldham, or Wigan or Huddersfield, or Widnes or St Helens, for that matter. It had to be Barrow, where they could watch him every week and where he would not have to leave home – where they could take care of him.

A week later Tommy was at Corporation Terrace again. Mr Summerscales wanted Willie for another trial, this time at Bradford Northern.

Willie and Alf repeated the journey to Yorkshire before catching a Bradford connection and taking a bus to Odsal stadium, a cavernous and frightening place, with rows of railway sleepers covered with black clinker reaching into the Yorkshire sky. Willie had been on night-shift the evening before so he tried to grab a couple of hours fitful sleep as the train steamed its way across the Pennines before they met the Oldham party. He had another wonderful game, destroying any doubts the more cautious directors may have held over his potential and the wisdom of making him a permanent member of the playing staff.

They had seen enough. Come back with us on the team bus, they told him. At the Watersheddings, Willie and Alf found themselves in the boardroom, confronted by two well-dressed men, men of breeding who talked pleasantly, the sort of people who expected to get their own way.

"Right Willie. You've had two good matches and we want you to sign for Oldham. We'll give you £350, right here and now," a director announced, pushing forward a piece of printed paper and laying an expensive fountain pen on top, as though agreement was automatic, refusal unthinkable. After all, times were hard.

"We'll come back next week with our father," said Alf seizing the initiative while Willie stared blankly, unnerved by the amount of money he could be taking home, his mind dancing with colourful images of the things it might buy.

In 1943, £350 would buy you a terraced house in Barrow town centre, Arthur Street, Monk Street or Dundonald Street, small but warm and comfortable. And you would still have enough left for a three-piece suite and a cushion or two.

Willie was excited by the money but he did not want to move to Oldham. He wanted to play for Barrow. So they came back home wondering if they had done the right thing. There might be another halfback Oldham were watching. What if they signed him and withdrew the offer?

They didn't have long to question the wisdom of their delay. The next day there was another knock on the door of 5 Corporation Terrace. Only this time Ethel was smiling. It would be good news. She knew that before her husband opened the door.

At last. Barrow RL wanted Willie.

★ ★ ★

Edgar Senior did not waste time explaining the reasons for his visit. It was obvious. So he got straight to the point. He liked conducting business like that – open and honest, nothing clever or devious. Barrow RL wanted Willie and Willie wanted Barrow RL. All that was left were loose ends, agreeing a fee and signing the form. It was over in less than five minutes.

"Whatever mam and dad decide is OK with me," Willie said, brushing past Mr Senior, keen to escape being the centre of attention, embarrassed by the mention of money, contracts and legalities. He left the house and headed for the skating rink to meet his pals and tell them his news. He was a Barrow player before he reached the end of the street.

"Money is tight," Mr Senior told Willie's father. "We can offer £100 now and another £150 at the end of the war." He was a shrewd and experienced negotiator. His manner and tone implied authority, leaving Alfred in no doubt it would have been foolish to haggle, to ask for more. So they shook hands and Mr Senior was gone leaving 20 neat, white £5 notes on the table. Training is on Tuesday, he called over his shoulder as he headed for the door. Willie can sign the forms then.

When he came back later that night Willie distributed the money among his family, enjoying the role of wealthy benefactor. He gave £60 to his mother and father, £12 to Alfred, everyone got something, until all he had left for himself was enough for a new pair of boots and a night out at the pictures. It wasn't the money that mattered. He would be playing for Barrow; that was all he had ever cared about.

The Evening Mail buried the news at the back of the paper using type so small anyone not blessed with perfect eyesight would have been hard pushed to read it without the benefit of a magnifying glass. There it was, on page seven, alongside a Reuter news report about Germany's dwindling U-boat fleet, under the headline OLDHAM MATCH OFF. *The signing of Willie Horne is certainly a good piece of business*, it read, with the sort of impact the Mail usually reserved for train derailments in Alaska or typhoons blasting the Malaysian coastline.

Other amateurs quickly followed – winger Jimmy Lewthwaite from local soccer, centre or stand-off Harold Kerr from Vickers rugby union and second-row forward Trevor Petcher from Barrow Island.

Willie couldn't wait for his first training session. There were so many players he had looked up to since he first began watching Barrow as a seven-year-old holding his father's hand at Little Park, Roose. When the club moved to Craven Park in 1932 he continued his support, always standing in the same place with his friends, on the Popular Side 25-yard line.

He admired the industry of the forwards, big men such as Alf Marklew and Alec Troop, who would break from a scrum with a sprinter's speed, ruthlessly pursuing halfbacks foolish enough to think they only had Barrow backs to worry about. But most of all he liked scrum-half Billy Little. He was his hero.

Billy created play with accurate passes, and he could kick drop goals and grubber kicks. But it was his defence that set him above other halfbacks. Friends said he was robust, enemies that he was dirty. It was all the same to him. Billy looked on the dangers of rugby league with cold indifference, in the same way a National Hunt jockey knows, eventually, he's going to fall off his horse and get hurt. Broken bones came with the job.

Billy was a hard man who admitted thumping the odd forward if he roughed up one of his threequarters. But he was never nasty. He didn't start anything. And after all the odd punch in the face was part of the game . . . especially if the referee was looking the other way. That was his style; play hard and play to win.

Sometimes he was on the receiving end, like the time a sadistic Keighley forward elbowed Billy in the face when the ball was on the other side of the field. Momentarily he was out cold. When the magic sponge brought him round he scratched his nose, looked up and spat out four broken teeth.

"Come on Billy," ordered trainer Hector Halsall. "You're coming off."

"Nay lad," he answered rolling up his sleeves, wiping the blood from his face. "It's nowt but a scratch."

Before the end of the game his eyes had swollen so badly he could hardly see. Later it was revealed his nose was broken in two places and he needed six stitches in the gash on the side of his mouth. The following day he played at Craven Park against Swinton as though he'd suffered nothing more painful than a mild headache. That was Billy Little – hard as nails.

Billy enjoyed being recognised. He liked people. Most Saturday mornings, when Barrow were playing at home, he walked along Dalton Road with his wife Madge, meeting people, breathing in the fresh air. It was good here in Barrow, he thought, living among so many friends. To him their regular walk was as much a social event as buying the weekend groceries. Enthusiastic fans stopped him on street corners, wishing him well, slapping his back as if they had known him for years. Billy liked talking to supporters, signing autographs and patting admiring children on the head like a favourite uncle.

There was something else too, something Willie admired almost as much as the uncompromising way Billy played. He was always smiling. It was clear he loved rugby. It was in his blood, something he was born to do.

Willie knew a few details about Billy's past, that he was born in a village outside Workington, that he had lots of brothers and sisters, that he didn't have much to eat when he was a little boy.

But he didn't know the real reason behind the beaming face. Billy owed everything to Barrow RL, not least his home in Cedar Road and the labouring job he enjoyed at the shipyard.

Billy is 83 now, an old man, but his memory is sharp and accurate and when he recalls his brief working life at Great Clifton he shakes with loathing.

For six awful years he worked 1,000 feet below ground in terrible temperatures, crawling on his hands and knees through deep pools of black water, the noise so dreadful he couldn't hear a colleague shouting less than three feet away.

Billy had been a coal miner.

CHAPTER EIGHT

LITTLE BIG MAN

IT IS impossible to watch miners at work without feeling a pang of envy for their toughness. It is a dreadful job they do, an almost superhuman job by the standards of an ordinary person. For they are not only shifting monstrous quantities of coal, they are also doing it in a position that doubles or trebles the work. They have got to remain kneeling all the while — they could hardly rise from their knees without hitting the ceiling — and you can easily see by trying it what a tremendous effort this means.

A coal mine is like hell, or at any rate like my own mental picture of hell. Most of the things one imagines in hell are there — heat, noise, confusion, darkness, foul air, and, above all, unbearable cramped space. Everything except the fire, for there is no fire down there except the feeble beams of Davy lamps which scarcely penetrate the clouds of coal dust.

All of us owe the comparative decency of our lives to the poor drudges underground, blackened to the eyes, with their throats full of coal dust, driving their shovels forwards with arms and belly muscles of steel.

THE ROAD TO WIGAN PIER by George Orwell

ANY attempt to remain anonymous was doomed from the start. Great Clifton Amateur Rugby League Club were accustomed to visits from unfamiliar men wearing expensive suits and puffing cigars. Barrow RL directors Wilf Gabbatt and John Atkinson watched the two teams troop out at Aeroplane Field knowing they had been detected, knowing the crowd and the players were aware of the real reason for their three-hour journey from Furness. They were the latest in a long line of wealthy men searching for young stars to entice away from home with a few pounds and the promise of a better way of life.

Cumberland had produced many world-class players – men like Egremont second-row Martin Hodgson, a massive man who signed for Swinton and went on to become one of the greatest forwards in the game. The coalfields on the county's west coast guaranteed its sons had abundant supplies of strength and bravery, qualities vital for a professional rugby league player. It was their birthright.

Billy Little was only 20 but reports of his fearless, almost reckless displays had drifted down to the rugby heartland of Lancashire. He was a wanted man. Normally Barrow monitored a potential signing for several weeks before making the player an offer, an offer they knew he could not refuse. But this was different. Delay could mean Little was lost.

The week before he'd been to Oldham for a trial. The match was the easy part. But the next day he was home, back with his family, a scribbled note left at the Watersheddings ground . . . *"Sorry, I missed my mum."*

Billy's brief flirtation with the unknown world outside his insular community had unsettled him and heightened his emotions. He'd always worshipped his mother and away from her his love deepened with an unexpected intensity. But it was coupled with the worrying realisation of how much he loathed the colliery, how much he hated the black, claustrophobic pit. He felt trapped, his future mapped out, a preordained life sentence.

Everyone knew they had come to watch Billy. He was the county half back and the inspiration behind the club's formidable reputation. Centre Billy Gunson joked about a cut of the fee if he set him up for a try, if he made him look good. Billy laughed as he prepared to kick off but he seemed unsettled and nervous. He was determined to impress the men with cigars, the men with the money, the men who could set him free.

★ ★ ★

Billy waved goodbye to his mother and set off for Allerdale colliery less than 400 yards from their tiny terraced home. It was almost four in the morning and though he felt sleepy and lethargic there were other more deep-rooted reasons for his laboured steps to the end of the street where twin brothers Anthony and Harry waited patiently.

They were accustomed to this early morning routine when they shared shifts with their brother. They detested the dreadful way of life but, unlike Billy, they recognised the futility of questioning their perilous occupation. It was as pointless as their future was inevitable.

Most Cumberland children grew up devoid of aspirations and ambition. From the day they were born their lives were inextricably linked with the black gold that lay buried deep beneath the green countryside. Men went down the pits. Women bore their children, children who knew where they would end up. If they didn't mine coal they didn't work and if they didn't work, eventually, they didn't eat.

Some escaped the mental pain by daydreaming perhaps of walking along picturesque Lakeland valleys, vivid images of children harvesting hay on hot summer days. They accepted the drudgery of their existence in the same way a Grimsby boy knows adulthood means facing a similarly hazardous career searching the icy waters of the North Sea for shoals of cod and haddock.

Mary closed the door of 20 William Street, whispering a silent prayer to God to protect her family but she had neither the time nor the inclination to debate her own miserable life. Two other sons would be home soon and daughters Lily and Agnes were awake, unable to sleep through the noise created by three men preparing for work. Mary had had it rough, even by the pitiful standards of Cumberland in 1932. She had lost her husband Tom 15 years before, his body riddled with cancer. His death left Mary with seven sons and four daughters to bring up. Now she was forced to work on the screens to help feed her family. It was backbreaking, dreary and depressing, watching coal rattle by on belts, black hands searching for lumps of granite that had slipped through. But Mary never complained.

The three men joined the crowd of workers arriving at the pit, instantly anonymous among cloth-capped heads bobbing up and down, the ground echoing to the sound of countless clogs tapping the cobbled street. Billy was carrying a large tin called a snap-can. It held his mid-shift meal – a large jam sandwich. In his other hand he carried a smaller tin of cold tea to help quench the awful thirst of the coal face where clouds of dust hung in the air so thick it was impossible to recognise a friend hammering at the rock less than three feet away. They passed the main gates dwarfed by the wheels of the headgear turning tirelessly first one way then the other, challenging the dawn to break through the miserable sky. Into the lamp house for the lights and brass coins that would enable accurate records of production to be kept. On a good day they could earn six shillings (30p). On a bad day a few coppers.

Already a long queue had formed by the steel cage that would take them on the first part of the journey to the coalface. Rain was falling gently, forming white specs on grimy faces constantly emerging from the mineshaft. It was a gloomy morning, more gloomy than usual, and the sombre mood deepened as waiting miners heard the news about Frankie Dempster.

It had happened during the night. Evening shifts are always more risky, more threatening as miners grow tired and careless. Everyone knew Frankie. He was only 16, though he looked four years younger, his thick mop of curly hair framing an innocent face. He seemed untouched by the oppressive power of the mine, his spirit unbroken. Now he was gone, crushed beneath a tub carrying half a ton of coal.

Deaths were common but every time someone was killed miners took it badly, as though fate was reminding them of their own mortality, their own uncertain future. They thought of the grieving mother or widow. And they thought of the funeral at St. Luke's on Chapel Brow, the church so full many mourners had to stand outside, heads bowed, mumbling prayers they'd heard so many times before.

Mary always called on the family with what little food she could spare. For a few short weeks they were singled out with collections from working miners, until the next time a victim of the black pit was dragged to the surface.

Billy began to feel cold as his thoughts turned to his own friends and family who had been hurt or killed in the mine. There was his brother-in-law Harry Owens who died instantly in a freak accident when a wooden prop snapped and broke his neck. And Jonathan Wilson who lost his arm the week before he was due to travel to Huddersfield Rugby League Club for trials.

The cage was designed to carry eight broad-shouldered miners. In practice, a dozen squeezed in as the operator worked his own short cut to a small bonus based on transporting workers to the face within a set time. Nobody said anything. To them it was just another day, another acceptable risk in a job where one miner in six was injured every year. Compared with the hazards of working underground, overcrowding was an irrelevance, a minor inconvenience unworthy of complaint.

A few seconds later they were 1,000 feet below, pushing to leave the cage as exhausted miners pressed forward to take their places and escape to the surface, away from the foul air, the stifling heat and the awful, deafening noise.

They were in a large cavern, around 12 feet square, the size of a modern living room, though miners had to crouch slightly. Two tunnels branched off in opposite directions, Greengill on one side, Birkby the other. Billy and his brothers turned right and began walking into the inky darkness, their lamps struggling to pierce the gloom. At first progress was quick as they moved silently, ever downward, regularly stepping aside as ponies slipped by pulling tubs laden with coal, egged on by teenage boys, grim-faced beneath black masks of dust, like old, lonely men who had long since forgotten how to smile.

On and on they trudged, steadily downhill, the tunnel narrowing all the time, until in places they had to crouch then crawl along rock smoothed by generations of miners. After 45 minutes they could hear picks hammering, dull sounds drifting along the shaft. Then they were there, at the face.

Shift changeovers were always chaotic. The last of the night workers were beginning their long journey to the surface, tools slung over drooping shoulders, spirits lifted with thoughts of the fresh, cool air less than an hour away. The face was called Ligbank. Its seam, two feet thick, stretched more than 100 yards into the darkness. Everyone hated working here – it was the wettest part of the pit.

Billy crawled on his hands and knees through pools of black grime, as drops of water cascaded endlessly from the roof, drenching his clothes. He reached his own section where his partner was already at work, stripped to the waist, loading massive rocks of coal into a half empty tub, his chest black from the dust hanging in the air.

Billy squeezed towards the face pulling his pick behind him. It was like lying underneath a small single bed, yet he began hewing the coal with remarkable efficiency, each blow a mirror image of the one before, its power never weakening. Every 20 minutes he stopped and pushed the rocks towards the tubs where fillers continued the process with the same skill and economy of effort. Despite the constant spiral of work, time drifted slowly, each hour monotonous and painful. And there was always the horrible noise, and the foul air filling their throats with black dust.

The only rest from the agonising labour was a short break in the middle of the shift, when they sat in darkness, lamps switched off to preserve power, eating meals in ghostly silence. Before long they were back, hacking away at the face again, thousands of feet below the rolling hills and the green fields. It was like working in hell.

Miners were paid only for what they produced and when they stopped they didn't earn any money. Sometimes, if the coal was as hard as iron or if there was a fault in the seam, workers failed to produce the minimum quota and they were paid the bare wage, less than a shilling (5p).

"They're here lads," someone shouted, announcing the arrival of the next shift. Word travelled fast. Billy crawled from the face, splashing through the same pools of filth he'd passed ten hours earlier. His whole body was hurting, aching from a thousand swings of the pick.

He joined his brothers for the slog to the surface, to safety, away from the black nightmare. It always took miners longer at the end of a shift. There was the gradient but that was only a minor factor. After the demands of the face the men were exhausted, shuffling along in single file, almost asleep on their feet.

Eventually, they reached the main shaft. Shivering with the sudden drop in temperature, the brothers squeezed into the steel cage. It had stopped raining as they emerged, gasping the clean air, coughing up balls of black phlegm as they dropped off lamps and tools without stopping.

Billy knew who the visitors were as soon as he turned the corner and saw the car outside his home, its fresh paintwork gleaming in the afternoon sun. Wilf Gabbatt and John Atkinson were sitting together on a small settee as Mary poured boiling water into a tin bath, dominating the room in front of the fire, windows steamed up, dripping with condensation.

"We want you to play for Barrow," Wilf said as Billy undressed and lowered himself into the soapy water with an almost childlike lack of embarrassment.

Ten minutes later they were gone, clutching a piece of paper that would enable Billy to play in the weekend fixture with Wakefield Trinity. Billy was smiling, holding a cheque for £70. It seemed an enormous amount but he handed it to his mother without hesitation or regret. The money wasn't important.

He was out. And he wasn't going back. Not for anything.

★ ★ ★

Every one of the 31,384 crowd will remember Billy's drop goal as long as they live, that split second of divine inspiration etched on their memory, untouched by time. The Halifax players too will carry that piece of rugby history to their graves, haunted by memories of the day their Wembley dreams were wrecked by a shy, simple Cumberland coalminer.

It was April, 1938, the semi-final of the Challenge Cup at Huddersfield. Barrow and Halifax were drawing 2-2 after 80 minutes of tough, uncompromising rugby. Thoughts of enterprising football had been suppressed, held in check, both teams almost paralysed by the fear of failure, the fear of making a mistake. So the ball was kept in the forwards, big men battering down the middle, neither side able to gain the upper hand. The threequarters were paid observers, jogging into promising positions, methodically, waiting for a pass, a chance to make the vital break. But the passes did not come.

Barrow were attacking the scoreboard end of Fartown, facing a huge white clock high above the crowd, its black hands tiptoeing past 4.30p.m. It was injury time when a Halifax forward knocked on outside his own 25. His colleagues weren't worried. Even if Barrow gained possession, the Halifax halfbacks would be out of defence quickly to snuff out any danger. By then the referee would blow for time. Everyone was thinking about the following Wednesday night, the replay at Wigan. Everyone except Billy Little.

The two packs locked together in a final effort to win the ball, groaning, panting, steam rising from 12 exhausted men. Barrow hooker Danny McKeating looked up to the sky, a prearranged signal to his scrum half – he wanted it thrown high, thrown to his knee. Billy fed the scrum, the ball deflecting at right angles, through the human tunnel and out the back. He looked at halfback Ieaun Lloyd and saw Halifax stand off George Todd charging forward, arms outstretched, ready to make the tackle.

Billy stopped, turned and drop kicked the ball. He caught it perfectly, his left boot following through to the white sticks 40 yards away. Immediately he was thrown to the ground by scrum half Jack Goodall and loose forward Harry Beverley, four hands thrust into his chest, pushing him into the mud. Billy looked up at their faces turned towards the posts watching the brown piece of leather spiralling into the distance. He could see their fear, sense their anxiety.

The timing of the kick had been so precise, so exact, the crowd realised instantly it had the length to be successful. Halfway through its journey the ball was still rising, soaring through the Yorkshire air, before banking left, spinning violently away from the posts, away from its place in rugby league history.

Then it straightened, snatched back on line by an invisible hand before grazing the inside of the left hand post and banging into the iron railings surrounding the pitch. St. Helens referee Jim Orford raised his left arm high, rigid, holding a white handkerchief signalling confirmation that the kick was good. Simultaneously he blew his whistle, two long blasts. The match was over. Barrow had won 4-2. Beverley helped Billy to his feet as Goodall walked to the dressing room in silence, holding back the depression, the disappointment.

"You little sod," Beverley said. "You cost me £20 winning money." Then he smiled sincerely. "Good luck at Wembley, Billy."

The Barrow team surrounded him, shaking his hand, slapping his back. Everyone was on a high, intoxicated by victory, by the fulfilment of a lifetime dream. It was pandemonium as thousands of supporters flooded the pitch, keen to touch the players and savour every last scrap of emotion. Billy was carried shoulder high in the middle of the human sea, protesting, a reluctant hero.

Three weeks later Barrow lost the final, going down 7–4 to Gus Risman's Salford. Billy kicked a drop goal in that match too. The players and supporters soon recovered from the disappointment. It was as though the final itself was an anticlimax, a wasted journey after the drama at Fartown.

When the season was over fans met in the working men's clubs of Barrow to analyse the previous year, to relive the golden moments. Nobody spent too long talking about the Wembley final. They were too busy savouring that unlikely goal, Billy's unforgettable drop of magic.

The Horne family outside 4 Middle Square, Roosegate. Doris, Alf, Dad, Florence, Ada and Mam. George is at the front left alongside Willie. The photograph was taken around 1928 when Willie was six. He had already begun to play rugby league, joining in with Alf and older children on the estate.

Class 1A, Risedale School 1933. Back: Albert Pearson, Edwin Babbs, Cecil Harkins, John Murray and John Todd. Middle: Bernard Sim, Reggie Woodend, Sid Grey, Eddie Worrall, George Bull and John Dewhurst. Front: Gordon Hackett, Willie Horne and Ted Pearson

PC 73, Nevile Lorain, the popular Barrow policeman who watched seven-year-old Willie playing rugby league and predicted he would play for England. Sixteen years later, at Central Park, Wigan, his prophecy came true.

Workers pour over the High Level Bridge on their way to Vickers shipyard. When Willie began his apprenticeship as a turner in 1937 more than 19,000 workers were employed at the shipbuilders.

A section of the Sub Engine Shop where Willie learned his trade from his father for 7/6 (37p) a week. The building produced engines for submarines.

Risedale Old Boys, 1938, at Craven Park. Back: Unknown, Barney Fogerty (front row), Billy Rose (centre), George Kennedy (wing), unknown, Hughie McGregor (loose forward), Harry Morrow (second row), Stan Ayres (front row) and Harold Egan (Risedale School games teacher). Middle: Norman Cassley (second row), Jackie Parker (centre), Tommy Milnnine (full back), Tommy Clark (wing) and Toby Mason (hooker). Kneeling: Ernie Baker (reserve), Billy Hopkins (scrum half), Willie Horne (stand-off half) and Bob Kell (reserve).

Willie when he was 17 outside his home in 5 Corporation Terrace with his best pals Joe McMurray, Billy Peters and George Troth.

Alf Horne when he was 14. In a four-year career his only losing contest was against Cumberland champion Billy Murdoch.

Freddie Cotton, Barrow's formidable featherweight boxing champion who fought a host of nationally-ranked fighters.

Risedale Old Boys in 1941 before the Lancashire Junior Cup Final against Barrow Island at Craven Park. Back: Tommy Roberts (trainer), Stan Ayres (prop), Billy Peters (full back), Bob Fallowfield (second row), Vince McKeating (hooker), Sid Ferguson (loose forward), Alf Horne (coach) and Fred McMurray (prop). Front: Doug Greaves (centre), Steve Turner (centre), Eddie Wilson (second row), Willie Horne (captain and stand-off half) George Troth (wing), Geoff Tweddle (scrum half) and George Keen (wing). Six of the team went on to play professional rugby league.

League official Mr Edmondson presents the Lancashire Cup to Willie after Risedale had defeated Barrow Island in the final 8–0.

Willie was one of the first players in rugby league history to kick goals "round-the-corner." In his career he converted more than 800 goals.

Bert Summerscales, Oldham RLFC's long-serving secretary, who came close to persuading Willie to come to the Watersheddings after two successful trials.

Barrow RLFC secretary Edgar Senior who signed Willie for £100 down and a further £150 if he survived the Second World War. Willie turned down £350 up front from Oldham.

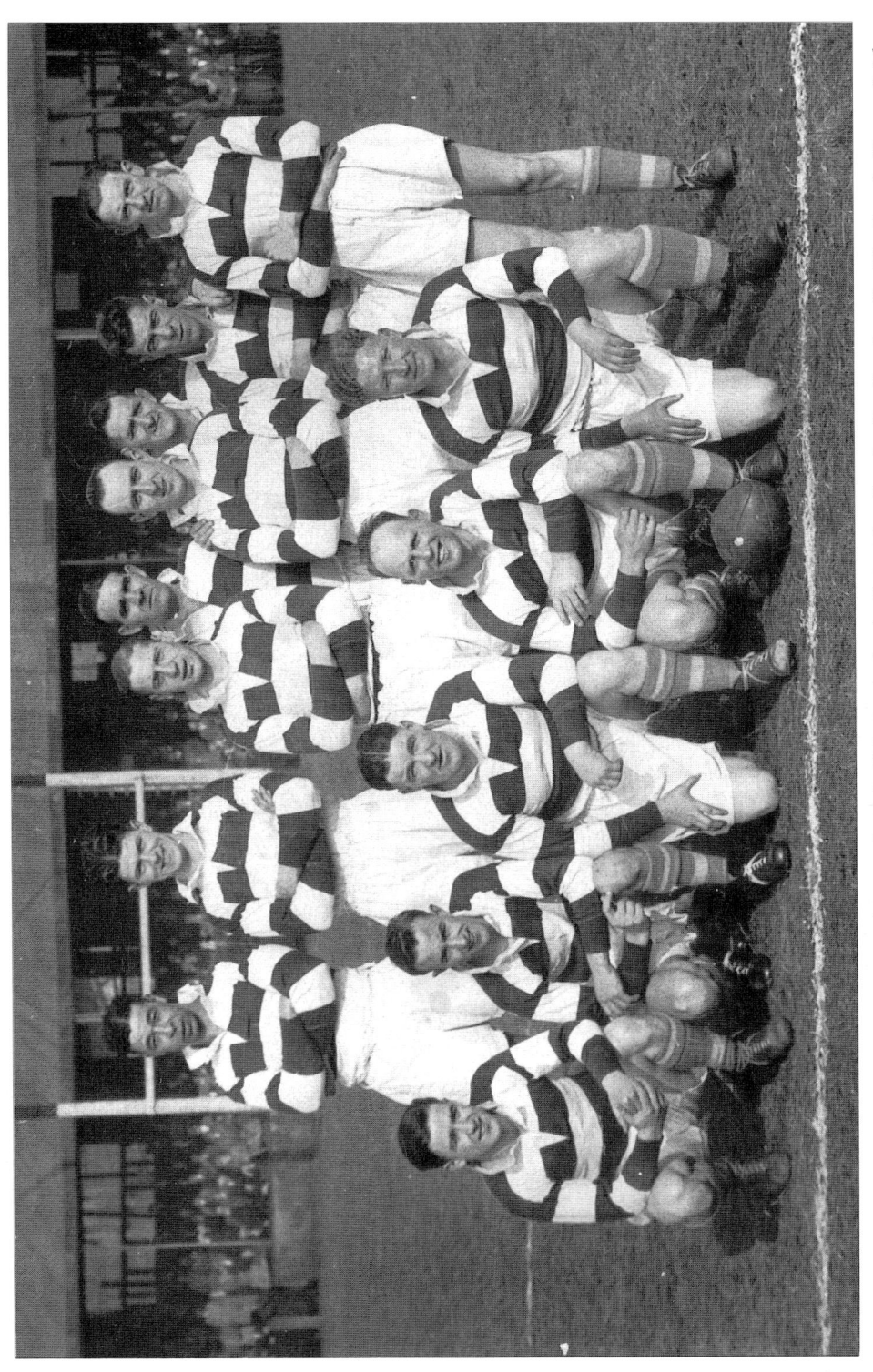

Barrow RLFC in early 1943, just after Willie had signed. Back: Val Cumberbatch, Jimmy Leathwaite, Jim Braeden, Freddie French, Trevor Petcher, Alf Marklew, Billy Woods and Vince McKeating. Front: Harold Kerr, Willie Horne, Billy Little, Bobby Ayres and "Ginger" Hughes.

William Street, Great Clifton, where Billy Little grew up with his mother, six brothers and four sisters.

Mary Little, Billy's mother, who was forced to work shifts at the colliery screens to help buy food for her family.

Billy Little, shortly after his move to Barrow in 1933. He was paid £70. He gave all the money to his mother.

A rare action photograph of the 1938 Challenge Cup semi-final between Barrow and Halifax with Billy Little in the foreground. Billy kicked an injury-time drop goal to earn Barrow their first Wembley appearance.

CHAPTER NINE

IF THE CAP FITS

WILLIE Horne has no superior in the game today. He is England's star back, a fine successor to Les Fairclough of St Helens, my ideal outside half. What a player Horne is for a big match.

JIM BROUGH, full back, 1936 Lions Tour captain,
Rugby League Review, March 28, 1946

WILLIE Horne was born to play rugby league in the same way L. S. Lowry was destined to paint artistic masterpieces and Wordsworth to write wonderful poetry. When Willie joined Barrow RL he was already an outstanding talent who knew pretty much all there was to know about the game. There was no need for him to learn the tricks of the trade from the club's experienced professionals. He'd done all that when he was five years old playing with the teenagers on the muddy streets of Chinatown.

Barrow supporters recognised his genius quickly. It took only a couple of matches before excited fans were predicting greatness with passionate confidence.

Of course, he had talented players around him. Billy Little was moved to loose forward strengthening a menacing pack that boasted the creativity of Alf Marklew and the sparkle of Bobby Ayres, a second-row forward with a childlike enthusiasm for confrontation. Bobby loved his rugby. He wore a permanent smile to prove his insatiable affection for tackling and running. Bobby played hard and he played to win.

Opposing forwards rarely risked painful retribution by slapping a Barrow back or tackling high and late. Bobby could dish out the rough stuff if it was required. The balding forward, Barrow's skipper, was an England international at the peak of his powers.

Cumberland wrestling champion and professional sprinter Jimmy Lewthwaite was scoring goals for a local soccer team so frequently his name was linked with Blackburn Rovers, Preston North End and Wolverhampton Wanderers. In three years he had hit the net 135 times. Then after a one-match trial, he joined Craven Park, inexperienced, green as grass, but fast and fearless.

Winger Lewthwaite was an instant success, scoring tries with a growing regularity. And when Bryn Knowelden signed from Morecambe Football

Club, Barrow carried deadly threats whenever the ball was thrown out wide, which was often. Willie made sure of that.

Wally Bowyer was scrum half. He was unspectacular but safe and dependable, the perfect foil for Willie's entertaining heroics. Wally was content to follow instructions that required him to give the ball to his unpredictable stand-off half quickly and frequently, tackle enthusiastically and back up. The rest he left to Willie, who gave coach Hector Halsall the flexibility of deputising at full back when injury forced team changes.

In March, 1943, the Evening Mail published a match report of Barrow's 13-2 defeat at St. Helens. Barrow missed chances, it said, and Lewthwaite caught the eye with his clever change of pace. Willie Horne made perfect openings cutting through with the ease of an invisible man, the report concluded.

Like all gifted sportsmen, Willie made everything look easy. Soon his reputation spread to other grounds, from Central Park to Belle Vue, Station Road to Crown Flatt, where knowledgeable men nodded in appreciation, making mental notes to monitor Willie's career.

In season 1943-44 he was the league's top points scorer with ten tries and 58 goals. Bryn Knowelden, who scored 18 tries, was selected for England's match against Wales, after fewer than 20 games in the first team. His recognition surprised Barrow supporters, many of whom were baffled by the omission of Willie, who was outplaying the best halfbacks in the game week after week. But his time was not far away.

Further Evening Mail match reports illustrate Willie's powerful influence on Barrow's performances.

ST HELENS 5, BARROW 24

Horne, who kicked five goals, made more openings than any stand-off half I have seen for years. – October 2, 1943.

BATLEY 8, BARROW 21

Barrow owed their success to Horne who played an outstanding pivotal game at stand-off. Even when things went wrong, Horne showed his opportunism. He played polished football, he has speed, is elusive and penetrative, breaking away time after time, getting clear of opposition to pave the way for dangerous attacks. He scored the first two Barrow tries and kicked the goals himself. – October 16, 1943.

WIGAN 16, BARROW 3

The full back position was filled splendidly by Horne. His fielding, no matter how the ball came, was faultless. He kicked strongly even against the wind and his touch-finding was, at times, uncanny. He was the outstanding Barrow player. – January 3, 1944.

In September, 1944, Willie and Knowelden were picked for an RL XIII friendly against Northern Command. It was an exhibition match with nothing at stake but the reputation of a dozen of the game's top players, stars such as Alex Fiddes, Dai Jenkins and Joe Egan. Northern Command had their share of formidable names, too – players such as Ernest Ward, Jack Brown and Stan Brogden.

The RL XIII won 27-23 in front of 3,500 spectators at Huddersfield's Fartown. Willie, who scored a try and kicked two goals, earned eulogistic notices, 1,000 pats on the back and the assured prediction that more representative football was just around the corner. You'll play for England before long, he was told as he set off for the station.

It was a magical experience for him to play alongside such great stars. But he was not unsettled or worried about the possibility of further honours. Like successful football managers in post-match interviews, Willie took one game at a time. Naturally, he wanted to play for his country. Who wouldn't? If he did, that was fine . . . and if he didn't, well, that was fine too.

So he returned to Barrow and continued building submarines, looking after his family and entertaining the Craven Park faithful with his daring exploits. England's next international was against Wales the following March. Willie wasn't wasting time in pointless speculation. Others were doing that for him. He was a certainty for the match if you believed the newspapers. Privately, Willie knew he was playing well and asking opposing stand-off halves questions they were incapable of answering. Sometimes, Willie Horne was almost literally unplayable.

It would have been foolish and naive for him to be unaware of his chances for selection. How nice it would be, he thought, playing for his country . . . the crowds, the atmosphere, the excitement. Then there would be the cap, maroon with a red rose, regal and imposing. Rugby League was not like soccer. One was all you got; after your first cap there were no others. If he was fortunate enough to be picked, his theoretical cap already had a home. There was only one place it was going to end up – with his mother.

★ ★ ★

There was an unmistakeable air of tension hovering over Craven Park that chilly March evening. Superficially everything was normal, people went about their duties the same way they had for the last couple of years. But those in the know, the coaches, the directors and most of all the players, sensed anxiety and apprehension. The reason, unspoken through superstitious fears of invoking bad luck, was the impending announcement of England's team to take on Wales at Central Park, Wigan.

Many Barrow players had been performing above themselves, perhaps as well as at any time in their careers. Now, privately, some dared hope they might be wearing the white shirt of their country.

Bryn Knowelden . . . he'd been there before. And Bobby Ayres, he too, had enjoyed the thrill of international football and the kudos that went with the public acknowledgement that for a few days he was considered one of the best second-row forwards in the country. Then there was Trevor Petcher and Jimmy Lewthwaite, young men who were automatic choices for Barrow, improving fast, so quickly there were those inside the game who were saying international recognition would be sooner rather than later.

They all had legitimate claims for selection. But there was another name more unanimously tipped in the pubs and clubs of Barrow. Willie Horne, they all agreed, was a certainty. Newspapers joined the pro-Horne lobby with editorials praising his creativity, speed and unquenchable thirst for work.

Willie had done everything for Barrow that year. He'd scored tries, made openings, kicked goals and tackled everything that moved, not arrogantly but with the assured confidence of someone who knew deep down that he was fortunate to have been blessed with a unique gift.

Rugby League is all about winning, coming out on top and earning money. So teams quickly recognised the threat of the matchwinner in a number six shirt. Opposing players left their dressing room with ears ringing from the repeated instructions of anxious coaches: "Stop Horne and you stop Barrow."

Ruthless forwards with thick arms, wide shoulders and broken noses, followed Willie around the field like shoals of hungry piranha. But he learned fast. It didn't take him long to recognise the dangers presented by less skilful opponents who, he knew, would shed no tears had he been carried off bruised and unconscious. They chased, they covered, they threatened but only rarely did they catch him. And when they did, an elbow or careless fist to the face only strengthened Willie's resolve and his persistent desire for victory.

Despite Willie's skill and commitment, Barrow supporters did not need reminding that outstanding performances were no guarantee of international recognition. The game was littered with ghosts of forgotten heroes robbed of their rightful reward by injury, bad luck or inter-club politics. So Barrow held its breath along with Craven Park officials, waiting for justice to be done, for Willie to receive the honour his talent demanded.

That March evening's training included several players whose minds wandered to the imminent announcement of the England team, how they would feel if they were chosen and how they would feel if they weren't.

Secretary Edgar Senior knew a journalist from a Manchester paper. He had promised to phone him with the team as soon as it was released. While the Barrow players sprinted and worked moves for the weekend fixture at home to Featherstone Rovers, coach Hector Halsall joined the directors in the boardroom for a cigarette and a medicinal glass of whisky. All they could do now was wait.

Training was almost over when Mr Senior's round shape appeared on the touchline, the twilight softened by the yellow light breaking through the stand entrance directly behind him. The players gathered around without waiting for an invitation.

"Right lads," he said, keen to share his news without delay. "Joe Jones, you're the Wales full back and Fred Hughes is in at prop forward. Bobby Ayres is in the England second-row with Bryn Knowelden at right centre." A slight pause, then: "Willie Horne is the England stand-off. The scrum-half is Tommy Bradshaw."

Ten minutes later Willie left the ground in a hurry, his hair still dripping wet from a hasty shower. He couldn't wait to get home and break the news to his family. Now he was an international. He was too excited to be nervous.

The following Thursday, two days before the international, Mr Senior was standing on the touchline again, beckoning Willie, this time with a more private message.

"You're wanted on the phone," he said, pointing towards the boardroom. Willie took off his boots and tiptoed along the narrow corridor, his wet, stocking feet making perfect footprints on the cold stone floor.

"Hello," he said nervously, holding the receiver in his left hand. Willie was uneasy, more edgy than he had ever been before a big match when 25,000 people watched every move he made. Rugby came easy. This was different. He was 23-years-old and it was the first time he'd used a telephone.

"Congratulations Willie," a voice crackled down the line. "It's Tommy." Silence. "Tommy Bradshaw," he went on. "I thought we should get together before the match. The Welsh will be no pushovers."

On Saturday morning, at Wigan station, Tommy was waiting to greet Willie as he had promised. They hit it off right away. There was a mutual respect, a general agreement that rugby was a game to be enjoyed. Willie had expected to like him. When Barrow played Wigan he'd remembered how much of their play revolved around Tommy's darting runs and how he'd tackled the Barrow forwards with the will of a snarling terrier. Then there was the way they shook hands and Tommy had always said "Well played," whatever the result. Yes, Tommy would be OK.

It was a short walk to Tommy's house, 21 Elm Avenue, where Willie met his wife, drank tea and nibbled a slice of toast, before being led into a back garden smaller than a family lounge but big enough to run through set moves, that, they hoped, would dupe the Welshmen.

★ ★ ★

England won the match but it had been touch and go. For Willie it was over almost as soon as it had started leaving him with fleeting, colourful images of the most wonderful day of his life. Back home he closed his eyes, reliving golden memories, new friends, how he felt when he pulled on the white shirt of England, the smell of victory and the firm handshakes of Welsh opponents who took defeat with honour.

Willie remembered the crowd, the dressing room tension, the team talk and the unity of 13 men hellbent on winning. He remembered the speed of the game, the ferocity of the tackling and the sea of red shirts who refused to give up. Most of all he remembered his try and how much he owed Tommy Bradshaw.

The match was only a few minutes old when the forwards locked for a scrum outside the Welsh 25. The front rows crunched together, legs driving into the ground, gouging great lines like a human plough as the packs strove for possession.

"Let's try the blindside move if we get the ball," Tommy Bradshaw whispered to Willie, before checking the position of the Welsh backs, calculating instantly the angle he would run and where he would go.

A moment later Tommy ghosted past the bewildered Welsh loose forward before slipping a perfect inside ball to Willie who skipped through a gap in the centres narrower than a half-open door. It was all he needed as he brushed by outstretched arms to the tryline.

The move was a perfect replica of their hurried lunchtime training session. England, spurred on by the early score, went on to win 18–8 with three tries from winger Eric Batten and three goals by Billy Belshaw.

Willie had much to celebrate that night, not least his own confident performance. He had eclipsed opposing stand-off Willie Davies so emphatically the Welsh threequarters spent most of the afternoon running backwards, exchanging worried glances, the kind tail-end batsmen make when their team is still 100 runs behind. The Welshmen wouldn't give in. They had too much pride for that. But they were never going to win.

The following day's newspapers were full of patriotic praise for the Englishmen's performance, in particular how Tommy Bradshaw and Willie had blended together so effectively. Had reporters known about the secret lunchtime rendezvous the headlines would have been less predictable than "**ENGLAND HALFBACKS QUENCH WELSH FIRE**." As it was they reached similar conclusions that the game was just the start of a long representative career for Willie.

Two weeks later Willie's cap arrived at Corporation Terrace. It was immediately placed on the mantlepiece over the clock where his doting mother knew visitors could not fail to notice her son's sporting trophy.

Willie finished the season as Barrow's top scorer with seven tries and 36 goals. Further honours came with appearances for Lancashire against Yorkshire and Cumberland and again for England against Wales and France.

LANCASHIRE 18, CUMBERLAND 3

Willie Horne was the cleverest player on the field in this county championship match at Workington. He kicked three goals and scored a try. The Lancashire half-back partnership of Horne and Tommy McCue was irresistible.

NORTH WEST EVENING MAIL,
Monday, January 28, 1946

In December 1945 Australian tour rumours began circulating northern towns. No one was surprised when Rugby League officials announced that the eighth British Lions would embark from Devonport in mid-April and that the 26-strong party would be named on March 11.

Newspapers were full of informed speculation on which players would be aboard the Barrow-built aircraft carrier HMS Indomitable, carrying a bag full of summer shirts, sun tan lotion and sun glasses. They all agreed with vigorous certainty on one thing . . . there were no automatic choices.

The last tour had been ten years before when Jim Brough led the 1936 Lions to Ashes victory with a gripping 12–7 decider at Sydney in front of 53,000 hostile Australians. Most of those fine players had retired or were too old, their youth lost on the battlefields of Europe.

Tour places were open to anyone. Selectors faced a difficult job with rugby league enjoying a spectacular renaissance as a new generation of thrilling players shook off the cobwebs of wartime inactivity to enthral record crowds.

The first tour trial was at Leeds on January 12 with Barrow men Jimmy Lewthwaite, Bryn Knowelden and Fred Hughes enjoying the chance to impress selectors receptive to classy performances. But no Willie. When the second trial was named two weeks later Barrow prop forward Trevor Petcher received a surprise invitation. Still no Willie.

The Evening Mail fulfilled its civic duty by backing Willie's cause when "Crusader" said: "National and local opinion seems to be unanimous that the British halves should be Willie Horne and Tommy McCue of Widnes. Neither player has been in a trial match. To me this indicates selectors already know who shall form the halfback line – Horne and McCue."

On Monday, March 11, Willie was at Vickers in the sub-engine shop working on a combination lathe. He found it difficult to concentrate, knowing as he did that the tour party would be announced that day.

"I'll go and see if the boss will let me phone the Evening Mail," said Albert Knowelden, Bryn's brother. A few minutes later he came running back, beaming with pride.

"You're going Willie," he said, hugging his young friend. "And so's our Bryn. Jimmy Lewthwaite and Joey Jones have been picked too."

The furthest Willie had travelled from Barrow was the tortuous five-hour journey to Hull's windswept Boulevard. Now he faced a long trip to the other side of the world, to a different climate, a different culture, an exotic country with place names he couldn't even begin to pronounce such as Mundiwindi and Meekatharra.

He didn't have long to worry about the long sea voyage. The Indomitable left Great Britain less than four weeks later.

CHAPTER TEN

INDOMITABLE

WILLIE HORNE is the best English five-eighth since Les Fairclough and Billy Rees. He is a greater menace than Stanley Brogden and Emlyn Jenkins. Horne moves very quickly, beats opponents with subtle changes of pace, and sidesteps off both feet. Horne and full back Martin Ryan promise to be the personality players of the tourists.

SYDNEY MORNING HERALD
May 23, 1946

MONDAY morning, April 1, 1946. The 9.05 train from Barrow's Central station crept from platform two with a familiar human cargo of servicemen, English, American and Scottish, the odd family on a shopping trip to the capital and six rugby league men beginning a four–week journey to the other side of the world.

Willie Horne, Jimmy Lewthwaite, Joe Jones, Bryn Knowelden, Fred Hughes – now with Workington Town – and tour manager Wilf Gabbatt smiled affectionately to the 100–strong crowd, snatching a final glimpse of their heroes, everyone waving, banners fluttering, wishing them well as the Jubilee Class locomotive puffed clouds of white steam into the still, spring air.

Ten hours later the Barrow party were watching Tommy Trinder and George Black in a West End theatre. At 3.15pm the following day they were taking uncertain steps up a swaying gangway, boarding the aircraft carrier HMS Indomitable, swallowed by Plymouth docks, bleak, grey and sinister.

The four Barrow players followed a sailor obediently through identical corridors, dragging shiny new suitcases behind them, alongside pipes, tubes and portholes through endless passages before arriving at a steel door with the number 81 painted at the top in large white letters.

Indomitable had slipped into Walney channel on March 3, 1940. The aircraft carrier weighed 23,000 tons, carried 1,700 sailors and 60 planes and was capable of a top speed of 32 knots — with a favourable wind. Of course they didn't know the technical specifications, only what their eyes and tired legs had already told them, that it was a big ship. Very big.

Captain Andrews held a welcoming party, where he told the non-nautical passengers the ship's immense dimensions — 754 feet long and 96 feet wide, he said, enough room to hold three rugby pitches.

During the sea journey players were to be paid 30 shillings (£1-50) a week, once ashore this would be increased to £2 10 shillings (£2-50). Cigarettes were 12/6 (62p) for 500 and, in an unusual act of generosity, tour administrators presented the squad with £10 each to help buy souvenirs for proud families expecting miniature Australian flags, postcards and photographs of their men patting kangaroos and holding cuddly koala bears.

5.30pm, Wednesday, April 3. The Indomitable left Plymouth harbour steaming south quickly passing the Channel Islands before darkness descended. It was the first night many of the passengers had spent at sea, under the stars, listening to the unnerving call of hungry gulls, watching the flashing lights of French fishing villages breaking the emptiness momentarily before disappearing into the void.

The carrier was alive with the babble of excited passengers – 2,000 Australian soldiers, 32 rugby league players and administrators and six Irish priests who were due to reveal an unlikely and wholly inappropriate reluctance to accept defeat in the games they were to share with their new sporting friends.

Back in cabin 81 the four Barrow players found themselves directly above the engine room, clanking with activity, driving vibrating propellers through the sea, pushing the carrier forward. The noise was loud and persistent and, combined with the constant lurching of the ship, it left the men seasick for days.

The Indomitable docked in Gibraltar on April 6, where passengers gorged themselves on oranges and bananas costing less than £1 for 100. Then on to Malta, Suez and Ceylon, the days all the same – training, playing cards, each evening the monotony broken watching flickering black and white films such as Brief Encounter and Scarlet Street.

The sailors organised a deck hockey tournament with Willie joining the Wigan Wallopers. Other teams were the Welsh Wizards, Cudworth's Cripples and the Tourist Terriers . . . Jimmy Lewthwaite, Bryn Knowelden, Arthur Bassett, Dai Jenkins, Bob Nicholson, Les White and journalist Eddie Waring.

The Irish priests, aptly named the Sky Pilots, proceeded to deliver passable imitations of Mafia hitmen as they tripped and blustered their way through the early rounds, only to lose a violent final to even more robust opponents in the shape of the Ship's Stokers.

The players were sunbathing every day now, the journey's time and the sun's relentless heat recorded in ever darkening skin. Bradford Northern winger Eric Batten was so brown everyone called him Abdul. Willie, too, was dark and healthy as the Indomitable arrived in Fremantle, Western Australia at 9am, Tuesday, April 30, behind them 27 days of unforgettable experiences.

Everyone had lost weight. But the players were in good spirits, anticipating the comparative luxury of a comfortable bed that awaited them in Sydney, four days sailing away. It would be wonderful they thought, to close their eyes and allow sleep to envelop them without hammocks swinging from the violent motion of an angry sea. They didn't know it then but their eventful journey was far from over.

An exhibition match was played between the Reds and the Whites to raise money for naval charities. Willie was stand-off half for the Reds who won 24-5. The result was not important but every player knew it was an early opportunity to impress captain Gus Risman who, it had been decided, would be in charge of team selection, in partnership with manager Walter Popplewell.

The match was low key, the tackling friendly and undemanding, and though it would be unwise to read too much into individual performances Willie was fresh and inventive, feeding rusty team-mates with accurate passes that impressed cigarette-smoking journalists, full of questions at the post-match interviews. Who was the unpredictable five-eighth buzzing round the field, they asked looking for a story for the Australian press.

The days drifted by, everyone wondering why there was a delay and when they would set off for Sydney. Willie and Jimmy Lewthwaite watched an Australian Rules match between Subiaco and East Fremantle; the next day they went to a trotting meeting at Gloucester Park. Back on the Indomitable bad news awaited them. The aircraft carrier was to return to the United Kingdom immediately. The party must travel across the continent by train, or rather by several trains – more than 2,600 miles across desert, wilderness and bush, stretching towards a distant horizon always so far away.

They assembled at Claremont station where everyone received tin cutlery, army-style, before boarding a troop train, already full, claustrophobic and suffocating. The train clanked and rattled ever eastward across the Nullabor Plain, the days unbearably hot, the nights unbearably cold, everyone sleeping in the clothes they wore, cramped in corridors and luggage racks. And always there were the swarming, biting flies.

At the gold mining town of Kalgoorie they were greeted by beer-drinking miners, their faces black, their bodies rippling with muscle, honed by the horrible work under the desert. There were more black faces at Port Pirie and Adelaide, where aborigines banged on the coaches selling trinkets, charms and cheap boomerangs.

The desert slipped behind them, the red sand turning brown before they passed through green countryside, wild and uncultivated. Another 500 miles to Melbourne, another sleepless night, another 500 miles, more stiffening muscles, then at last to Sydney, aching, exhausted and relieved, looking more like bearded, emaciated convicts than professional rugby league players.

Everyone headed for the Olympic Hotel before collapsing into a deep sleep they desperately needed. Willie shared a room with Jimmy Lewthwaite, Bryn Knowelden and Leeds scrum-half Dai Jenkins. The next day they slept late, surfacing for lunch, rejuvenated by a hot bath and a much-needed shave.

They were feeling better now. The nightmare journey had failed to weaken the players' will to defeat the Australians and answer the prayers of a nation huddled by crackling wireless sets 12,000 miles away. There was only one thing that mattered . . . bringing back the Ashes.

★ ★ ★

Daily training sessions soon breathed fresh life into tired bodies. For the first two days players attempted nothing more energetic than a jog around the field and a few simple stretches. Slowly the work got more taxing as the squad came to terms with the pitches that awaited them, hard as iron, baked under the Australian sun, ready to rip flesh from British bodies more familiar with the mud and rain of a European winter. It was like being tackled on concrete.

After the workout the squad split into two groups, forwards and backs, to gain familiarity, to get used to playing with each other's different styles, different ideas, thrown together from all parts of the country to take on the formidable Australians, regimented and predictable, but certain to be super-fit and frighteningly passionate. In the background always Popplewell marching up and down urging the defensive line to move up quickly and straight.

The halfbacks, threequarters, full backs and loose forwards stayed late to run through set pieces they hoped would fox the Australians who had a traditional weakness under the pressure of defending their own line against skilful players whose actions they could not predict, men such as Willie Horne and Ike Owens.

Scrum-half and vice-captain Tommy McCue took charge, collating suggestions from other players keen to contribute their own club's unique plans. He pieced them together and came up with four moves, to be called by number by the stand-off half whenever he felt the opponents' defence was liable to be breached.

Number one, to be used in the centre of the field, was a decoy run by the stand-off half, leaving the way clear for the full back to receive the ball and continue through a gap in the middle. The second was a slight variation; this time the outside centre was the receiver. The third move involved the stand-off half receiving the ball and preparing for a runaround with the inside centre. Then instead he passed to the full back, unmarked and in the open. In the final move of the Lions' box of tricks the winger cut inside the centre on the blindside to make the extra man.

At first the players were unco-ordinated, dropping passes and mistiming runs but each man quickly understood his role and when they were executed successfully, it made an imposing sight, seven or eight men darting around randomly, each one independent, but part of the whole, the ball placed beneath the sticks before bemused defenders knew what was happening.

The first match was at Junee, where the Tourists crushed Southern Districts 36-4. It was an awesome performance but Australia's coach Rick Johnston was arrogantly unimpressed. Puffing on a long, fat cigar he bragged to the press, through a blue haze, that he'd seen nothing to worry about.

"The Englishmen played a fast open game," he said. "But the opposition was terribly weak. I followed the match very closely and I saw nothing I did not know before. They played spectacular rugby but we'll see how they get on with those reverse and long passes when they play the Test match.

"They weren't tackled and they did as they liked. It is still too early to form an opinion and I admit they look a smart side. I think Australia can put a Test team together to win the Ashes."

Further results gave Australian supporters reassuring indications that the Tourists were far from invincible. The Lions were defeated, first by South Coasts, then Newcastle, fuelling patriotic flames of optimism. To add to the Lions' problems, the injury list was growing alarmingly. Wakefield Trinity loose forward Harry Murphy broke his collar bone after only 20 minutes rugby, Martin Ryan had a groin operation and was out for the rest of the tour, Trevor Foster suffered strained knee ligaments, Joey Jones a twisted ankle, Bob Nicholson caught the flu, Jimmy Lewthwaite had calf problems and Fred Hughes a sprained ankle. The Test side was now anybody's guess.

Willie had played well but so had Willie Davies, the Welsh stand-off half who had the advantage of playing for Bradford Northern, behind a dominant, threatening pack, massive forwards, like the men who stood on street corners when you were young, faces rough and unshaven, smoking cigarettes and growling at passers-by. That was the Bradford pack . . . ruthless and intimidating.

Willie had looked up to Davies, a more experienced man with a dazzling side-step as good, it was said, as any that had graced the game before him. Now that respect had turned to affection. They were close friends but Willie Horne had tasted the big time and he wanted that Test shirt badly. Willie had played for Lancashire. He had liked that. He'd played for England. He'd liked that too. This was different. A full Test appearance, against the old enemy. That was every player's dream.

CHAPTER ELEVEN

ASHES TO ASHES

IF AUSTRALIA can bottle-up Willie Horne at five-eighth our prospects in the Test match will be much brighter. This bottling-up process will, of course, be a great undertaking.

AUSTRALIAN WESTERN DAILY LEADER
Saturday, July 6, 1946

7.30pm, Sunday, June 16. The players sat in the Olympic Hotel lounge drinking orange juice, chatting, laughing nervously, the way one might behave before a dental appointment or a driving test. No one knew the Test side, least of all the Australian papers, who were reaching wildly differing conclusions on the likely line-up.

It didn't matter much now. They were about to find out. Walter Popplewell walked boldly into the room, clutching a piece of paper, Chamberlain-like, flanked by Gus Risman and Wilf Gabbatt a respectful distance behind. The players waited for the announcement, no one talking, each man concentrating on the three faces of stone before them.

Popplewell coughed slightly, catching his breath before reading out the names to a murmur of approval, pausing between each one as he stared over horn-rimmed spectacles. When loose forward Ike Owens was confirmed at number 13 everyone clapped, breaking the unsettling silence before shaking hands, the omitted players concealing personal disappointment to wish the team good luck.

"Well done, Willie," said Willie Davies, patting his young rival on the back. "You deserve it. I know you're going to have a great game." "Thanks very much," Willie Horne answered quietly, the responsibility of his selection sinking in slowly as a line of smiling faces waited to offer individual congratulations. He was glad Willie Davies had taken his exclusion so graciously. He had expected that.

That night sleep would not come to exorcise the ghost of self doubt that haunted him as he sat gazing out of the hotel window at the blanket of stars in the black Australian sky, the faint scent of freshly-cut grass drifting into his room. Willie closed his eyes and listened to the hum of droning insects and the repetitive snoring of other players apparently untroubled with thoughts of failure in the most important game of their lives now just a few short hours away.

★ ★ ★

The match was tense, action-packed and compelling entertainment for the 64,527 fans who packed Sydney Cricket Ground waving green and gold flags, yelling for the slaughter of the white-shirted Lions. The 8-8 draw left players drained and exhausted. It will forever be remembered for three reasons: the dismissal of British centre Jack Kitching, appalling goal-kicking and the devastating form of Willie Horne, Tommy McCue and Ike Owens.

Kitching was sent off after 28 minutes for punching Australian captain Joe Jorgensen. It was a nasty incident ending with Kitching led reluctantly from the field, holding his side and shaking his head as the crowd howled their support for the referee defying the agitated English and pointing to the dressing rooms.

At first it appeared Kitching had simply lost his head after being roughed up. But the next day newspapers published graphic pictures showing Kitching's angry face, a stubby finger pointing to a strange mark, brown indentations in the skin, as a small boy might leave a half-eaten apple. He had been bitten.

Jorgensen and Lions captain Gus Risman missed 13 goal kicks between them, some so close to the sticks a schoolboy would have been embarrassed at such dismal failures. Jorgensen was so upset he sat mournfully alone in the dressing room for more than ten minutes, still and thoughtful, before changing and telling journalists brave enough to inquire what had gone wrong: "My goal-kicking let Australia down. I have never had a worse day."

Willie, who scored the Lions' first try, had a marvellous Test debut, prowling behind his forwards, sending spiralling passes to hungry threequarters, missing men out, first to the open then to the blind, always inventive, never predictable, and so calm and graceful, as though he was doing nothing more difficult than waving to a friend across a crowded street.

When it was over a strange atmosphere hung over the Lions' dressing room as aching players seemed unsure what to do . . . whether to celebrate or commiserate. Risman thanked everyone for their courage and fortitude, handicapped as they were playing for more than 50 minutes a man down against such dogged opponents, united by the blind belief that honest endeavour and brutal power could achieve anything.

Above all, they looked forward to the Second Test with no fears or insecurity. If they won that they kept the Ashes. And that was why they were here.

★ ★ ★

Two days later the Tourists, patched up and weary, hammered Tamworth 61-5. Further victories against Widebay, Central Queensland and Mackay ensured they would not question the policy of open, thrilling and sometimes risky rugby. They all felt it would prevail against the crashing, lifeless tactics of Australians who preferred made-to-measure forwards bashing into defences who, they believed, were bound to buckle eventually. The Mackay result was a personal triumph for Jimmy Lewthwaite who scored seven tries in the 94–0 drubbing, with Ernest Ward's 17 goals also entering the record books.

The opposition for most of these country matches was weak and unchallenging but often teams contained a sprinkling of large, ambitious forwards hoping to make a name for themselves by intimidating the British players. Refereeing was, to put it charitably, weak. More significantly, it was biased. Sometimes the men with the whistle were so patriotic and partisan, matches finished with the Lions recording ludicrously high penalty counts while the home 13 managed to go through the entire 80 minutes without once prompting the angst of a referee seemingly blind to Australian offsides, late tackles and scrum infringements.

Usually the British had too much speed and guile to be caused anything but the mildest inconvenience. And with hard men like Ken Gee and Joe Egan monitoring challenges that might be construed as dangerous, the Tourists warmed up for the Second Test with a string of high-scoring walkovers.

Four days before the match the latest pile of post was delivered to the Olympic Hotel. Willie received his 206th letter, a record that colleagues saw as a good excuse for some harmless mickey-taking.

Back in his room he sorted the letters into sections — family, friends, neighbours, workmates and, finally the slanted writing he knew was from Bessie Irwin. They had been going together for more than two years when he was selected for the Tour. They had been in love for a long time but now, away from her, absence had strengthened his affection. Bessie, who lived in Marsh Street, was an office worker at North Lonsdale Hospital. Before her there had been other girlfriends, nothing serious, a walk home from a dance, a peck on the cheek, the occasional Sunday dinner, mums and dads asking endless questions about his rugby career. Most were like that, seeing his sporting talent first, his personality second. Bessie was different. She liked Willie because he was good, honest, trustworthy, hardworking, sincere, affectionate, generous, modest, reliable and loyal – not because he could run quickly and throw a leather ball about.

Willie kept his place in the Test side, though his selection was in no way remarkable. His form had been consistent and eye-catching, the weaker defences of the modest opposition were highly vulnerable to his jinking runs and accurate passing.

The Brisbane authorities were unprepared for the fever of expectancy that was gripping the city. Crowds began gathering at the Exhibition Ground at four in the morning, not just isolated groups of rugby league supporters but whole families, mums and dads carrying impatient children wearing green bobble hats, office workers, labourers, teachers, managers, men and women, young and old, united by a fierce obsession to witness what was certain to be a historic event when the rampant Kangaroos routed the Lions.

The gates opened at 7a.m. before closing four hours later, more than 60,000 supporters hemmed in, many more than was thought prudent. They spilled onto the field, forcing red-faced policemen wearing white shirts and sweating uncontrollably, to dart around clearing the playing area lest the kick-off be delayed.

They waited expectantly, glancing at watches, willing time to pass quickly, and for each minute that slipped by they grew more excited and steadfast in their support, the noise rising to a symphony of cheering, everyone yelling, producing a wall of sound designed to carry the team to victory on a deafening chorus of jingoism.

In the British dressing room the din washed over players busy tying boots, taping ankles and wrists and rubbing vaseline on knees reddened and cut from a 1,000 tackles on the concrete-hard pitches. Then the knock on the door signalling the kick-off was less than five minutes away. Captain Gus Risman shook everyone's hand as they lined up jogging on the spot, keeping loose, failing to quell the overwhelming nervousness and all the time hearing derisory jeers filter through. In the face of such remorseless, tribal hostility who wouldn't have felt intimidated, vulnerable and alone?

Out they went, Risman leading the line of men into the afternoon sun, hot and blinding, the crowd's taunts growing in volume as the players stood together preparing for the challenge before them.

The Australian players appeared to a simultaneous roar of approval. Willie had played before big crowds before but he'd never experienced anything like this. A few good-lucks from nervous team-mates and the two captains met in the middle of the field, the noise briefly subsiding.

Willie took a deep breath, rubbed his hands together and moved into position. It was almost time now.

★ ★ ★

Halifax winger Arthur Bassett dived over the Australian tryline for the third time at precisely 4.26pm on Saturday, July 6, before turning towards euphoric colleagues and raising his arms in celebration, acknowledging his personal triumph.

Bradford Northern centre Ernest Ward was the first to arrive, picking up the ball to prepare for an irrelevant kick at goal as Arthur jogged back to the Lions half to join the early celebrations of what was sure to be a long evening of collective backslapping and, for some, heavy drinking.

Great Britain were leading the Second Test 14–5. There was no time for the exhausted Australians to mount a comeback. With the First Test drawn the Ashes were safe. The Lions could not be beaten.

The Australian players were inconsolable, lined up in their green and gold shirts beneath the posts, dejected and weary. Some stared at the ground, others towards the blue sky as if seeking divine intervention to rescue them from humiliation in front of patriotic, vocal and soon to be deeply depressed home supporters. No one spoke. They had wanted to win so badly. Now it was all over.

High in the stands, typewriters clicked across white pages as dozens of international reporters put the finishing touches to match reports that would flash the news across the world. The newspapers that arrived on the doormats of English homes the following morning all told the same tale . . . the Aussies simply were not good enough. They offered power, industry, speed and an indestructible will to win but they lacked the sparkle and ingenuity of the Tourists, who, when it mattered, had been too clever in attack and too resolute in defence to contemplate defeat.

As Ward walked slowly back to take the kick, the crowd, who earlier, when the result was in doubt, had shouted and jeered, were now deathly silent realising the Ashes were irretrievably bound for Great Britain where they had been kept since 1922, the year Willie Horne had been born.

Ward's kick whistled wide. Seconds later the Australians were deep in their own half, weary forwards lumbering into a wall of white shirts, still determined their line would not be breached.

When Queensland referee Stephen Chambers blew his whistle to end the game British halfbacks Willie Horne and Tommy McCue embraced in communal admiration before joining loose forward Ike Owens and shaking hands, tired, bruised, proud and most of all honoured to maintain the Lions' 24-year domination their own efforts had done so much to secure.

And the Australians? Some marched petulantly to the dressing room, to bathe exhausted bodies and broken hearts, escape questioning reporters and the glare of morose supporters. Others congratulated their opponents. Stand-off half Pat Devery made a point of clasping Willie's hand firmly, powerfully, as a father might welcome a wounded son home from a bloody war.

"Well done, Willie," he said. "You played well and the best team won."
"Thanks Pat," Willie replied before trotting to the dressing room and into the history books as one of the most complete halfbacks Australia had ever seen.

★ ★ ★

That night the British party celebrated like never before, ecstatic and raucous. Rivers of free champagne were laid on by Western Suburbs Rugby League Club at Brisbane Town Hall. Not one Australian player turned up. The stress of failing their nation was, apparently, too much to take. They stayed in their own hotel, coming to terms with defeat privately, unwilling to watch the Britons drink themselves firstly to merriment then incomprehensibility and finally to the grinning stupor that comes to all drunks before exhaustion brings on a deep, contented sleep.

The next day Australian papers reported that top clubs were offering huge sums to entice the cream of Britain to stay for a lucrative few months. Frank Whitcombe, Martin Ryan, Ike Owens and Ernest Ward were among those ready to sign, it was claimed. Willie, the reports went on, was considered the star man. The Sydney club Newtown had reputedly offered him 300 dollars for a handful of matches.

Eventually reports subsided as Great Britain warmed up for the Final Test at Sydney with four comfortable victories against Brisbane, Ipswich, Toowoomba and North Coast.

After the euphoria of Brisbane, the Third Test was an anticlimax. Some Australians, acutely aware that the destination of the Ashes had already been decided, let frustration get the better of them. Arthur Clues was sent off and with full back Dave Parkinson breaking his leg after only seven minutes, the Lions' 20–7 victory was scant reward for the remaining 11 Kangaroos' brave defiance.

Willie and Pat Devery exchanged shirts as the British celebrated quietly behind them, without enthusiasm as if they had been drained of emotion by the drama at Brisbane. It was a tradition, changing shirts like that, one that Willie was happy to maintain. The Australian shirt was a nice memento, something tangible, something to give his mother. But losing that Lions shirt, grass-stained, soaking with his own sweat, a red number ten on its back, personal, unique . . . well, he'd rather have kept that.

Nine days later a Sunderland seaplane took off from Rose Bay, Sydney, carrying the Tour party on an eight-hour trip, 1,200 miles across the Tasman Sea to Auckland, New Zealand. The players enjoyed the pleasant drop in temperature and the encouraging feel of softer grounds. Long studs were inserted into boots with cheerful anticipation.

The Kiwis played spirited rugby winning the solitary Test 13–9 on a pitch so muddy and wet only the most biased home supporter could claim it should not have been postponed. The Lions were strangely lacklustre. Australia had taken too much out of them.

3pm, Wednesday, August 14. The New Zealand liner Rangitiki left the sanctuary of Wellington harbour and sailed into the Pacific Ocean. The tour had been a privileged experience for the tired players who waved goodbye, taking a kaleidoscope of memories with them . . . the friendship, the tough matches, the endless desert, red sand and spasmodic bushes, biased refereeing, hostile crowds, the fierce, burning sun and most of all the Test matches, violent, passionate and victorious. Now it was time to go home, time to be reunited with families.

The Rangitiki ploughed eastwards through turbulent waves, 300 miles a day, clocks turning forward a few minutes each night. Fred Hughes organised a sweepstake, participants attempting to predict the ship's daily progress, the winner taking the pot of 10 shillings (50p).

After 21 days the liner drifted through the Panama Canal before short refuelling stops at Curacao, a Dutch island in the Caribbean and Nova Scotia on the east coast of Canada. Then into the Atlantic, three more weeks, everyone thinking of loved ones waiting, counting the days slipping by slowly, until the outline of the English coast came into view on Sunday, September 23.

Passengers gazed at Hastings and Dungeness, leaning over railings for a clearer view, then they were gone, hidden behind the headland as the ship sailed through the English Channel, by Dover cliffs, white and magnificent, on and on, everyone excited now, up the Thames estuary, past ports and towns, preserved sailing ships clear against a welcoming background of green hills, long masts reaching to the sky, until at last they reached Tilbury Docks, bustling with sailors and dockers swarming along the quayside like colonies of ants.

Quick farewells, handshakes, sincere signs of friendship and respect, then they parted for different train stations, the final leg of the worldwide journey, behind them a 40,000-mile voyage and a nation still mourning the Test defeats and wondering what went wrong.

10.25pm, Monday, September 24. Home at last. Deputy Mayor Ald. Mrs Ward greeted the Barrow players at Central station, joined by other politicians, officials from Craven Park and a large crowd, joyous, welcoming smiles staring at the dark faces they had missed so badly.

Willie's family were all there of course – mum and dad, proud and happy, sisters and brothers cheering with all the others. Back at Corporation Terrace a large poster had been draped across the road: "Welcome home, Willie," it proclaimed, everyone in the street waiting, clapping hands enthusiastically, each one waiting in turn for a personal handshake and to pose a host of questions he was too tired to answer. But he did, with patience and without complaint.

The next night Wilf Gabbatt gave a moving speech at a town hall civic reception, paying tribute to the spectacular play, sportsmanship and impeccable manners the Barrow players had shown throughout the tour. "Willie was particularly popular with the Australian crowds," he said beaming with pride, talking to the hushed audience. "He played wonderful rugby on hard grounds, never shirking a tackle, no matter how heavy the opposition might be."

Barrow RL had made a mediocre start to the season, stripped as they were, of four star players. Willie and the others were welcomed back both as conquering heroes and timely saviours.

Another winter beckoned, more late tackles, more broad men with hate in their eyes. Only now it would be worse. Now he was the best stand-off half in the world. No question.

More than 10,000 supporters turned up at Craven Park the next Saturday, to be enthralled by Willie's dazzling display of evasive running and thundering tackles. Barrow beat Rochdale Hornets 30-19 with Willie scoring three tries, making the others and still finding time to kick two goals.

Business as usual.

Tommy Bradshaw, Wigan's superb scrum-half who partnered Willie in his first England international against Wales at Central Park, Wigan.

The England team when Willie made his international debut in the 18-8 victory over Wales in March 1945. Back: linesman, Willie Horne, Bryn Knowelden, Ernest Ward, Eric Batten, Tommy Bradshaw, Billy Belshaw, George Phillips (referee), linesman. Front: Albert Johnson, Bobby Ayres, Cyril Stansfield, George Brown, Joe Egan, Harry Wilkinson and Billy Hutchinson.

The 1946 Tourists at Barrow's Central station on Monday, April 1. Ahead lay a four-week sea voyage to the other side of the world. Joey Jones, Willie Horne, Jimmy Lewthwaite, Wilf Gabbatt, Bryn Knowelden and Fred Hughes.

101

The tour party aboard the Barrow-built aircraft carrier HMS Indomitable shortly before the ship sailed from Plymouth.

The Lions in training at Fremantle, Western Australia. Willie with Bryn Knowelden, Arthur Bassett and Albert Johnson.

Willie and Albert Johnson take a break in Fremantle joined by Tour Manager Wilf Gabbatt.

Great Britain crushed Southern Division 36-4 in the opening match of the 1946 Tour. Willie, who scored two tries, receives close attention as Trevor Foster looks on.

The Tourists stop for a meal at Callgooly, midway through their five-day train journey across the Australian continent.

Willie and Leeds loose-forward Ike Owens at Brisbane Zoo. Welshman Owens destroyed the Australians with his direct running and unpredictable distribution.

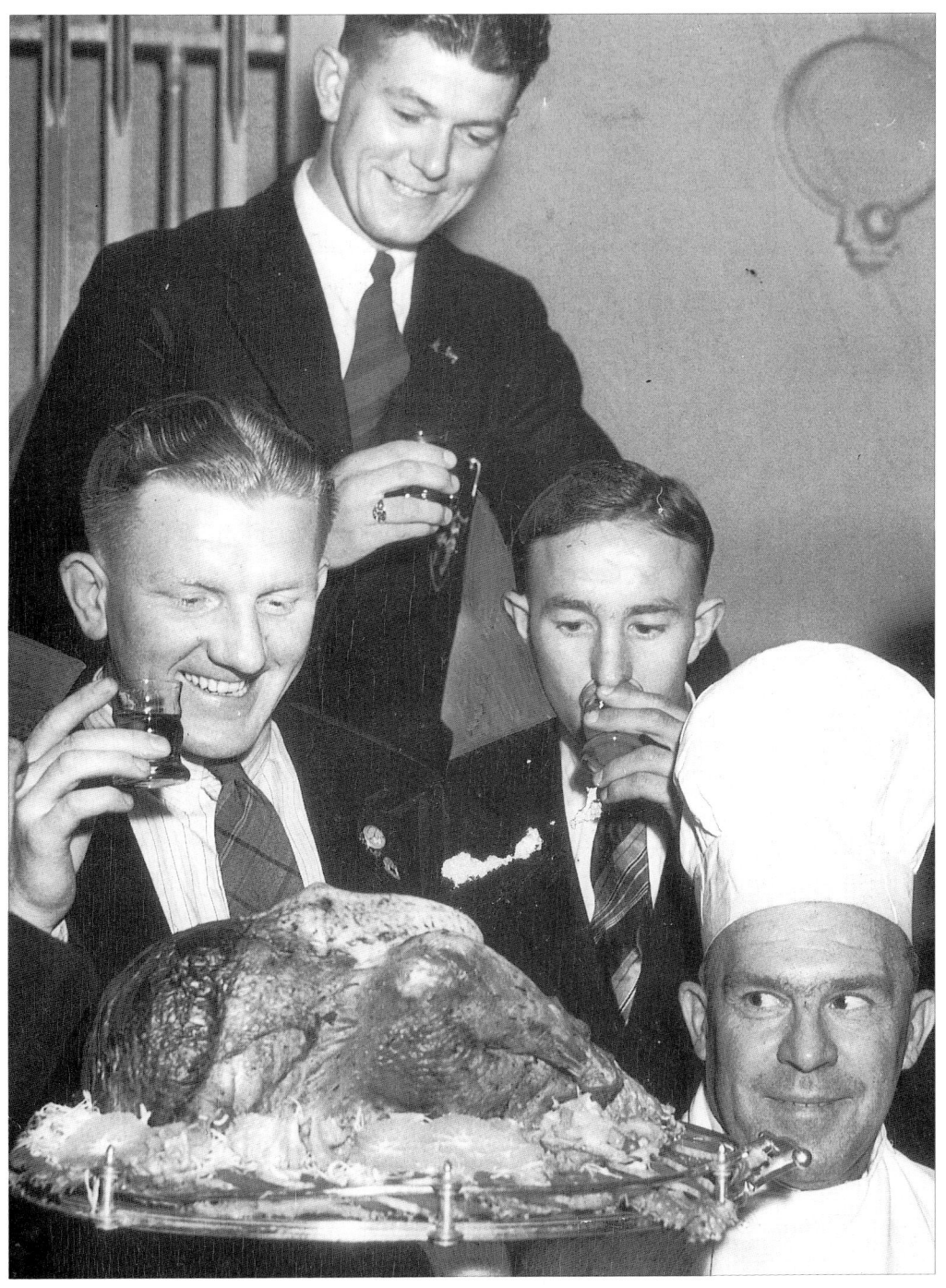

Bob Nicholson, Jimmy Lewthwaite and Willie can't wait to get their first taste of roast turkey since the start of the Second World War seven years earlier. The banquet was organised by Consolidated Press at the Australian Hotel, Sydney.

Willie, Bryn Knowelden, Joe Egan, Tommy McCue and Jimmy Lewthwaite join an Australian girl for a stroll around a cherry orchard in Orange.

The Tourists watch New South Wales v Queensland at Sydney Cricket Ground.

Willie evades Australian winger Edgar Newnham in the Second Test at Brisbane. The Tourists' 14-5 victory meant they could not lose the Ashes.

Balmain full back Dave Parkinson tries to clear the danger as Willie closes in during the Second Test which was watched by an unofficial crowd of more than 50,000.

Willie makes a break and looks around for support in the Brisbane Test.

Opposing stand-off halves Willie and Pat Devery. Pat, who later joined Huddersfield, swapped shirts with Willie after the Third Test at Sydney following the Tourists' 20–7 victory. The Indomitables are still the only British side to remain unbeaten in a Test series in Australia.

Walter Popplewell and the triumphant 1946 Tourists with the Ashes Cup at the City Tattersalls Club, Sydney.

Willie at a play-the-ball behind Warrington winger Albert Johnson during Great Britain's 9–7 victory against Auckland at Carlaw Park. Two weeks later the Lions lost the New Zealand Test 13–9.

The conquering heroes of the 1946 tour were welcomed home by hundreds of proud Barrovians at the town's Central station.

Willie was in big demand for autographs following his superb performances in Australia. A few weeks into the season the Barrow board were preparing to put him on the transfer list for a world record fee.

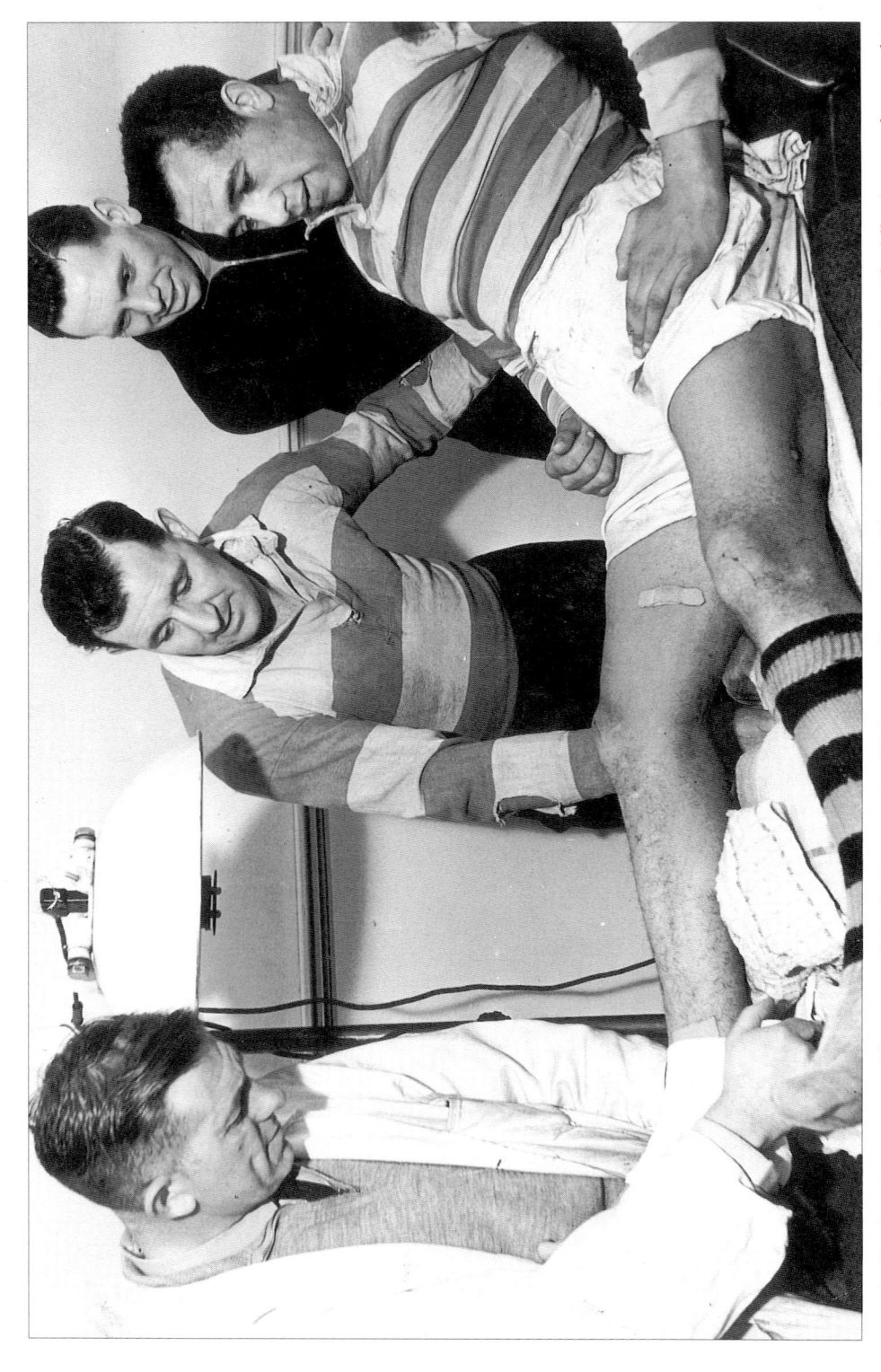

Maurice Hughes, the masseur with a great gift for healing, saved Willie's career after treating his ruptured achilles tendon. The following year he moved to Wigan RLFC. Here Maurice treats legendary winger Billy Boston as Great Britain centres Ted Ward and Ernie Ashcroft and look on.

CHAPTER TWELVE

HOME AND ABROAD

MOST rugby league men will agree that the best half-back combination England can muster today is Tommy McCue and Billy Horne. Both are masters of their craft and have earned international honours. Billy signed for Barrow in 1943 and in two seasons had made such a name that he was an obvious choice as an international. His tactics and style have made him England's number one out-half. He plays brainy and constructive football and the Craven Park club have had good occasion to realise their bargain. One of his greatest assets is an ability to sidestep an opponent and seize opportunities whenever and wherever they present themselves. He is well-known, yet Billy is an unassuming young man of 5 feet 8 inches, weighing about 11 stones.

NORTH WESTERN EVENING MAIL
October 2, 1947

TIME is not predictable, rhythmic and unchanging – not if you are watching a rugby league match. It moves at two opposing speeds, each dependent on the fortunes of your team. The more precarious the scoreline, the more pronounced the variation.

If your team is hanging on to a slender lead, defending their own line against powerful opponents threatening to overwhelm your men, who are tackling heroically with unwavering courage, time ticks by slowly. So slowly, when you look at your watch convinced at least five minutes have gone, hoping seven, the hands have barely moved and as your eyes return to the game the players appear to be running in slow motion like an action replay on Match of the Day.

Yet when you are behind and attacking, relentlessly seeking the winning score, time races away uncontrollably in great gulps, so quickly that if you dare glance around you there will be other supporters troubled by similar fears, shaking watches violently before holding them against disbelieving ears, convinced they must be broken. And again you'll stare at your watch, at the sweep of the second hand rushing towards the final whistle in the hope that your concentration can somehow control time, slow it down.

April 12, 1947 was such an afternoon. Barrow were playing mighty Wigan in a league match with close on 14,000 supporters squeezed into every corner of Craven Park straining for a clear view of the dramatic confrontation. Wigan were much as they are today . . . full of internationals, never unentertaining, always exciting and formidable. Barrow were a point behind after two goals by Wigan's Cec Mountford and a try by Johnny Lawrensen were followed by three Willie Horne goals bringing the game to a crescendo of expectation as the blue and white shirts poured forward.

There was less than a minute left as the home pack made a last, furious attempt to breach the defiant wall before them, driven on by Willie flicking passes left, then right, short, then long. Suddenly play halted and tired men shuffled into position. There was too much noise to hear the referee's whistle but the manner and direction of those movements told knowledgable eyes that Wigan had wandered offside giving Barrow a penalty kick wide on the right hand touchline.

Everything happened quickly now. Willie balanced the ball on the pitch, laces facing the posts where the referee stood surrounded by breathless Wigan players mumbling encouragement about the acute angle and the substantial distance. It's too hard they concluded . . . even for Willie Horne.

Willie walked backwards staring at the ball before looking up at the white sticks so far away he was leaning on the concrete wall that surrounded the playing field. A sea of hands brushed his sweat-stained shirt, human talismen, hushed and hopeful. This was Barrow's last chance. Everyone knew that.

Five long strides, a swish of the boot and away it went, drifting to the right at first, off line and to defeat before curving inwards and dropping sharply near the bar. It was touch and go. The crowd waited in silence, a moment's pause before the referee held up his hand confirming the two points. The kick was good. Barrow had won.

The two teams shook hands before leaving the field, Barrow skipping over the ground elated, victorious, Wigan dragging their feet, physically shattered by the game, mentally broken by the harrowing manner of their defeat.

Willie tried to ignore the adulation of euphoric fans, some moved to tears by the emotion of the previous few minutes, as he walked to the dressing room, unconcerned by the game's unlikely and thrilling conclusion. After all, he thought, that's why I get paid, to make tries, tackle and kick winning goals. Mind you, it's always good to beat Wigan.

★ ★ ★

Three weeks after the Tourists' spectacular reappearance in Barrow colours, secretary Mr Middleton left a crisis board meeting at Craven Park, grim and deliberate, the time well beyond midnight. When he arrived home the director pondered momentarily before telephoning the Evening Mail reporter known to the paper's readers as "Sentinel."

"Barrow Rugby League Club have an important statement to make," he told the journalist without apology, the words bereft of accent, as though they were strangers.

"Willie Horne, Bryn Knowelden, Jimmy Lewthwaite and Joey Jones have asked for an increase in playing wages," he went on as the reporter searched bleary-eyed for a pencil and notepaper, still half asleep. "The board offered very good terms. Lewthwaite and Jones accepted but Horne and Knowelden did not.

"As a consequence the board are considering placing Horne on the transfer list but the final decision has been delayed in the hope commonsense will prevail. Horne and Knowelden are not included in the team to play Liverpool Stanley on Saturday."

The next day, Wednesday, October 16, 1947, the Evening Mail reported the sensational news with typical brevity in small serif type commonly used to announce railway timetables . . . "**DEADLOCK AT CRAVEN PARK**" the headline stated dryly.

Two days later the entire playing staff pledged their support for the two internationals who were making the claim on behalf of all the Craven Park squad. Before the Tour, first team wages were £4 10 shillings (£4-50) for a home win, £2 10 shillings (£2-50) for a home draw or defeat, £5 for an away win or draw and £3 for an away defeat. The players wanted £6 for a win and £4 for a defeat plus moderate increases for the 'A' team which stood at 25 shillings (£1-25) for a win and 15 shillings (75p) for a defeat.

The board faced an awkward dilemma. Willie was one of the most exciting and gifted players in the world. They knew that and privately many directors were prepared to make an under the counter payment to their unsettled star in the mistaken belief that without Willie's involvement the dispute would fold. Even if they had made the offer it would have been respectfully refused. Willie and Knowelden were insisting everyone should profit from any revised terms.

Headlines barked across the national press with many papers speculating that the world record transfer fee would be smashed. Earlier that year full back Bill Davies moved from Huddersfield to Dewsbury for £1,650 but now that figure was under threat with knowledgeable writers predicting Barrow's asking fee would be a minimum of £2,000. Officially, the Craven Park board were denying any offers but several clubs had already been in touch, including Workington Town, Warrington, St. Helens and Hunslet who went public saying they had offered "a substantial fee."

Despite these dramatic events Willie was named in the Lancashire side to play Yorkshire the following week as the Barrow directors tried to pressure his colleagues by threatening to drop the entire first team squad unless they agreed to accept the revised offer.

Then, in an impressive show of solidarity, captain Jack Bowker said his players would not talk to the Press. Hours later, after another hasty board meeting, Middleton told waiting reporters that the first team had agreed to make the trip to Warrington, pending further discussion.

Three days later, Wednesday, October 30, it was over with neither the board nor the players publicly revealing the final settlement. The Evening Mail stated boldly "**HARMONY AT CRAVEN PARK**," leaving readers to decide for themselves the terms their heroes had settled for.

That night supporters across Furness toasted the health of the Barrow board grateful for the prudence of their decision to keep Willie at the club. It didn't matter to them how much it had cost. Whatever it was, he was worth it.

The 1947 season finished with Barrow in the top half of the table following a number of encouraging performances suggesting the long process to assemble a side capable of winning the Challenge Cup was off to a positive start. Scrum half Ted Toohey had been signed from Wigan for £1,000 and Dennis Goodwin, a huge centre threequarter from Walney ARLC, was a late season arrival amid quiet optimism that he had limitless potential. The two men were destined to play leading roles in Barrow's quest for greatness but for the moment they were just new faces overshadowed by Willie's customary dominance that was enthusiastically reported in the Evening Mail:

BARROW 8 LEIGH 0

At the outset I would like to pay tribute to Horne for the way in which he led the home side to victory and for his Trojan efforts in opening out the game and engineering Barrow's attacking moves. Horne and Francis made a brilliant pair.

MONDAY, JANUARY 13

BARROW 17 BELLE VUE 10

Horne played a grand game and had a great deal to do with Barrow's victory. Not only did he land four goals, one from near the halfway line, but he played with praiseworthy dash and engineered nearly all Barrow's brightest moves.

MONDAY, APRIL 18

The 1947-48 season began with the exciting announcement that Barrow were poised to sign Australian Harry Bath, Balmain's second-row forward, who had been selected for New South Wales many times. The players welcomed the news as further confirmation of the board's vigorous attempts to create an entertaining and successful side. But newspaper reports claimed Bath's £750 signing-on fee was coupled with a lucrative contract that guaranteed a weekly wage far higher than anyone else.

The squad were unsettled and bitter, despite repeated denials by a succession of pleading directors desperate to avoid another wages' row. "Bath will not receive a penny more than any other player," pledged chairman John Atkinson as the players' smouldering resentment slowly subsided.

On Wednesday, August 13, with the opening match against Salford less than three weeks away, Willie made his own headlines, though this time it had nothing to do with rugby league.

He was riding along Risedale Road on his secondhand 500cc BSA Gold Star with his girlfriend Bessie Irwin on the pillion, heading for the Coast Road. They enjoyed walking along the shore, holding hands and watching terns glide overhead before the chattering birds began their astonishing flight to Africa and the Antarctic. Willie was a safe driver who did not like going fast or taking chances. He overtook a corporation bus opposite the Pavilion Cinema as a daydreaming cyclist wandered into the main street from Roose Road. A moment later Willie, Bessie and the cyclist, Donald Cameron, a 24-year-old rugby supporter from Eskdale Avenue, were lying on the ground unconscious, surrounded by spinning wheels and shattered pieces of machinery.

Bessie and Willie awoke in adjacent beds at North Lonsdale Hospital. Bessie had nothing worse than mild shock and a black eye but Willie's collar bone was broken. Later that night they were sent home clutching bottles of aspirin and sick notes for the next four weeks.

Bath arrived in the United Kingdom on Thursday, October 2, sporting a six-inch gash above his left eye. The violent Bon Voyage inflicted by his compatriots in his final match was to delay his Barrow debut by more than a week. He was enthusiastic, fit and eager, quickly impressing his new colleagues in his first training session with his speed and the way he adapted to Barrow's moves and style of play.

Barrow supporters were delighted with the arrival of the 16-stone forward. After all, the team's mediocre start to the season had brought just three wins from nine games. On October 10, a crowd of 3,644 watched Bath make his debut in Barrow 'A's 21-18 victory defeat of Oldham. Alongside him Willie, now fully recovered, made an energetic return kicking a penalty goal in the first minute and dominating the game as you would expect from an international playing in second team football.

Willie was back in the first team the following week, continuing his sparkling displays, his courage and skill unaffected by the self-doubt that often haunts players recovering from broken bones. Physically they are strong but mentally, large forwards and gang tackling are experiences to avoid when the spirit is weak. Willie had always enjoyed the rigours of battle as much as the instant drop goal or the match winning pass. Now he was fit again and his determination to assist Barrow's stumbling attempts to produce a top team earned him two more England caps and a fourth Test appearance when Great Britain defeated New Zealand 25-9 in front of 42,680 fans at Odsal stadium. But the season that had promised so much ended empty and frustrating. Barrow finished near the foot of the table with the gloom darkening further when Willie missed the last few games after cracking bones in his back playing against St Helens.

Bath was transferred to Warrington following the arrival of his Australian girlfriend who was stricken with boredom after a few days in Furness. Long country walks, Cumberland mountains and sailing on Walney Channel did not appeal to a young woman who yearned for concerts, famous dance bands and the big-city atmosphere. Bath, who had played only 17 games for Barrow, was joined at Wilderspool by Bryn Knowelden who was replaced as Craven Park captain by Joey Jones. He was a popular choice with the players and supporters but Willie was already being mooted as a future skipper. His time would come.

In June Willie and Bessie were married at St George's Church. After a short Lake District honeymoon they returned to Dumfries Street, a comfortable row of terraced houses a short walk from the town centre.

Willie began the 1948-49 season with a string of masterful displays that earned him Test cap number five when Great Britain defeated Australia 23-21 at Headingley in a match described by most newspapers as the most thrilling in rugby league history. *"Fifty years hence the recital of this story will be a sore trial to bored grandchildren,"* Alfred Drewry wrote in the Yorkshire Post.

Barrow had their best season for many years finishing in the top four, spurred on by an average attendance of more than 10,000. The highlight of the year was the Challenge Cup third round match with Wigan at Craven Park. A gate of 21,900 watched Jimmy Lewthwaite score two outstanding tries after Barrow had finished the first half 7-0 down. Six minutes from time Willie kicked the winning penalty goal to propel the club into a semi-final date with Bradford Northern. But Barrow played poorly, missing out on a Wembley trip after an emphatic and dispirited 10-0 defeat at Station Road, Swinton. The Yorkshire Observer reported Willie posed the only threat to a Bradford side who overran off-form Barrow with internationals Willie Davies and Ernest Ward dominating the tie.

In October, 1949, an unknown winger scored two tries on his Barrow debut in the 21-3 win over Bradford Northern. Frank Castle was an instant favourite with the Craven Park fans, making the number five shirt his own for the next 11 years. Willie later described Castle as "the fastest rugby league player I have ever seen," and the former Coventry union star was to share in and contribute to Barrow's greatest triumphs, still a few years away.

The next season Barrow were inexplicably at the wrong end of the table and although Willie's reputation as one of the best number sixes in the world remained undisputed, the club plummeted to 20th in the league despite being supported by an average crowd of close on 11,000.

As the club drifted into mediocrity, Furness fans turned their attention to the impending Australian tour and the chances of Craven Park representation. In Barrow, everyone believed Willie was the best in the business. That was a result partly of civic pride and partly of informed opinion.

Yes, if you asked 100 rugby league supporters across the country who was the leading stand-off half the chances were that more than 90 would name Willie Horne. But history also taught them that athletic excellence had never been a guarantee of selection. Many times leading players who were considered Tour certainties missed out, their places taken by mediocre unknowns who, more often than not, went on to make isolated and unspectacular appearances for the Lions before returning home with a healthy sun tan and a priceless Tour cap their talents did not deserve.

In 1914 the best rugby league player in the world was Hull's dynamic centre-threequarter Billy Batten. Yet he was not chosen for the 1914 Tour and he was overlooked again in 1920. Sixteen years later Billy Belshaw would be the first name down for the 1936 trip to Australia. That's what all the papers were predicting with passionate harmony, opinions endorsed when the full back was transferred from Liverpool Stanley to Warrington for £1,450, then a world record fee. Again he missed out on the original party before being called up as a last-minute replacement when Jim Sullivan withdrew.

So no one in Furness was taking anything for granted. They mistrusted selection committees as aging middle-class businessmen making deals behind closed doors . . . "you pick my man and I'll pick yours." On March 2 the party was made public after a long meeting at the Palace Hotel, Birkdale, near Southport. Willie was in.

The news was no less sweet for the second time of asking. And it was received with great relief, coming as it did with Willie's hand still in plaster following a mistimed tackle against Featherstone Rovers in February. He was to play just one more match before boarding the Himalaya for the four week voyage to the other side of the world. Two days after arriving in Fremantle the Lions defeated Western Australia 87-4, with Wigan winger Jack Hilton scoring seven tries.

Five weeks and nine unbeaten matches later the Lions kicked off against Central Queensland with Willie at stand-off half. He had much to think about. He sensed a good performance might earn him a place for the Test match, now barely a week away.

Ninety minutes later he couldn't walk. His Tour was over. All he would bring back from Australia were broken dreams, a well-used stick and the gloomy prognoses of perplexed doctors.

He might never play again.

CHAPTER THIRTEEN

ACHILLES HEEL

IT ALL HAPPENED about 15 years ago when I hurt my knee at work. I didn't think much of it at the time but the following day I couldn't walk. I went to the hospital where a specialist said there was nothing he could do to help me. He said it was wear and tear and it might get better in time but a bad knee was something I was going to have to live with. He gave me two walking sticks and sent me home.

Four weeks later, when I still couldn't walk, my wife suggested I try Maurice Hughes. I hobbled in on my sticks and sat on his treatment table. He flexed and pulled my knee, first one way, then the other, saying something about a trapped cartilage. After a couple of minutes he told me he had put it right and that I was OK. Of course, I didn't believe him, but when I got off the table and walked around the room it was as though there had never been anything wrong. I left my sticks at his house and I've never had any trouble with the knee since. It was like a miracle.

PERCY YATES
Furnace Place, Askam-in-Furness, August 1993

IT HAD been a good afternoon's work, thought Willie, catching the ball tossed gently his way by winking Lions' winger Tommy Danby as he trotted towards the halfway line. Tommy had just scored his fifth try and, like most of the other 17 tries the Tourists had recorded, it had been created by the magical skills of a stand-off half from Barrow-in-Furness.

Willie's dominance had been so emphatic, his partnership with scrum-half Tommy Bradshaw so productive that the Central Queensland threequarters were given to ambling around the field wearing the dejected look of criminals embarking on long-term prison sentences. They had accepted the futility of trying to analyse or anticipate where Willie was going and what he would do when he got there. So they had given up.

The opposition had been inept and embarrassingly keen to accept the inevitability of defeat. The forwards were too big and too slow, the backs too small and too predictable, but nevertheless Willie's own performance had been so faultless, in attack and defence, he hoped it would be enough to earn his place in the Test team for the forthcoming international at Brisbane, now less than a week away.

The Lions had won the First Test at Sydney 6-4 with two tries from Wigan winger Jack Hilton. Heavy rain had made the pitch a mud heap that reduced the British backs' superiority in speed and imaginative handling. But the close result had encouraged patriotic papers to claim that the British were weak and lacking the spirit needed to hold onto the Ashes. They were there for the taking, it was said as Australians prepared for the confrontation with the same fervour that possessed them when they fought hordes of Japanese fanatics pointing bloody bayonets their way six years earlier.

Willie placed the ball casually in front of the sticks but before he could register his tenth successful conversion that afternoon a loud buzzer echoed across the ground. It was a familiar noise, not unlike the shipyard buzzer that told Vickers workers when to start, when to brew up and when to turn off their lathes and head for home. Willie knew it signalled the end of the match and that under international rules he was allowed that final kick at goal. He took one step forward, tapped the ball a couple of inches and shoved it under his shirt, simultaneously turning towards the touchline where the rest of the team were already standing pouring cold water over red legs and drinking glasses of orange juice to quench the awful thirst brought on by the scorching heat.

It was an unwritten rule among the players that whoever had possession of the ball at the end of the game kept it to take home as a souvenir of the trip. His mother would be delighted with that ball, Willie thought as he struggled to pull off his shirt before throwing it on top of a mounting pile of sweaty kit in the centre of the dressing room. Around him naked men wandered around boldly, the hiss of gushing showers audible above the excited chatter. Then he took off his boots.

His right heel was swollen, the skin red and inflamed. And it had started hurting, not badly at first, more like the dull pain that precedes toothache or a mild migraine. But it was getting worse and when he tried to walk to the showers the ankle gave way beneath him.

On the bus journey to the hotel Willie went over the game methodically, searching for an incident that could have caused the injury, as one might look back over a misplayed hand of whist, with regret and annoyance. But he could find no explanation for the fierce pain that was now shooting up his leg.

Tour manager Tom Spedding sent for a physiotherapist that night. A torn Achilles tendon was diagnosed. There was no treatment, he said. Rest was the only cure. It was a career-threatening injury, thankfully very rare. Your tour is over, he was told. As for the chances of a complete recovery . . . touch and go.

So Willie hobbled his way around Australia, the pain in his ankle equalled by the pain of defeat as he watched the Tourists, robbed of his services, lose the Ashes they had held since 1922. Willie had been in the Lions' dressing room in Sydney four years before, drinking champagne, slapping backs and shaking hands, basking in the thrill of victory. Now he was forced to witness different emotions, tired, forlorn expressions on gaunt faces, the empty silence of strangers who had become friends united in common purpose, whose dream had been shattered. To make matters worse, just a few feet away Australian voices were raised in celebration as the team toasted their historic victory. Great Britain went on to lose both Test matches against New Zealand too.

The next chance to beat the Australians would be two years later when the Kangaroos toured the United Kingdom. All Willie could think about as the Mataroa steamed home was regaining his place in the side and getting back those Ashes. But first he had to get better.

★ ★ ★

Maurice Hughes had always sensed, deep down, that he had been born with a unique gift, an extraordinary skill that could not be learned from textbooks or college courses. He was as much faith healer as qualified masseur. Not that he didn't have an alphabet of initials after his name and an exhaustive knowledge of muscles, bones, ligaments and joints. There was something else he could rely on when science failed to provide the answer. Maurice knew instinctively what was wrong and how to put it right. He never questioned where his powers came from or how they worked. All that mattered was that he did not waste them.

There was nothing in his childhood or family history that suggested he might pursue a career in medicine. Maurice was born on November 24, 1908, at 21 Smeaton Street, a small terraced house close to Barrow town centre. His parents were humble, working-class people who looked no further than where the next meal was coming from. Fourteen years later Maurice began an apprenticeship as a Vickers shipwright, a precision trade that involved building ships' hulls in wood and steel. He was a tall, muscular man who played moderately well as a front-row forward for St. Matthew's Rugby League Club. Maurice was reliable and hardworking, the sort of player everyone respected, though he lacked the power and pace to become a professional. He had large hands, so big it was said he could hold two pints of beer in each palm and cross a crowded dance floor without spilling a drop.

Maurice's life was mapped out before him like other young men born in Furness. He would walk across Michaelson Road bridge to the shipyard for nine hours honest work each day, earning enough to get married, rent a house, raise a family, enjoy a night out at the pictures and the odd pint of beer. It was all so predictable.

Then Maurice began to heal people. Nothing too grand at first, sprained ankles and sore backs, but the manner of his patients' recovery and the gratitude they showed spurred him on to learn more. He became friendly with an orthopaedic surgeon from Liverpool. Maurice continued working at the shipyard but most weekends he travelled to Merseyside to watch the doctor and learn from the way he examined patients and his analytical method of treatment. Maurice qualified as a masseur in 1932, though it would be many years before an overflowing waiting room finally forced him to down tools and wear his white, starched coat permanently.

During the uncertain years of World War Two Maurice spent his spare time at North Lonsdale Hospital, helping overworked doctors deal with victims of the German Luftwaffe. It was bloody and stressful, but all the time he was developing his instinctive feel for how the human body worked and what made it better.

Maurice did not specialise as most masseurs did. He never turned anyone away, whatever the problem, wherever the pain. But it was sporting injuries he enjoyed healing the most. He found it refreshing and invigorating when a young man limped into his Hartington Street surgery, frightened and confused then walked out confidently a few minutes later, mumbling a hurried thank you before rushing off to tell friends that he would be playing at the weekend after all. Maurice refused to cash in on his gifts, charging everyone 2/6 (12p) regardless of time or cost of materials. And they kept on coming . . . young and old, with bad ankles and knees, backs and necks, hips and elbows. Furness sportsmen associated doctors with walking sticks, operations and sick-notes. When they spoke of Maurice they talked of bandages, caressing hands and quick recovery.

Maurice joined the Craven Park staff in 1948 where he was an immediate success, known for his dedication and patience. His abilities as a masseur were accepted without question. Maurice was a popular man who adapted easily to the bawdy atmosphere of a rugby league dressing room. Everyone liked him as much for his charm and sincerity as for his amazing gift for healing. He had read newspaper reports about Willie's ruptured Achilles heel. Experience told him it was unwise to dismiss those reports as dramatic speculation. It was a serious injury that was never guaranteed to respond to treatment.

Barrow RL's directors had bought players wisely, producing an air of expectancy in the town, an optimism that an outstanding team was taking shape, a team with the skills and enthusiasm to win the Rugby League Challenge Cup. Barrow RL were on the brink of greatness.

But what if Willie's career was over? Barrow were never the same without him, as though his presence was so overwhelming, other players were incapable of overcoming the handicap of his absence.

The future of the club lay in the large hands of a tall shipwright in Hartington Street.

★ ★ ★

Willie stepped off the 7.16 from London Euston and walked through the billowing clouds of steam to a hero's welcome. He had expected a large welcoming party after what had happened in 1946. But not this. They had lost the Ashes and instead of moving confidently across the platform towards a proud family elated by his arrival he was limping noticeably, even though the injury was now nine weeks old.

Bessie was carrying their 15-month-old daughter Brenda, who dutifully kissed her father before the trio boarded a taxi to speed home to Dumfries

Street to unpack and enable Willie to recover from his five-week journey.

The heel had improved dramatically in appearance. The swelling had gone and to the naked eye there was nothing wrong. But Willie had worrying fears that his career might be over. The heel was sore to touch and anything more taxing than a light jog was difficult and painful. As for sidesteps and sudden turns – not a chance.

He had missed an eventful start to the season. Barrow could manage only three wins from their opening nine matches. It was time for a change. Despite being on the injured list Willie was appointed club captain, replacing Joe Jones, who was quickly put on the transfer list after the full back had intimated he might return to his native Wales.

Directors had tried to entice Trevor Foster from Bradford Northern, a bold invitation that failed only at the eleventh hour when the Yorkshire club realised how much the loss of the international forward would scupper their own hopes for success. It was planned for Foster to take control of Barrow's first team as player-coach and though directors were naturally disappointed, further, more successful, moves into the transfer market followed.

Second-row forward Jack Grundy was signed from St. Helens for £1,000 and Phil Jackson, an 18-year-old centre threequarter, joined the club from Vickers Rugby Union. Barrow hit the national headlines when they swooped for Hugh Lloyd-Davies, the Welsh international full back who was thought to be the first Cambridge Blue to play professional rugby league. After just one game he disappeared amid rumours that he had gone to live in London. Although Lloyd-Davies returned briefly to play four more matches, he soon vanished yet again – along with his £1,000 signing-on fee.

The directors' tireless efforts to create a winning line-up did not trouble Willie. He was more concerned with saving his own career. And that meant seeing Maurice Hughes.

CHAPTER FOURTEEN

SKIPPER

EVERYONE in Barrow was talking about Willie's injury in Australia. Thinking he was going to miss the start of the season was a big worry, especially at Craven Park. Willie was the inspiration behind Barrow. We had plenty of great players but we were nothing without him. He made us all.

If he passed the ball and it was a yard in front or above we let it go. It would have been meant for the next person in the line. That's how accurate he was. I played with a few good stand-off halves but no one was in the same class as Willie. He was a complete player who had everything, kicking, passing, tackling. He had the lot. And, of course, he was such a marvellous person.

So all this talk of him having a bad injury was unsettling as you would expect. After all, as far as the rest of the Barrow players and myself were concerned, he was the greatest player in the world. That's how highly we thought of him.

DENNIS GOODWIN
Centre threequarter (Barrow, Lancashire, England & Great Britain)
1947 to 1964

WILLIE had been on Maurice's table many times, closing his eyes while gentle, educated hands eased the pain from sore muscles and aching joints. He trusted Maurice and his method of healing. So he felt irrationally optimistic as he was ushered into the front room, smelling as it always did of sweat and wintergreen. It didn't look much, not compared with the gleaming hospitals and surgeries of Australia. He watched Maurice putting on his white coat, framed by a dozen diplomas, long lines of mysterious letters, imposing and comforting, red ribbon hanging down over colourful maps of the human body. In a corner, a large lamp as high as a tall man stood, begging to be used.

"Let's have a look at you," said Maurice as Willie took off his shoes and socks. Maurice began applying olive oil, softly at first, feeling his way, searching for scar tissue and burst vessels. Willie had expected to feel pain but there was none, only a pleasant, numbing sensation as Maurice massaged the heel, his face flushed with effort. He began describing what was wrong and why the injury had taken so long to get better, speaking confidently in a reassuring voice explaining how he planned to treat it. After 20 minutes Maurice cleaned off the oil and strapped the ankle tightly but not so as to cause discomfort and rigidity.

"Come back tomorrow," he said as Willie forced his shoe over the bulging bandage. "We'll have you playing again within a month."

Already the ankle felt less painful. The strapping gave it a strength he had not felt before when applied by other, less skilful masseurs. Four times a week Willie visited Maurice for treatment. Each time the injury felt better. This would be no instant recovery but a gradual improvement, accompanied by an encouraging resumption of light training and a slow, noticeable return of the quicksilver speed and agility.

The directors had wisely resisted the temptation to interfere and hasten his return to the team. They wanted him back but not until he was ready, not until Maurice said it was time.

On Monday, October 2, 1950, Maurice Hughes made the announcement all of Barrow had been waiting for weeks to hear. "Willie's ready," he told club chairman John Atkinson. "He can play in the next match against Liverpool Stanley." The following Saturday a crowd of 9,221 watched Willie fulfil a childhood dream when he led Barrow onto the field at Craven Park. It was a proud moment, the blue and white line of expectant players trotting a respectful distance behind their new skipper, his face straight and serious, failing to mask the uncertainty, the fear, the doubts. Would his ankle hold up and if his team would respond to his leadership.

Competitiveness glowed in him. Before, when others had been official captains, Willie was the leader. He was respected, followed and obeyed by the players, whose admiration was subtle yet unmistakeable. His enthusiasm was infectious, his energy and spirit easily conveyed to others. Willie appeared impervious to adversity, reacting to the highs and lows of life with a fateful shake of the head, never shouting, always calm, encouraging others with sensitivity and understanding. Yet he could be forceful, demanding and unforgiving if he felt players had let the team down by being lazy or irresponsible. They did what he told them or the following week they would find themselves in the 'A' team.

Being captain was something Willie had wanted for a very long time, not out of conceit but because he sensed it was a job he could do well. It felt good, as he knew it would, and that elation was so pronounced it had not been surpassed by Australian tours or international call-ups. Willie was the star player, someone whom it was said was incapable of playing badly. Now it was time to see if he could inspire others. The team was ready; the town was ready. The rest was up to him.

★ ★ ★

Barrow were dramatically inconsistent in the 1950-51 season. Supporters were often drained of emotion after watching a magnificent display full of flowing rugby and brave commitment, only to be rendered despondent and gloomy a few days later after an inexplicable defeat by a moderate side. Barrow beat great teams such as Leigh, Workington and Hunslet then somehow managed to lose against the likes of York and Rochdale Hornets – basement clubs with mediocre players offering nothing more threatening than endeavour and team spirit.

Barrow saved their best for the Challenge Cup, carrying Furness with them in a magical trip to the Wembley final. The opening round was an undemanding win over the Welshmen of Llanelli, setting up a second round derby tie with Workington Town, a young team propelled into the top flight by the mercurial talents of captain and coach Gus Risman and an ambitious board of directors generously supplying him with handfuls of cash to buy success. Craven Park was bursting with 21,389 fans who watched Barrow come out on top 12-5 with tries from Frank Castle and Hughie McGregor and a penalty and two drop goals from Willie.

Another 21,000 crowd saw Barrow defeat Bradford Northern 5-4 with Evening Mail headlines proclaiming **"HORNE AGAIN HERO OF CUP WIN"** after he had kicked a late penalty goal to earn the club a semi-final date with Leeds, the league's wealthiest club. Another huge attendance of 57,729 was enthralled by one of the most exciting cup games in history. Leeds held a two-point lead with two minutes left when full back Harry Stretch forced a replay with a wonderful touchline goal, tying the score 14-14.

The Leeds players were visibly shaken by Barrow's unlikely comeback. They shuffled off the Odsal field in small, bemused groups, their energy lessening with every step as though that late penalty had sentenced them to inevitable defeat in the replay. And while the Yorkshiremen tried unsuccessfully to recover their composure, the Barrow players headed towards their supporters, bristling with confidence, each man applauding the intense, vocal support they had fed off when all looked lost. For the Barrow fans the trip to Wembley was beginning to appear a formality.

Barrow's cup fever was heightened by the fact that the club occupied such a low league position. The replay was at Fartown, Huddersfield, the following Wednesday, kick-off 5.30pm. Lakeland Laundries gave their workforce the afternoon off with the Steelworks allowing its workers an early finishing time as thousands of supporters made plans for the cross-Pennine trip for the match everyone wanted to see.

Leeds were disorganised in attack and careless in defence, while an unstoppable power emanated from every Barrow player. Willie's side won 28-13, but even that comfortable scoreline did not accurately reflect their dominance. The Evening Mail reported: "We were complete masters, superior in every department."

The Barrow squad arrived at Central station at 1.20am – 82 minutes late. But the town was far from asleep as thousands waited patiently to greet their conquering heroes. The Evening Mail reported: "The noise defied description with wild, excited supporters waving rattles, blowing bugles and cheering madly until the police were able to get their favourites away."

There is a picture in this book of Barrow-born referee John Jackson shaking hands with Willie, surrounded by his team, everyone smiling. John, too, was delighted with the team's advancement to the final, although Barrow's presence meant he would not be in charge at Wembley stadium. It is a tradition, some say a foolish one, that referees are not placed in control of matches involving teams representing the town of their birth. Sadly John did not go on to earn the ultimate honour, despite his reputation for excellence.

Two weeks later the Barrow players were enjoying a taste of the good life at Gilston Park Country Club, an Elizabethan manor house in the Essex countryside, preparing to face cup favourites Wigan in the Wembley final. Again Furness responded with 14 trains pulling 132 coaches packed with supporters leading the exodus to the capital. At 2.30pm on Saturday, May 5, more than 12,000 Barrow fans stood shoulder to shoulder, praying that Willie would once again weave his magic and inspire the team to the ultimate victory.

The game had been billed in the national press as a David and Goliath confrontation, a description that did not unsettle the preparations of the Craven Park men, still euphoric after their semi-final triumph. But Barrow proved strangely off-form, unable to overcome the considerable handicap of losing scrum possession time and time again to Wigan's wily international hooker Joe Egan. Starved of the ball, they could not prevent Wigan winning the cup 10-0 in a dour, lifeless match devoid of flowing rugby.

Barrow had not been expected to win. And though each player had performed with admirable effort they were not good enough to take on the best side money could buy, a team boasting no fewer than nine internationals. The final had come too soon. Barrow had not been ready. Not yet. The after-match dressing room scene was like any other in the shadow of defeat – unopened bottles of champagne, grey faces at regrets of what might have been.

Back in Furness the next day an open-top bus took the team around the streets of Ulverston and Dalton before slowing along Barrow's tree-lined Abbey Road, flanked with flag-waving children and men and women wearing blue and white scarves under the lengthening shadows of elm and sycamore. Willie acknowledged the tributes respectfully but when he looked into the fans' faces he saw disappointment not celebration, sadness not jubilation. At a town hall civic dinner Mayor Ald. Winn welcomed the party among small-talk about how they would win next year and what a commendable achievement it had been to reach Wembley. International scrum-half Ted Toohey delighted the crowd with a tuneful rendition of Silver Dollar while an exhausted policeman was quoted in the Evening Mail as saying: "If a Barrow team ever comes back with the cup they will have to barricade the town hall." All Willie wanted to do was go home and forget the lost hopes of a community that had wanted to win the cup so badly.

The following year saw another season of unfulfilled expectation. Barrow feared no one but they lacked the consistency to press for the league title, finishing nine places behind champions Bradford Northern. In the Challenge Cup there was more heartache when Willie's men lost a semi-final against Workington Town 5-2 in a heated match full of controversy. Prop forward John Pearson scored a late try for Barrow but it was disallowed by the referee, a decision photographs later cast considerable doubt upon.

Willie began the following season playing brilliantly, regaining his place in the Lancashire side as captain. He finished as the league's top scorer with 313 points, eight ahead of Joe Phillips from Bradford Northern. Willie's total smashed the Barrow record, previously held by Fred French with 190 points in 1937-38.

The record meant little to Willie. He was driven by thoughts of helping his country regain the Ashes he had watched wrestled from Great Britain's grip by passionate Australians while he leaned helplessly on a walking stick at Sydney Cricket Ground two years before. He was desperate to get back in the Test side. This time Willie was fit and eager, his efforts concentrated on one, overpowering thought. The Kangaroos were coming.

★ ★ ★

Barrow began the 1952-53 season with a heartening run of victories that suggested the club was at last beginning to jettison their unwelcome reputation for inconsistency. Leeds, Wigan and Hull Kingston Rovers were defeated as the pack, led magnificently by Hughie McGregor and Jack Grundy, reliably provided Barrow's dazzling backs with plentiful possession they enthusiastically turned into an avalanche of points.

Meanwhile, Britain awaited the arrival of the eighth Kangaroos, making the 13,000-mile journey on the Barrow-built Strathnaver, smarting from a crescendo of cruel criticism on the back of an inept display against New Zealand.

The Kiwis had crushed Australia in both Tests, running in 49 points in the second match, a game which left Sydney journalist Jim Mathers echoing a country's shame when he wrote: "Australia were spineless and demoralised, the players crushed and defeated. They shamed the men who selected them. This was not only the worst defeat in Test history, it was surely the worst-ever effort by an Australian side."

The 1952 tourists contained 21 players from New South Wales and seven Queenslanders but there were those who said better men had been left behind, that the Kangaroos could not recover from the New Zealand debacle and the Ashes, recovered so emphatically in 1950, would soon be back in British hands.

But five weeks together on the long sea voyage had allowed the players time to nurture an energetic spirit, everyone vowing to regain the country's honour amid nightly bouts of patriotic singing that meant everything to the Australians . . . Waltzing Matilda and My Mabel Waits For Me.

Captain and full back Clive Churchill sensed the communion of purpose, and wisely cultivated the power emanating from the party. He was one of the world's leading players, someone everyone looked up to. They did not want to let Churchill down or misplace the trust placed on them by nervous selectors desperate to drive away the Kiwi demons still dancing painfully on a nation's grave.

The Kangaroos quickly banished the myth of mediocrity, criss-crossing the Pennines to run in tries effortlessly with a brutal combination of fearless defence and fast, open rugby. Keighley, Hull and Barrow were hammered as the Tourists ran in 106 points in the three matches, without a hint of a try being scored against them, dominating arrogantly, remorselessly and showing a cruel lack of respect that bordered on conceit. But there was a price to pay, one that did not trouble the consciences of players or officials.

The Tourists were rough, even dirty, it was said. After each match dazed Englishmen limped off the field as partisan crowds spat out abuse. But the green and gold machine rolled on. Willie missed Australia's match against Barrow when he failed a late fitness test on a badly sprained ankle. He was forced to watch his team crushed 26-2, the 16,044 crowd wincing as the Kangaroos dominated absolutely. But again late tackles and merciless defence tarnished the result. The Evening Mail was full of angry letters, with Brian Boast of Dalton summing up the town's fury, when he wrote: "May I express my disgust at the exhibition given by the Australians. The forwards employed the worst tactics I have ever seen. I have always been under the impression touring teams were ambassadors of goodwill chosen not for ability alone but also for fair play. It seems I was wrong."

Whitehaven, Halifax and Wigan were dispatched with no let-up in the vicious tactics. And each win made any modification of belligerence less likely. The Australians were not here to win friends and enhance Australian-Anglo relationships. They simply did not like getting beaten – especially by Englishmen. Retaining the Ashes was all that mattered. That was the only reason they were here, laughing in the faces of those doubting supporters back home.

On Thursday, September 5, Willie Horne was named England captain for the forthcoming international against Wales at Central Park, the selectors simultaneously announcing that the Great Britain side would be picked the following day. Willie was understandably delighted but unsettled when he read newspaper predictions that his appointment for the Test match was automatic barring a disaster against the Welsh.

Play it safe, he was told. Don't take any chances – cautious advice he was incapable of following even if he had wanted to. Willie liked to take risks – that was part of his daunting talent. So he played the same as always, as if the pressures of leading his country were no greater than turning out for Risedale Old Boys on Holbeck Park in front of a few dozen cloth-capped supporters all those years ago. The effect was the same. Willie was heroic in defence, flamboyant and inspiring in attack, sprinkling spinning passes to busy threequarters and willing forwards hungry to impress watching selectors. He made two tries for Alf Burnell and one for Charlie Pawsey as the English swamped the Welshmen 19-8.

The next day selector Gideon Shaw announced the Great Britain team to take on the Australians. As expected Willie was skipper with Barrow further honoured with the inclusion of winger Frank Castle and scrum-half Ted Toohey. There was a worrying apprehension in the response from the British media who collectively labelled the side "experimental," questioning the forwards' capacity to withstand the perpetual bombardment expected from the Australian six. Bookies rated the Kangaroos five points better. But these bleak predictions did not affect the British players as they readied themselves for the challenge before them.

The squad met on Wednesday at Castleford, running through moves and set pieces, taking time off to watch the Australians humble Featherstone Rovers 50-15, a game that was a personal triumph for Toowoomba winger Des McGovern who ran in six tries. And the side that demolished Rovers was very much a second-string outfit, with only three players having previous Test experience. Rovers were a typical Yorkshire team with courageous forwards and capable backs, yet they had been smashed easily, without remorse as a bored child might throw away an old toy. How on earth could Great Britain hope to quell the Australians' unquenchable thirst for domination?

Leeds winger Drew Turnbull withdrew from the British squad as the big match approached, his place taken by Halifax's Arthur Daniels. On Friday night the Australians rejected an invitation to attend Pontefract races, unwilling to distract players' concentration from the task ahead. The British party had one final low-key training session before a light evening meal, a team talk and the traditional early night. Outside their hotel bedrooms Leeds police implemented town centre traffic restrictions designed to cope with the expected influx of thousands of supporters.

It was the game everyone wanted to see. The BBC television cameras would be at Headingley hoping to entertain an audience thirsty for a home victory. But the morning papers dampened enthusiasm, casting doubt on the British players' ability to provide it. The Kangaroos were too big, too fast, too strong, some said invincible.

Willie's only pre-match quote stated simply: "We have a good chance." Meanwhile a nation waited impatiently for the kick-off as Willie and his team pulled on the white shirts they would die for. Defeat would almost certainly mean the Ashes were lost.

They had to win. It was that simple.

In 1947 Barrow signed Australian Harry Bath from Balmain for £750. Here the second-row forward introduces his fiancee to his new team-mates. After only 17 games 16-stone Bath was transferred to Warrington.

Great Britain receive a pep-talk the day before the Test against Australia at Headingley in 1948. Great Britain won 23–21 in a match dubbed "the greatest rugby league game in history." Standing: Ken Gee, George Curran, Bob Nicholson, Stan McCormick, Willie Horne, Dave Valentine, Jim Ledgard, Albert Pimblett, Johnny Lawrenson, Trevor Foster, Jim Featherstone and Ernest Ward (captain). Kneeling: Gerry Helme, Joe Egan and Russ Pepperell.

Skippers Wally O'Connell and Ernest Ward lead out the two teams before the historic 1948 Headingley Test.

Frank Castle scored two tries in his Barrow debut in October 1949. The former Coventry rugby union winger earned every top honour in the game including selection for the 1954 Australian Tour. He was described by Willie Horne as "the fastest player I have ever seen."

Bobby Ayres well wrapped up by scrum-half Donald Ward in Barrow's 1949 semi-final defeat by Bradford Northern at Station Road, Swinton. A crowd of 26,900 watched the Yorkshiremen win through to the Wembley final 10–0.

Five of the 1950 British Lions at Port Said, Egypt, midway through the sea journey to Australia. Willie Horne, Jimmy Featherstone, Ken Gee, Tommy Bradshaw and Jack Cunliffe.

Willie in action during the Lions' 23–13 defeat of Riverina at Cootamundra.

Tom Danby bursts through the Queensland defence on June 17, 1950. The Salford winger was to set a Lions try-scoring record with 34 in 18 matches. A week after this game Willie limped off the field to be told by specialists he might never play again.

The 1950 Tourists prepare to board the seaplane Teal at Sydney for the air journey to Auckland, New Zealand.

Wife Bessie and toddler Brenda welcome Willie from the 1950 Tour at Barrow Central station.

October 7, 1950 – Willie leads Barrow out against Liverpool Stanley at Craven Park. It was his first game back after his ankle injury in Australia. It was also Willie's debut as Barrow captain.

Jimmy Lewthwaite tackles Workington winger George Wilson during the Challenge Cup second-round tie in March, 1951. A crowd of 21,389 fans crammed into Craven Park to watch Barrow's 12–5 victory.

Willie leads Barrow on to the field for the 1951 Challenge Cup semi-final against Leeds at Odsal, Bradford. The Leeds captain is Welsh international Dickie Williams.

Barrow's 1951 semi-final team. Back: Dennis Goodwin, Phil Jackson, Jimmy Lewthwaite, Frank Longman, Jack McKinnell, Ralph Hartley and Harry Atkinson. Front: Tommy Ayres, Harry Stretch, Willie Horne (captain), Ted Toohey, Frank Castle and Jack Grundy.

Leeds Kiwi full back Bert Cook brings down Barrow scrum-half Ted Toohey during the 1951 Challenge Cup semi-final at Odsal.

Barrow full back Harry Stretch kicks a last minute penalty goal to bring the semi-final score to 14–14. The match was watched by 57,729 fans.

Barrow second-row forward Ralph Hartley scores Barrow's first try in the Challenge Cup semi-final replay against Leeds at Fartown, Huddersfield.

Harry Atkinson dives over for another Barrow try in the semi-final replay victory over Leeds.

Barrow's victorious cup squad arrived home at 1.20 in the morning. Here Willie is congratulated by Barrow referee John Jackson who would have officiated in the Wembley final had his home team lost to Leeds.

The Barrow Challenge Cup Final party prepare to set off for the capital. More than 12,000 Barrow supporters made the trip to Wembley.

CHAPTER FIFTEEN

AGAINST ALL ODDS

GREAT BRITAIN 19 AUSTRALIA 6

IT WAS clear the Australians had met their masters in the First Test. Great Britain skipper Willie Horne was man-of-the-match, his breakthroughs paving the way for constant attacks, and he and Ted Toohey outplayed the Australian halfbacks Greg Hawick and Keith Holman. Horne tackled magnificently and, with Ernest Ward, gained precious ground with well-judged kicks to touch.

SPORTING CHRONICLE AND ATHLETIC NEWS
Monday, October 6, 1952

THERE WAS something menacing in the way he moved, arms swinging robotlike, head turning first left, then right, ever alert, ever vigilant, amassing information.

Greg Hawick was a young man with an unquenchable thirst for confrontation. Watching him it was hard to tell if it was something he had been born with or if his aggression had been acquired, as one might develop a taste for malt whisky or Panama cigars. Hawick was only 19 yet he thrived on responsibility, discharging authority with intelligence and understanding, never worrying if he had been hasty or made a mistake.

Confidence burned inside him and the responsibility of making his Test debut for Australia against Great Britain rested lightly on his broad shoulders. He was a brave man who gave the impression of being untroubled by self-doubt. That was how Hawick appeared on the rugby field – brazen, some said arrogant.

He was encouraged as he looked towards the other end of the Headingley pitch, watching the slim man he had to mark, flicking passes to white-shirted colleagues with a graceful, easy rhythm. Hawick liked what he saw. His eyes confirmed what he had read in the programme an hour before, that, statistically at least, he was in for an easy afternoon. Willie Horne was two stones lighter, 11 years older and two inches shorter.

Briefly Hawick recalled the pre-match talk from Australian captain Clive Churchill who had warned him of the calamitous consequences of underestimating Horne, who, Churchill had said, was quick, fearless and creative with a dangerous flair for the unexpected. The purpose of such dressing room analysis is to sharpen players' awareness of the task before them and to manufacture confidence. Hawick did not require either. He played as if he believed intimidation must always prevail. Even the 33,000 crowd, yelling impatiently for the kick-off, could not dent his wall of self-belief. Hawick was frightened of nothing or anyone, his courage wild and limitless.

Two years before he had broken his jaw playing for South Sydney against St. George, but Hawick had carried on for more than an hour before the team doctor led him from the field, still protesting. He was like that in everything he did . . . bold and reckless.

As Great Britain prepared to kick-off, Hawick glanced across the divide to Willie, less than 20 yards away, hands on hips, looking gaunt and nervous. Then the referee blew his whistle and he was gone, lost in a blur of white and the clatter of loud voices: "Come left," "watch the blind," "up in a line." Twenty six gallant men going to war.

Noel Pidding kicked a penalty goal to give the Kangaroos an early lead, which was greeted by the muffled applause of a small, isolated pocket of Australian supporters. Great Britain ignored the early setback, Willie leading his troops expertly, driving the forwards, taking turns to hurtle into the buckling green and gold line with a power that, close to, was awesome and frightening.

Hawick took his turn to repel each probing attack, taking pleasure in his power and fortitude and all the time searching for a big hit on Willie who patrolled behind the British pack, seemingly everywhere.

When a stand-off half receives the ball he has less than three seconds to pass or he will be buried beneath huge men with a painful affection for controlled violence. In Test match football he has less than two seconds, two blinks of an eye. Good stand-off halves learned this lesson quickly or they were likely to be carried off bloody and comatose.

Hawick was a wonderful defender. He relished conflict and the opportunity it gave him to test his manhood by meeting the opposition head on, bravely, without a backward step. Everything happened quickly, the ball gone, Hawick on top of the runner, shoving him, hurting him, so the poor man finished dazed and shaken, as if a small wall had fallen on top of him.

The British pack ignored the Australians' threats and punches, frustrating them with tenacity and valour, led by the Herculean efforts of Ken Traill and Charlie Pawsey. After 32 minutes a magical move inspired by an unexpected blindside pass by Willie gave Barrow winger Frank Castle the ball inside the Australian half. Seven seconds later the former rugby union star touched down beneath the sticks as Noel Pidding and Clive Churchill grasped the cold Yorkshire air, wondering how they could have missed their tackles. The game looked lost for the Tourists. But they were not ready to give up, fired up as they were with the pre-match patriotic talk of Australian soldiers dying on the beaches of Gallipoli and Ned Kelly's violent resistance to British authority.

Some Australians began adding verbal taunting to their defence, blurting out threats and insults as they became more and more ferocious, their rage boiling over. Willie was familiar with tough opponents. Violence came with the territory. But they did not trouble him. It was part of Test match football and he was equal to it. He had been marked by hard men before and experience taught him there were ways of dealing with players whose prime objectives were not always open play and secure defence.

Often such opponents are slow to recognise the dangers posed by long passes or inviting dummies offered and, more often than not accepted, by men whose naivety was easily exploited by artists such as Willie Horne. The pain inflicted by a punch to the face was soothed with the knowledge that a colleague was scoring a try, while the other defenders stared accusingly at the player who had been tricked, easily, like a puppy chasing a stick.

"This lad's getting a bit naughty," Ernest Ward, the British vice-captain told Willie as half-time approached, his voice firm, heavy with understatement. "Next scrum you stand out wide. Leave him to me."

Hawick caught the ball from scrum-half Holman as the Australian centres peeled off in support, watching his every move, hoping a running opportunity might come their way. Willie stood ten yards in front, shepherding Hawick towards the centre of the field where the British second-row forwards had already broken from the scrimmage searching for a Kangaroo to bury.

Fleetingly, Hawick wondered why Willie was fractionally out of position. Perhaps this was a chance of a break. Then he was down. Ward did not so much tackle Hawick as devour him, enveloping the half back with his long arms, throwing him over his hips effortlessly. The tackle had been so perfect and unexpected Hawick had already begun a brief acquaintance with oblivion before he hit the ground. Somehow he played the ball but he did not know where he was and why he was there. He meandered around the field bearing the look of a drunk labouring in the black despair of a hangover.

Slowly he began regaining his senses but his contribution to the Australian cause was spasmodic and unreliable. Just before halftime Alvin Ackerley won a scrum on the Australian 25 that led to a soft try created by the Kangaroos' panic-stricken attempts to close down Willie's sparkling distribution. Toohey took the ball but instead of passing to Willie he fed Ron Ryder who slipped through to score without suffering the inconvenience of being even partly tackled.

Behind him four Australians were lying on top of Willie, each man convinced the move had been prevented, that underneath their human pyramid the British captain was holding the ball, winded, and, like as not, hurt. The referee blew his whistle to signal a try as the Australian quartet turned, not believing what they saw. How did he do that, their inquisitive expressions asked as if they were small boys watching a magician pulling a rabbit out of a hat.

Early in the second half winger Arthur Daniels propelled the British to a 13-point lead with a typically evasive run and with Willie kicking five goals from as many attempts the Australians finished beaten, demoralised and exhausted.

Daniels' try was a mortal blow that eradicated any lingering doubts the more tenacious Australian players might have had of a miraculous comeback. There was a finality in their weary attempts to tackle the Halifax threequarter that told those experienced enough to recognise such things that they knew they could not win. The Australians had been beaten in every department, even their powerful, intimidating pack, accustomed to the less demanding challenge of club football, were weak and disorganised. Police escorted Willie and his triumphant team from the field before the crowd went home jubilant, believing the Ashes were as good as back in Great Britain.

In the Australian dressing room the Tourists bathed their bruises and went through the traditional routine to ease the pain of defeat. But there was a resigned sadness in the way they talked as though players sensed that the mountain they were summoned to climb in the Second Test would be too high.

Hawick, now recovered from Ward's ferocious tackle, was like everyone else in that room, quiet and depressed. He had been outplayed by Willie Horne's dazzling performance. Hawick was dropped for the next two Tests, a predictable decision that brought no protest from him. Back in Australia he matured into a wonderful stand-off half, playing a further ten times for his country.

He would never forget that First Test at Headingley. The despair of defeat, the cauldron of international rugby and the tackle from Ernest Ward. He was still sore two days later.

★ ★ ★

Australians have never needed much encouragement to entertain pompous opinions that they are the best, that greatness is somehow ingrained into the psyche of their country. This conviction produced rugby league players who embraced the philosophy so completely that they were incapable of doubting their ability to get the job done, priding themselves on frontier qualities such as courage and unbreakable spirit. They were intimidating and oppressive. Australians were born with an ego.

The First Test was a crushing blow, the defeat comprehensive and complete, but it was never in danger of suppressing these inbred qualities. The players had been hurt by the loss but the performance was soon forgotten as the Kangaroos turned their attention to the destruction of English club sides, still confident that belligerent aggression would retain the Ashes so that they could return home conquering heroes. The British press reached a different conclusion. On Monday morning the Australians were slated as passionately as the British were praised, and the Aussies chances of winning the remaining two Tests were considered at best fragile, at worst non-existent.

Nevertheless, there was no shortage of admiration for the Kangaroos' fortitude as they continued to humiliate the best teams in England. Bradford

Northern, Warrington, Leigh, Swinton, Hunslet, Workington Town, Doncaster and Huddersfield were all powerless to stop the Australian machine rumble on. So they arrived at Swinton for the Second Test with confidence high, the dramatic happenings at Headingley forgotten. Each man knew this time that victory was certain, as sure as night follows day. Of course there were casualties. Seven new faces were drafted in with only Clive Churchill, Noel Hazzard, Brian Carlson, Kevin Schubert, Duncan Hall and Brian Davies retaining their places.

Great Britain brought in centre threequarter Duggie Greenall for Ron Ryder and forwards Alvin Ackerley and Bob Ryan were replaced by Tom McKinney and Dave Valentine. But the British too were convinced they would win at Station Road, a ground where Australia had never won a Test. And they were right.

The game was a personal triumph for Ernest Ward. Great Britain won easily 21-5 with Ward having a hand in all five tries and tackling the Australians with such ferocity even their brave forwards finished weary, wisely avoiding Ward's uncompromising defence. The Kangaroos were eight points down after 30 minutes and 16-2 adrift early in the second half without a hint of breaking the British line. When the referee blew the final whistle some Australians shook hands sportingly with their triumphant opponents while others left the field petulantly, with a simmering anger, harbouring grudges which were to surface uncontrollably in the Third Test at Odsal five weeks away.

Again the Kangaroos put the Test defeat behind them, maintaining their domination of the rest of the country so emphatically that they arrived at Bradford still optimistic they could rally together and prevent the shame of a whitewash. They were the most successful Australian tour party of all time. Not counting the two Tests, they had played 23 games and amassed 778 points at an average of 32 a match, suffering a solitary defeat at St. Helens. But they were going home as failures. They had lost the Ashes. There would be no celebration party. The return voyage would be a long one, not helped by the knowledge that gloom and recrimination awaited them. Australians did not like their heroes losing.

The British players arrived at Odsal stadium mentally drained from their exhausting efforts in winning the first two Tests. They wanted to win this one too, but there was something missing in the pre-match talk, not in the things that were said or the things they did. The change was one of mood rather than preparation. There was a relaxed atmosphere that verged on complacency, as if the knowledge that the Ashes were safe somehow stifled the will to win. Players spoke of pressures lifted, optimistic plans of open play and how they were going to enjoy themselves.

So jokes were shared as the British taped wrists and ankles and smeared Vaseline on knees and brows unfurrowed with the discomfort of tension, ignorant of the stifling, oppressive atmosphere that hung over a very different Australian dressing room. The Kangaroos wanted revenge. And victory, sweet though it would taste, was not likely to satisfy the hunger of outraged men craving vengeance.

Before the game Willie was presented with the Ashes Cup by Australian Tour Manager Doug Maclean as the crowd screamed their approval. A few yards away the Kangaroos watched, simmering with hostility before readying themselves for the kick-off, forwards grunting like wild animals.

The match was a disgrace to rugby league. Australia won 27-7 but the headlines the next day hardly gave the scoreline a mention. Stories even crept onto the front pages, relegating to the inside the lengthening strike by Yorkshire miners and tentative moves to end the Korean War. **SHAME AT ODSAL** and **FIGHTING MARS AUSSIE VICTORY** were typical as Fleet Street flashed the news across the world.

Australian prop forward Duncan Hall was sent off after 52 minutes, the first Kangaroo dismissed in a Test in England. But he was not the worst offender. There were mass fights, assaults and dangerous late tackles as the Australians mercilessly pursued an orgy of mayhem, plunging the game into the gutter. Had these attacks been carried out away from the sporting field, the perpetrators would have been arrested and charged with grievous bodily harm before receiving lengthy prison sentences normally reserved for bank robbers and arsonists.

The following comments illustrate the extent of the violence:

KEN TRAILL (Great Britain loose forward): *"No one could say our forwards or the Aussie pack were footballers today. We acted like 12 animals, like 12 busy bears fighting for a bun. I have never played in a rougher match."*

SYDNEY MORNING HERALD: *"Veteran pressmen who have been reporting Test matches since the First World War said this was the worst example of unruly and disgraceful football they had ever seen."*

RUGBY LEAGUE REVIEW: *"What might and certainly ought to have been a grand game of rugby quickly degenerated into an ugly and unseemly brawl which almost ended in a bloodbath."*

CANON LOWE (Bishop of Bradford): *"The game developed into a free-for-all. The crowd turned up to see good football but all that was offered was a prize-fight."*

The Kangaroos let the criticism wash over them as they headed for France and another Test series defeat before that long journey home where they could start repairing wounded pride and count the days until 1954 when the Lions toured Australia. Willie's personal contribution and inspirational effect on those around him had been apparent to the British public and fickle journalists keen to report the achievements of a team they had predicted would lose.

Willie would lead the 1954 British Lions, they said. It was a certainty.

CHAPTER SIXTEEN

AN IDOL OF THE CROWD

IN REACHING the exalted rank of one of Britain's best, Willie Horne has been no weakling, in character or body. No man without initiative, resource or drive could have recorded the wonderful achievements which stand to his credit, but his greatest achievement of all did not come from any of these attributes.

Willie will stand out in my memory not just as one of the greatest players I have seen but because of the things I have not seen. In no match I ever watched, where he played, did I ever see him do a mean or petty action. How proud would we be if we could sincerely say the same.

TOM REYNOLDS
Rugby League journalist, March, 1953

WILLIE returned to Craven Park proud of Great Britain's destruction of the daunting Kangaroos and his own considerable contribution towards retrieving the Ashes. Nationalist euphoria echoed across the north of England for weeks in newspaper editorials and radio broadcasts. Willie was in perpetual demand answering predictable questions . . . why had we won? . . . who were our most outstanding players? Dealing with the media was something he had reluctantly grown accustomed to. He was always polite, patient, helpful and liberal in his praise of the British players he had been so honoured to lead. But it was part of the job he did not enjoy. All Willie had ever wanted was to play rugby.

In January, 1953, he was 31 years old but his powers remained unaffected by the passage of time. The game was changing. Many stars who had toured Australia with Willie seven years earlier had retired. Wonderful players such as Tommy McCue, Willie Davies and Dai Jenkins were gone, replaced by a new generation of exciting young men, eager, gifted and ambitious.

Of course, it was not inconceivable that Willie would be outplayed, one day. But it would take an extraordinary man blessed with a remarkable array of skills. He would need to be able to kick for position, near and far, drop goals and convert penalties; he would need to be able to pass, long and short, to backs and forwards with unerring accuracy; he would also need to inspire those around him with a potent combination of personal excellence, sincere respect and gentle encouragement; finally he would need to tackle opponents, big and small, fast and slow with a bewildering economy of effort, so victims finished dazed and demoralised in a crumpled heap as if they had been crushed under a grand piano. Yes, one day. But not yet.

As captain of Great Britain, England and Lancashire, Willie, like it or not, was looked upon with admiration combined with a touch of jealousy. Not for the first time in his career, he was burdened with the handicap of a reputation for distinction sustained by his own continuing brilliance and repetitive newspaper stories claiming he was the best in the business.

More often than not, teams facing Barrow contained halfbacks grateful for the opportunity to outshine Willie and accelerate their own careers. Outstanding young men such as David Bolton, Harry Archer and Ken Rollin came to Craven Park saturated with youthful arrogance, confident they could quell the master. They came, they saw and they were conquered. Willie beat them all, his skill, courage and leadership undiminished.

Barrow were respected by everyone, feared by most. No one came here underestimating the task before them. Craven Park was the graveyard of many championship aspirations as Wigan, St Helens, Leeds and Workington Town all tasted defeat in front of large crowds still faithful and expectant that Barrow would get their hands on some silverware eventually. It was just a matter of time, they said, with a conviction unshaken by years of disappointment, the average gate still more than 10,000.

Willie was much more than an outstanding individual player. He scattered confidence around lavishly, so that players looked up to him in the same way a loyal soldier obeyed a commanding officer, without question. It was like that when he played for Great Britain, for England, for Lancashire and, of course, for Barrow. His influence was so all-consuming that supporters were becoming fearful of a mediocre future without him. In April, Barrow drew with Rochdale Hornets. This report illustrates the team's inability to perform even moderately without him:

The 10-10 draw with Rochdale Hornets proved how Barrow are all at sea without skipper Willie Horne. Willie, who must now be regarded as an automatic choice for any big game for which he is eligible, was absent in France, where he led England to victory. Barrow felt his absence so much they were obviously without a leader. It says a great deal for the capabilities of Horne; it does not say much for Barrow.

It is high time Barrow sought a deputy for their captain. There is far too much reliance on one man and I hate the constant reiteration of the excuse: "If only Horne had been playing."

There is no doubt he is one of the greatest halfbacks in the game today, if not the greatest. Should Horne retire — and I hope he will not for some time – do we close the Craven Park gates? Obviously not. But it is high time we set about the job of building up the reserves.

NORTH WEST EVENING MAIL – Monday, April 13, 1953

The Mail's hard-hitting comments were favourably received by fans who prayed directors would respond and look to the future and the chasm that lay waiting to engulf a town craving for success. What would they do without him, they asked.

Willie had other things on his mind. He was granted a testimonial. Furness responded with rampant generosity, supporting a host of jumble sales, dances and raffles with an intensity that had not been seen before. Willie had always been considered special. He was coveted and admired not just for his bravery, influence and heroics on the field. There was something else. He had an aura, a presence about him that moved Barrow supporters to adoration for the way he acted, always with dignity, never losing his temper or reacting to intimidation. His testimonial brochure, aptly called An Idol of the Crowd was full of eloquent and sincere tributes to his genius:

> *Fame has sat lightly on Willie Horne's shoulders. He is not one of those men who knows he is good and never hesitates to tell you. Rather he is the quiet, unassuming fellow who realises he has a gift and a brain for football, who shuns rather than welcomes the limelight thrust upon him. He has his rivals, naturally enough, but it would not be exaggerating to suggest everyone in rugby league today knows Willie, likes Willie, and realises what he means in the code. He will always know that what he has done he has done well – for Barrow, for Lancashire, for England and for Great Britain. Good luck Willie.*
>
> SENTINEL, North West Evening Mail

> *To know Willie Horne the player is to know Willie Horne the man. I have almost everyday contact with this young man who has done more than make a name for himself in our game. He has made a name for Barrow and brought great honour on both himself and his native town. Willie Horne is as quiet and unassuming off the field as he is frequently brilliant on it. Who would think that in this slip of chap we have a Great Britain star, or that quiet spoken manner hides a football brain of inestimable value to Barrow RLFC. Willie Horne deserves to rank alongside the great in the history of rugby league.*
>
> JOHN ATKINSON, Chairman, Barrow RLFC

> *I am fortunate and proud to call Willie Horne a friend. He is one of the best tacticians I have seen in either code of rugby and he will never be able to appreciate how big a part he played in Great Britain's regaining of the Ashes this season. I can, without fear of contradiction, name him Footballer of the Year. His captaincy, knowledge of tactics and fearless tackling rightly earn him that title.*
>
> BILL FALLOWFIELD, Secretary of the Rugby Football League

When Willie Horne changes gear from brilliant into superb, well the fellows on the other side can just call it a day. Bamboozle isn't the word. Willie Horne has all the tricks of the halfback's trade, and he uses them often, with the slight variations that go towards the complete bluffing of the chappie who thinks he knows how to "put Willie Horne in his place." He isn't merely an individualist who shines as a player, he imparts his genius to the rest of the team.

Never was the opposition more thoroughly hoodwinked time and time again than the Australians in the First Test at Headingley. It was Willie's match from start to finish. To see him break through a defence which thinks it is something out of the ordinary is a rich experience. The Aussies were reduced to impotence by his artistry. As a maker of openings he's matchless; as a snapper of half chances he's unequalled; as a captain he has every quality to produce a 100 per cent team. For all his prowess you won't find a more modest fellow anywhere. There's your Master of Rugby Football Arts.

ALLAN CAVE, Daily Herald

Fund-raising culminated in a league game with Warrington, watched by more than 12,000. Barrow won easily 30-17 with Frank Castle scoring three tries as overflowing buckets were filled with copper and silver among talk that the final figure might reach £1,000. Barrow finished the season fifth in the league but despite all the splendid games and flowing rugby that delighted a nation, the club had nothing to show for their efforts. No cups, no titles, no trip to Wembley. Willie was briefly linked with the vacant coaching job at Wigan but the Craven Park board responded swiftly, appointing him player coach on a three-year contract. Barrow without Willie Horne was unthinkable.

On June 13, 1953, at a presentation in the Washington Hotel, Roose Road, Barrow, Willie received a cheque for £950, then the second largest benefit in the history of rugby league. The money was a catalyst for a major change in his life. He opened a sports shop.

★ ★ ★

Looking back, it is difficult to calculate the enormous gamble Willie and Bessie were taking as they walked around Aldridge's, an old paint shop in Paxton Terrace, holding hands, trying to imagine how it might look packed with sporting equipment.

The town centre premises needed a lot of work. And it wouldn't be cheap. They would rent at first, hoping the business prospered and produced the capital necessary to secure a mortgage, so they could call it their own. Local joiner John Stringer began the renovation, installing a large front window before building shelves, new counters and increasing storage space. Willie painted while Bessie bought stock, preparing for the opening day still weeks away. Rugby balls, cricket bats and shirts were easy but many wholesalers refused to supply goods, reluctant to jeopardise lucrative links with Barrow's other sports shops, Cliffes, Winters and the Co-operative.

Times were hard. Modernising the shop had to be done but the work was expensive, putting a strain on their meagre capital and forcing them to fill shelves with empty boxes to give customers the impression of variety and quality.

They had three children now: four-year-old Brenda, toddler Billy and baby Ada. Somehow Bessie managed on her own while Willie worked overtime and played rugby helping to sustain the fledgling business. Back at Craven Park fans began thinking about the 1954 Australian Tour. Willie was sure to be picked, they said. And he'd be captain.

★ ★ ★

Barrow started the 1953-54 season by signing hooker Vince McKeating from Dewsbury and loose forward Bill Healey from local amateur club Walney Central. McKeating, brother of Danny, who played for Barrow in the 1938 Challenge Cup Final, was experienced and industrious while Healey, a formidable amateur boxer, was fearless beyond the substantial limits normally displayed by professional rugby players. They were expected to be important members of the first team squad.

In November, Barrow beat Featherstone Rovers to register their tenth consecutive league win. Two weeks later Willie was at Central Park captaining England against Other Nationalities. The English won 30-22 with Willie giving one of his greatest performances in front of a devoted crowd, spellbound by his play. The Great Britain selectors were there too. And everyone reached the same conclusion. He was still the best, not just in England but in the world.

In defence Willie was faultless, tackling the green shirts courageously and with such chilling efficiency that the English forwards frequently accepted his invitation to rest on the blind side, secure in the knowledge the line could not be broken. Willie would see to that.

With the ball, confidence radiated from him. He set up abundant scoring chances effortlessly, casually as if the opposition were weak and inexperienced. But they were not. Other Nationalities had expected to beat England not because they were arrogant but because they were good. Very good.

In the backs they had Brian Bevan (Warrington and Australia), Tony Paskins (Workington and Australia), Pat Devery (Huddersfield and Australia) and Lionel Cooper (Huddersfield and Australia), while their forwards included Arthur Clues (Leeds and Australia) and Dave Valentine (Huddersfield and Great Britain). Not surprisingly they started the game as favourites.

Their attack was threatening, unpredictable and fast, as you would expect. The surprising thing was the feeble way they buckled under the onslaught of dangerous attacks all set up by Willie's elusive running and dazzling distribution. Centre threequarters Eppie Gibson and Duggie Greenall helped convert this harvest of opportunities as the English backs ran in seven tries including four by winger Peter Norburn, normally a second-row forward with Swinton. After the game Greenall told reporters Willie had been a centre's dream, that England's success was all due to the shy, slim turner from Barrow-in-Furness. Newspapers confirmed his spectacular contribution:

> *Without doubt Willie Horne is the greatest strategist in rugby league football and always on his best in big occasions. He did even more than four-try Peter Norburn to bring about England's unexpected defeat of Other Nationalities and make them international champions and holders of the Jean Galia Memorial Trophy for the first time in four years.*
>
> TOM LONGWORTH, News Chronicle

> *Barrow captain Willie Horne proved for the umpteenth time that he is the best we've got, and a rattling good best at that. What's more, he'll skipper the 1954 Tour party.*
>
> ALLAN CAVE, Daily Herald

The Yorkshire Post ran a poll in their weekend paper asking readers to nominate who they thought should make the Australian trip. Ninety six per cent picked Willie Horne as stand-off half with Warrington's Ray Price a distant second. The Rugby League Gazette published results of a similar survey. Again Willie was overwhelmingly supported as number six, this time Peter Metcalfe of St Helens was runner-up, a long way behind.

At lunchtime, Wednesday, March 10, the selectors emerged from a Southport hotel to announce the names of the 1954 British Lions. Willie hadn't made it. And he wasn't the only one. The news was received with unexpected hostility, frustration and, for some, uncontrollable anger.

The captain was Dickie Williams, a stand-off half who, four months before, had threatened to quit the game before moving from Leeds to Hunslet for £3,000. Some newspapers attacked his appointment, saying he lacked the physical presence to resist the expected Australian onslaught. They said he was too thin, too weak, too injury-prone. Such criticism was emotional and absurd.

Williams was a fine player, a 1950 tourist who had played many times for Great Britain with skill and exceptional courage. He was quick and he would not shirk in defence. Yes, he was good. Some said great. But Willie was better. Willie should have gone. And there were other more surprising choices. As well as Williams, Hunslet were represented by scrum half Alf Burnell and second-row forward Geoff Gunney. Informed opinion said they were all lucky, that better players had been disregarded, and the fact that the chairman of selectors Hector Rawson was also chairman of Hunslet did not help dampen rising suspicions of treachery and masonic-like deals behind closed doors.

No Alvin Ackerley. No Eppie Gibson. No Ted Toohey. No Stan Kielty. No Billy Banks. No Glyn Moses. No Johnny Whiteley. The party contained only four 1950 tourists: Dickie Williams, vice-captain Ernie Ashcroft (Wigan), Ken Traill (Bradford Northern) and Jack Cunliffe (Wigan). Many claimed it was the weakest team Great Britain had ever sent to Australia, and that the Ashes were as good as lost.

Jim Brough, a 1928 and 1936 tourist, said: "Twenty of the 26 players were chosen from clubs with representatives on the selection committee. These selectors must have found it most embarrassing to pass over several men who have been such consistent performers for club and country throughout the season. The constructive genius of Willie Horne will be sadly missed."

Willie was understandably disappointed. Only four men had previously been honoured by representing Great Britain on three Australian Tours – Jonty Parkin (1920, 1924 and 1928), Jim Sullivan (1924, 1928, 1932), Joe Thompson (1924, 1928 and 1932) and Gus Risman (1932, 1936 and 1946). There was nothing he could do. Resentment and envy were emotions he was incapable of feeling. So he concentrated his efforts on helping Barrow RL while the 1954 Tourists went on to fulfil the weighty expectations of disaster. The Ashes were lost. Outside the Tests, Great Britain were defeated six times. Stories filtered back of dissent, of dressing room rows, players not speaking and constantly mourning the absence of so many great stars, men capable of inspiration and leadership, men such as Willie Horne.

★ ★ ★

Barrow began the 1954-55 season in the same frustrating way they had so many before. They won games they should have lost and lost games they should have won. The team blew hot and cold, irritating supporters with inexplicable extremes of performance. Barrow were capable of wonderful, flowing rugby. Supporters knew, on a good day, they could beat anyone. There was a feeling in the town that this could be the season when potential was turned into success, promise into victory, expectation into glory. After playing for 54 years without a trophy, everyone was hoping this team had the capacity to provide one.

In the first round of the Lancashire Cup, Barrow defeated Rochdale Hornets 13-10 with Willie kicking two goals and scoring two tries. On paper it had been anybody's match and the narrow victory did little to dispel lingering fears over Barrow's varying levels of competence. The second round certainly did. Widnes, conquerors of mighty Warrington in the previous round, were thrashed 36-0 with Barrow running in ten tries. It was a brilliant, awesome display. Widnes, who had themselves harboured hopes of a successful season, were crushed mercilessly to set up a semi-final with Leigh at Kirkhall Lane. Now it was getting tough.

Leigh, coached by Great Britain international hooker Joe Egan, were top of the league. Away from home they were difficult to beat. At Kirkhall Lane the chances were that they would be invincible. But Barrow won 7-2 with

Willie scoring the only try of the match to earn his side a place in the final against Oldham at Station Road, Swinton.

Being underdogs was a condition Barrow were accustomed to that season. And it was to be the same in the final. Beating Leigh was something of a shock, received in the rest of the country with surprise and disbelief. But it was being said they could not raise their game sufficiently to vanquish Oldham. That would require a miracle. The board responded by announcing the players would receive £25 if they won. But financial incentive was not necessary to fuel their craving for victory.

Oldham had taken over from Leigh at the top of the table. They had won 11 games on the run. They had international forwards, international half backs and international threequarters. They had a full back, Bernard Ganley, who was considered the best in the game. They had money. And they had a proud heritage of greatness. Oldham had played in ten previous Lancashire Cup finals. Barrow had played in one. Oldham had won the Challenge Cup three times, Barrow never. Oldham had won the Championship three times, Barrow never. Everything was against them – form, statistics and history.

So the smart money was on Oldham, who were not merely expected to win. The word was Barrow might be out of their depth. If they were not careful, defeat might be severe and cruel. Oldham were that good. But Barrow prepared for the match with more noble aspirations than just keeping the score down. They wanted to win. They too had internationals. And with Willie at stand-off half such optimism was more than positive mental preparation. Informed opinion suggested if the Barrow pack could somehow cancel out the Oldham forwards, the outcome of the game might rest on the centre threequarters.

Oldham had Alan Davies and Roley Barrow, big men who enjoyed combat, welcoming the confrontation of rugby league. Davies, at 22, was already an England international. He was elusive and fearless while Barrow was even bigger, revelling in his formidable reputation for direct running and immaculate defence. They were daunting opponents, as tough as they came.

Barrow had Phil Jackson and Dennis Goodwin, locals who went into the final unnerved by the responsibility thrust their direction by newspaper talk. Besides, Oldham did not have Willie Horne. Nevertheless, the task before them was formidable and a touch frightening.

Willie never asked for the impossible. His pre-match instructions to Goodwin and Jackson were simple. Enjoy yourself and try your best, he said.

"We will," they promised respectfully.

But would that be enough?

CHAPTER SEVENTEEN

GENTLE GIANTS

WHEN WE found out Oldham were playing Barrow in the final of the Lancashire Cup it was a game we all looked forward to. Any match against Barrow was a pleasure. They were a great footballing side who always threw the ball about.

Of course that meant taking on Phil Jackson and Dennis Goodwin, two of the biggest centres in the game. It was always a challenge, yet I have to say that nine times out of ten they got the better of us. A lot of good centres don't go looking for the ball. They wait for it to come their way. But Phil would be all over the field searching for possession. That's why he made so many breaks close to the pack. He was a well-built, heavy player and that weight gave him confidence to do those things. Phil was a remarkably good centre.

As for Dennis, well it was the sheer size of the man. One player just couldn't get him down. That meant others had to come in to help, so gaps appeared all over the place and Dennis was so good at getting the ball out to his winger under those circumstances. If he stood with his feet a yard apart it was like trying to tackle a Manhattan Skyscraper.

Only one word comes to mind when I think about playing against Phil and Dennis. Awesome.

ALAN DAVIES
Centre threequarter and captain of Oldham RLFC

AN INTERNATIONAL centre threequarter is an outstanding athlete even alongside the daunting standards of physical excellence expected from all professional rugby league players. The top-ranking centre needs pace to support half backs. He must also be elusive, creating chances where they are least expected to break down resolute defences trained to perfection. And he must be strong and brave to endure the crunching tackles of not just one but two, three and four opponents, determined men not unfamiliar with coercion and intimidation. But above all he must manufacture a plentiful supply of running opportunities for his winger.

Wingers are a breed apart. If an average winger raced against an international second-row forward he could give him ten yards start and overtake him before reaching the halfway line. Often wingers are moderate tacklers woefully short of skill. Frank Castle was like that. If you questioned him about support play or the nuances of a defensive line, you would see his eyes glaze over and his face turn blank as if he was back at school pondering the capital of Afghanistan or the mysteries of calculus. But he could run. He was born to run. Frank had an almost boyish naivety about his play. But if you gave him the ball in open space nobody would catch him. In 1954 he was without question the fastest rugby player in the world.

Jimmy Lewthwaite was different. He too was quick but he was a complete player who tackled forwards without invitation, faultlessly and always with a frightening, mindless courage. He could also score tries by running round, through and over defenders, when you would think no man alive could do so. But he was missing for the final, dropped after playing with an injury, his place taken by Derek Hinchley, normally a back-row forward.

A good centre threequarter will voluntarily withstand the brunt of physical violence to protect his winger. But it will not be with bad feeling. He will perform this selfless act willingly, without complaint, as a shepherd watches over his sheep, with devotion and commitment. And when such a centre decides the time is right to present his winger with the ball there will be no broken-nosed loose forward closing in with mayhem in his eyes. There will be open space; and plenty of it. A good centre would rather create tries for his winger than score them himself.

If a centre-threequarter is to be considered truly great he will be a man of extraordinary physical qualities. He must combine the size and strength of a second-row forward with the speed and agility of a winger – rare attributes when you consider how evolution normally produces big men who are powerful and slow, and small men who are fast and fragile. Typically, a man who is either very strong or very quick pays too high a price in the reduction of the other requirement. So a centre threequarter who weighs more than 13 stones, who can run, kick, pass and tackle is considered a big man. In 1954 Barrow's centres were massive.

Phil Jackson weighed in at 15 stone. He had strong legs, his thighs thicker than the trunk of a small oak tree. His waist was narrow and fat-free, his powerful, muscular shoulders so wide that viewed from a certain angle his shirt appeared too small.

When he ran with the ball Phil could sidestep off both feet and he had a terrifying hand-off he used repeatedly, its effect never weakening, thrusting a hand as large as a dinner plate into the faces of opponents who fell down momentarily unconscious, waiting for logic to dislodge blackness, before picking themselves up numb and a little wiser, re-establishing where they were and what they were doing.

Phil had returned from the 1954 Australian tour with an enhanced reputation. He was respected as a creative footballer, a man with no obvious weakness, someone who could perform everything asked of him with style and efficiency. His partnership with a then unknown winger called Billy

Boston was fruitful and exciting as Boston broke the tour try-scoring record with 36 touchdowns. "Phil made 30 of them," he told reporters on his return to the United Kingdom. "He is a superb centre."

Phil Jackson was something of a showman. He enjoyed playing to the crowd, entertaining. Yes, Phil was a big man. But Dennis Goodwin was bigger. He weighed 16 stone and was 6 feet 4 inches tall. Dennis too was strong and imposing. Watching him play left you thinking how convenient it would have been having someone like him as a friend when you were at school and how the bullies would have left you alone.

Phil had a more celebrated reputation but Dennis was quicker and though he did not employ a sidestep, when the occasion demanded it he substituted this omission by running through players, knocking defenders aside like a large boulder rolling down a steep hill. His tackling was impeccable and he had an immense capacity for work. Add to this his exquisite passing, long and short, and you are left with a very fine centre-threequarter indeed. On his own Dennis was a dangerous opponent, as was Phil Jackson. Together they were, at times, unplayable.

Looking at photographs of the Barrow team with Phil and Dennis in the back row, towering over the forwards, it's easy to imagine how intimidating they must have been. There will be a young centre warming up in the middle of the field, jogging lightly on the spot, glancing towards the dressing rooms nervously, perspiring in anticipation. He'll have heard about the size of Dennis and Phil but he draws an uneasy comfort from his lack of faith in newspaper stories and though he knows such speculation is neither wise nor necessary he will not be able to stop himself staring, waiting for the blue shirts to appear.

When they do, he'll watch the team trot onto the field, Willie at the front, head down, carrying a ball, looking as he always did, slight and innocuous. The 13 players scatter as the young centre begins scanning black numbers on broad backs, his eyes inextricably drawn to the biggest men, not daring believe they will be wearing numbers three and four. But they are. He turns away, wincing slightly as if he'd just seen someone drop an antique vase, and he will mutter something, not to anyone in particular, whoever may be listening: "I might need some help."

Off the field Phil and Dennis were amiable and popular, making friends easily, so that, if you had a mind to, you could picture them helping old ladies across busy streets, or striking up pleasant small talk with strangers on trains, or queuing for weekend shopping. But once they pulled on the Barrow shirt their walk and presence implied belligerence and hostility, sending a subtle warning to opponents: taking them on was likely to be a risky business.

Oldham centres Alan Davies and Roland Barrow were in for a tough afternoon.

CHAPTER EIGHTEEN

UP FOR THE CUP

FIRST let there be praise for Willie Horne. If ever a man laboured mightily behind a hard working, grafting pack it was the Barrow skipper. His forwards never once let up in their great-hearted attacking and covering but their captain was everywhere. Oldham battered away but never found a chink in Barrow's armour. Our forwards were magnificent. Oldham had nothing to outdo Horne and no one to soften the punch of Phil Jackson and Dennis Goodwin. Willie Horne earned his triumphant moment when he received the cup. It was the grandest moment in a grand performance.

SENTINEL
North Western Evening Mail, Monday, October 25, 1954

THE RAIN battered violently against the dressing room windows forming a vocal background to Barrow's pre-match preparations. Jittery players sat wearing apprehensive masks of fear as the kick-off, now less than five minutes away, loomed ominously nearer. It had been raining throughout the day, alternating between furious downpour and light drizzle, the kind that appears inoffensive when seen through a living room window, yet if you venture out it will soak you in minutes unless you wear a thick, waterproof gaberdine. Rain was never welcomed by rugby league players. Rain meant mud and mud meant the ball would be heavy, hard to hold and easy to drop.

An abrupt clap startled the men into concentration. Willie stood rigid in the middle of the room, arms folded, behind a wooden table full of half-empty tins of Vaseline and long rolls of white tape.

"Right lads," he began. "We all know why we're here. We're here to win. I don't want any mistakes especially early on. People say Barrow are the underdogs, that Oldham are too good for us but I'm not interested. We all know we can win. Let's get out there and prove it." As he finished there was a polite knock on the door signalling, with perfect timing, that they were expected on the field.

The players walked out in single file, studs clattering on the stone floor, the crowd's roar washing over each man, the pressure mounting so you would expect dismay to turn to self-doubt rising to the appalling fear of failure. Yet it did not happen. Not to one man. Willie's talk had settled the mood, directing energies into the task before them. It wasn't the words, which were predictable, but the manner in which they had been delivered, by a man they believed was capable of achieving anything.

Onto the pitch they marched accompanied by the distant rumble of thunder, sheets of rain drifting through the damp air instantly drenching them, the mud heavy and cumbersome, clinging in lumps to boots as Willie tossed up in the middle of the field, the crowd yelling beneath a thousand black umbrellas. The teams changed ends jogging by each other, squelching through the treacherous and deepening puddles, no one talking, faces turned towards the ground. Willie glanced around him, a final check that everyone was in position before rubbing his hands together vigorously, raising his arm, stepping forward and kicking the ball deep into the Oldham half. Next birthday he would be 33. It was said his best years were behind him. This could be his last chance. Barrow had to win.

★ ★ ★

The pattern of the game was set in the first ten minutes. Conditions were grim and unpleasant but even allowing for them, Oldham's handling was appalling. It was rare for them to put together more than two passes before the ball bobbled forward as if it was a bar of soap, the guilty player staring through empty fingers bewildered by the error. To make matters worse, Oldham did not contemplate moderating their attacking plans of open rugby. That was the way they had played all that season. That was why they were top of the league.

So while Barrow sensibly restrained their own creative flair in deference to the dreadful weather, Oldham kept up a fruitless quest for superiority with the emphasis boldly resting on quick hands and tireless support play. In all probability such tactics would have been wise and dangerous had the final been played in August, on a firm, fast pitch by sun tanned players. But it wasn't.

So Barrow kept the ball in the forwards, who relished the extra opportunity for work, each man driving forward, making a yard here, a yard there, and when the time was right, Willie called for possession standing a shade deeper, hands outstretched, before kicking long and true, the ball soaring through the relentless downpour before spiralling into touch.

Such accurate kicking often demoralises teams on the receiving end, forcing forwards to wear dejected looks of discouragement as they shuffle back, heads bowed. But Oldham had come too far to give up. They continued tackling and running with the same enthusiasm as they had started, full of optimism and hope as if they were programmed like machines.

After 15 minutes Harry Ogden knocked on outside the Oldham 25. Ted Toohey picked up the ball and fed Dennis Goodwin who took the pass in a position that could only be described as unpromising, standing as he did with 13 opponents between him and the tryline. But a second later Goodwin slipped through a gap created by threatening to pass to winger Castle, an act guaranteed to generate panic so near the line. Forward he went, everyone in the stadium, including the Oldham players, convinced Castle would receive that pass. But the pass never came. Goodwin splashed over the line with three defenders clinging to his shirt like small boys trying to hold onto a kite on a windy day.

Soon afterwards Willie effortlessly dropped a goal, ignoring the presence of Oldham forwards, arms groping in the air, hoping forlornly to intercept his kick. Moments later Barrow were threatening again, penning Oldham back deep in their own half, defending tenaciously, big men sliding forward briefly before being driven back as Barrow sensed another score was likely.

Winger Dick Cracknell, a £4,500 signing from Huddersfield, was the unfortunate player who fumbled precariously close to the line. Second-row Reg Parker pounced quickly, diving on the loose ball for Barrow's second try as the Oldham players stood rigid, ponderous and sluggish, as if the strain of all that tackling had begun to diminish their spirit, as if, deep down, they knew the match was beyond them. Willie converted and though Ganley briefly heartened his team by kicking a penalty goal, Oldham left the field at half-time wearing stubborn expressions of defiance while Barrow changed shirts and drank tea, chattering excitedly, sensing the cup was almost won.

"Keep it up lads," Willie said. "Keep tackling and play safe. We've no need to take chances."

Even the most dutiful Oldham fan knew a comeback was unlikely. On the day they had not been good enough. So the second 40 minutes was a pleasant wait before an historic celebration. Willie kicked a late penalty to put Barrow ahead 12-2 as referee Ron Gelder blew his whistle signalling a pitch invasion no one had anticipated considering the quagmire underfoot. But most of the 4,000 Barrow fans did not want to miss the opportunity of sharing their heroes' euphoria and savouring every last drop of excitement by patting soaking shirts and yelling passionate gratitude.

Willie wiped his hands before walking up the steps to receive the cup from Mrs Spedding, wife of the County President. Three hours later the team strode from Barrow's Central railway station, through a human sea of supporters, clapping and cheering, even the awful rain failing to dampen their rampant jubilation. A team bus whisked the party to the Washington Hotel in Roose Road, escorted by two police cars, their presence signalled by wailing sirens.

The next day there was a civic reception at the town hall where the players were each presented with inscribed ash trays by the Mayor, Coun. T. A. Tyson. And while they were enjoying a five-course meal, a crowd began to chant outside, faintly at first, but rising steadily until the noise became an insistent roar . . . "We want Willie. We want Willie." At last, he appeared, embarrassed and uncomfortable, cup in hand, flanked by his fellow conquering champions.

It was an emotional moment, especially sweet, coming as it did at the end of a career that had seen Willie achieve almost everything. He had captained his home team, his county, his country and Great Britain. He had been on two

Australian tours and he was assured of a place in history as one of the greatest stand-off halves the world had ever seen. There was just one thing missing – winning the Challenge Cup at Wembley. This year would, like as not, be their last chance. Many of the players, like Willie, were growing old. He dared not think how it would feel to realise that dream. To think of it — two cups in one season. Perhaps not. That was too much to expect.

★ ★ ★

Four weeks after the thrill of the Lancashire Cup, Barrow had been beaten by St Helens, Wigan and Warrington. These defeats were narrow but nevertheless the lost points all but destroyed hopes of a championship title or a place in the top four play-offs. All they had left was the Challenge Cup.

In the first round Barrow scraped through 11-8 at Dewsbury, a struggling side more familiar with embarrassing 30 point drubbings. Both teams made so many mistakes the game was strewn with penalties and scrums. But at least Barrow had won. And any disappointment at their poor performance was consoled with the knowledge that the victory earned them a second round trip to Salford, festering in mid-table, a great side in decline.

The Willows pitch was more like a ploughed farmer's field than a sports arena. Nevertheless Barrow were superb. Led by dedicated forwards, they crushed the opposition 13-0. The third round meant further travelling, this time to Rochdale Hornets, another challenging match with an uncertain outcome. But Willie's team were again inspired, winning 13-2 with tries from Les Belshaw, Frank Barton and Jimmy Lewthwaite. There was a measured determination permeating through the Barrow side, a confidence and security that was increasing with every game. It was as if the players sensed they were going all the way, that Wembley was their ultimate destiny, that they were unbeatable.

Such excited anticipation was mirrored by eager supporters who had begun making tentative inquiries as to the chances of time off work on Saturday, April 30. The semi-final paired Barrow with Hunslet at Central Park, Wigan.

It was the draw no one had wanted. The other semi-final, to be played at Headingley, was between Workington Town and Featherstone Rovers, both tough, respected sides. But they had been fortunate to avoid the might of Hunslet, powerful, clever and bristling with internationals.

Away from Craven Park no one was giving Barrow much chance of reaching the final. Hunslet had so many good players, brave forwards such as Arthur Clues and Geoff Gunney complemented by fast, gifted backs such as Dickie Williams, Great Britain's 1954 tour captain, and Alf Burnell. More than 7,000 Barrow fans travelled from Furness, disregarding newspaper predictions that Hunslet were strong favourites to get to Wembley. This was our year, their faith still undiminished. Yes, Hunslet were a great team. But we had Willie Horne.

★ ★ ★

Willie's reputation for greatness would have destroyed a lesser man. He had an engaging capacity to produce the unexpected at just the right time, an uncanny gift that rarely failed him when his team needed it most. And the Barrow players had come to rely on it too, perhaps unreasonably so. But they had anyway.

As half-time approached, Barrow held a 4-2 lead. There was a scrum on the Hunslet 25 and you could tell from the manner the Yorkshire forwards packed down, slow and deliberate, that they were happy with their efforts despite the scoreline. Hunslet had attacked often and boldly. They had looked ominously dangerous, kept out only by desperate defence. For the moment, the blue line remained unbreached but you had the feeling that unless Barrow could scramble a try all might be lost, that Hunslet were preparing to swamp them.

Willie stood on the open side, his threequarters alert and prepared. Ted Toohey gave him the ball quickly as he had been instructed by his captain while the Hunslet pack scattered into space to assist the backs.

Everyone was marked tightly. Dickie Williams waited five yards in front of Willie, arms held out stiffly, shuffling sideways like a crab, shepherding him, mindful of the unexpected. He had played against Willie many times, enough to be cautious and patient, enough to respect what his opponent could do. Williams's face was etched in concentration when it happened. The move was half sidestep, half body swerve, a gift that is impossible to teach, something you are born with. One second they were together, almost touching, the next Williams was lying on the ground fumbling for something solid to grab, but failing, fingers stretching into emptiness.

Willie was gone, darting forward, glancing around, calculating instantly the position of the Hunslet defenders, their direction, angle and where they would be two seconds later. Loose forward Granville James was closing in fast but Willie was thinking quickly now.

"I'm here," barked Phil Jackson as the Hunslet centre prepared to make the tackle, knowing he was outnumbered. Yet all was not lost, not yet. Behind him, sprinting flat out, full back Arthur Talbot was moving across the field.

Drawing defenders and parting with the ball is something internationals do effortlessly, making a mockery of the precision of such an act. If you pass too early your advantage is lost, too late and you are tackled with the ball. You're dealing in fractions of a second, the difference between success and failure, victory and defeat, Wembley or the tears of broken dreams.

Almost on top of him now. Surely he's left it too late. A blur of movement. Willie and the Hunslet centre are down in a crumpled heap, dazed from the collision but Jackson has the ball now, similarly drawing the winger before feeding Jimmy Lewthwaite 20 yards from the Hunslet line . . . the cover is almost across. Talbot makes the tackle, the two men locked, striving for domination as they crash across the line, Jimmy grounding the ball before sliding off the field, as he has done for Barrow 100 times before. A middle-aged woman wearing a light brown coat and a black hat runs on and embraces him as he picks himself up, covered in mud and glory, the crowd wild, howling their approval.

It was a dramatic score that was to have a terminal effect on Hunslet's hopes of victory. And there was worse to come as the Yorkshiremen stood beneath the sticks, the rain still falling in great sheets while Willie prepared for the conversion attempt, a yard from the touchline. It was the sort of distance and angle a good kicker might be happy to make perhaps one in five on a still, dry day. Then there was the pressure – you know, Wembley just 40 minutes away. In this weather it was bordering on the impossible.

Willie walked backwards, quickly, as he always did, until he was lost in the crowd briefly before emerging, coming at the ball in a half circle, unique, like no one had ever done before. Away it went, long, straight and true, dropping over the sticks for two more points. If you were close enough you would have seen the anguish on the Hunslet players' faces as they jogged to the halfway line like mourners at a funeral.

Willie was back in position now, waving away the congratulations of his comrades with an impatient shake of his arm, ordering players to concentrate and prepare to receive the kick. The previous two minutes had changed the complexion of the game. Barrow were on top, confident, aggressive, fired-up. No one was going to stop them making that Wembley trip. Not now.

Hunslet rallied in the second half. Two penalty kicks from Talbot brought them within three points. One converted try and Barrow were out. On came Hunslet in waves, pouring forward relentlessly, repeatedly and with such determination there seemed at times no way the blue shirts could hold out. Forwards crashing, backs jinking, searching everywhere for a weakness, trying the open then the blind, like a tide rolling in, persistent and mighty. Intermittently, when Barrow had the ball, Willie cleared the threat with long kicks, but then they were back, the green shirts pummelling Barrow's line tirelessly. But they did not cross. When at last the final whistle came, players shook hands and embraced, mutual respect flowing like an electric current.

Later that night a crowd started to form at Barrow's Central railway station, a handful at first, then more as the evening wore on, until there were hundreds waiting to greet their heroes. The players signed autographs patiently, the way they always did, before disappearing into the night, home to recover and prepare for the final, four weeks away. Workington Town had beaten Featherstone Rovers. The Cumberland team, captained by Bill Ivison, had won the cup three years before. But now, it was said, they were even better. It wasn't going to be easy. But the drama at Central Park had fuelled great optimism. Barrow were going to win. And everyone wanted to be at Wembley to see it.

★ ★ ★

They sold jewellery, furniture, clothes and tools, anything they could get their hands on. Books, bikes, toys and paintings all ended up in Furness pawn shops as houses emptied to raise the cash needed to make the long journey south. Everyone seemed to be going. It was like a crusade. Teachers, dockers, fitters, joiners, mechanics, young and old, rich and poor – were all making plans for the big day. Houses were decked in white and blue, and everyone was talking about little else but the final, our chances of winning and how a town would celebrate the victory. Locomotives began arriving on Monday, pulling empty coaches from Crewe and Chester, Rhyl and Birmingham, long, black lines snaking through the Barrow sidings until it seemed the station could take no more. A seat cost 55 shillings and threepence (two pounds 77 pence).

The first train steamed out of Barrow at 7.15 on Friday morning, packed with 670 fans bound for Euston station. Every half hour the trains left, until finally the town fell silent and ghostly, stripped of more than 17,000 inhabitants. Then there were buses, motor cycles and cars, meandering along the A590 sounding horns, waving flags, everyone cheering, united in expectation.

The players and directors were staying at the Riviera Hotel, Maidenhead, 26 miles from the capital, cocooned from the excitement. But they knew what was happening, anxiety accelerating with every passing hour. At 10 o'clock on Saturday morning a Dakota plane left Walney Island carrying 34 supporters. Half an hour later another plane took off also heading for Bovington Airfield where a luxury coach awaited them.

Wembley was beginning to fill when the team bus arrived at the stadium an hour and a half before the kick-off, the sun shining from a cloudless sky. Workington Town were already there, safe in the dressing room. The minutes ticked by slowly until someone said it was time to get changed, not into their usual blue and white hoops. A clash of colours had forced Barrow to wear red shirts with a white 'V'. But no one was thinking about colours then.

This was it. Willie's last chance. Losing was unthinkable.

Willie introduces prop forward Ralph Hartley to H.R.H. the Duke of Gloucester before the 1951 Challenge Cup Final.

Willie closes in on a Wigan forward in the 1951 Challenge Cup Final. Barrow could not overcome the handicap of limited possession. Wigan won 10–0 with tries from Ken Gee and Jack Hilton.

No way through for Wigan front-row forward George Curran wrapped up by Harry Atkinson in the 1951 Challenge Cup Final.

Thousands welcome the Barrow Wembley party home to a civic reception at Barrow town hall.

Barrow prop forward John Pearson plunges over the Workington tryline during the epic 1952 Challenge Cup semi-final at Central Park, Wigan. The referee disallowed the try and Workington hung on for a 5–2 win.

Barrow's Great Britain halfbacks Willie Horne and Ted Toohey.

Australian skipper Clive Churchill and Willie lead the teams out for the 1952 First Test at Headingley.

Willie presents Bradford Northern's brilliant loose forward Ken Traill to Lord Derby.

Greg Hawick, the Australian stand-off half in the First Test. A strong, fearless opponent.

Hunslet full back Jack Evans is brought down by Mick Crocker during Great Britain's 19–5 First Test victory.

Willie kicks for position in the First Test despite the close attentions of an Australian defender. Bob Ryan, Warrington second-row forward is in support.

Australian Tour Manager Doug McClean presents the Ashes Cup to Willie Horne before the Third Test at Odsal. The Australians won 27–7 in a battle dubbed by the Sydney Morning Herald: "The worst example of unruly and disgraceful football anyone had seen."

The Lancashire line-up who defeated Cumberland 19-11 at Whitehaven in May, 1952. Back: Ike Fishwick, Eric Ayles, Charlie Pawsey, Alan Prescott, Jack Cunliffe, Austin Heathwood, Jack Grundy, unknown. Front: Jack Hilton, Alan Davies, Willie Horne (captain), Gerry Helme, Albert Naughton and Laurie Platt.

Dickie Williams, the Hunslet stand-off half, who was chosen as the 1954 Great Britain Tour captain.

Phil Jackson, Barrow's international centre threequarter, who played 27 times for Great Britain.

Dennis Goodwin, at 6 feet 4 and 16 stones the biggest centre threequarter in the game.

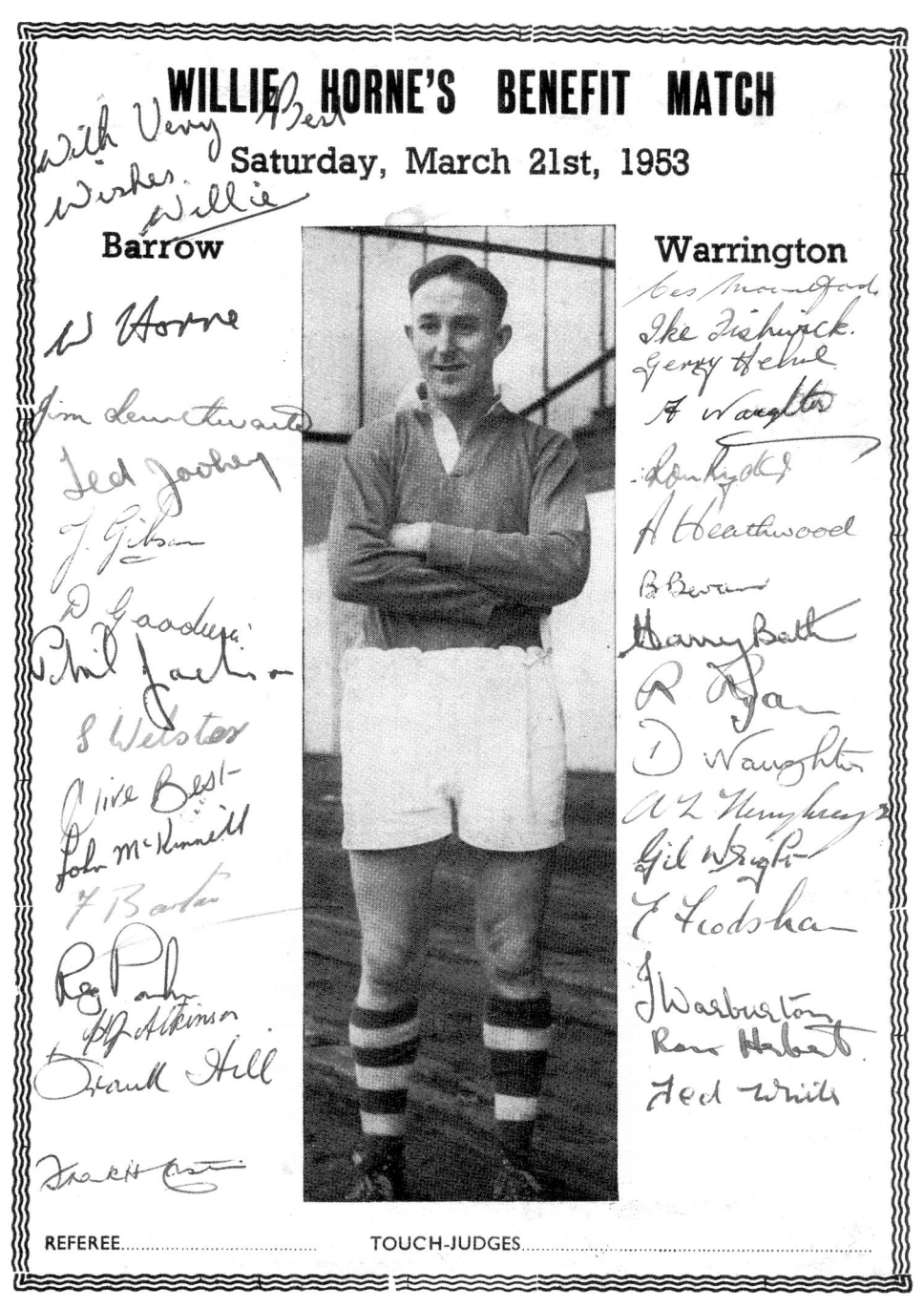

WILLIE HORNE'S BENEFIT MATCH
Saturday, March 21st, 1953

Barrow — **Warrington**

With very best wishes, Willie

Part of Willie Horne's testimonial brochure signed by the players. Barrow defeated Warrington at Craven Park 30–17 in front of a crowd of 12,192. The final total of Willie's benefit was £950, the second highest in rugby league history at that time.

Barrow winger Derek Hinchley, between Oldham's Great Britain internationals Terry O'Grady and Frank Pitchford during the 1954 Lancashire Cup Final.

Oldham second-row forward Sid Little in the skull cap and record signing Dick Cracknell, number two, anxiously watch a loose ball during the Lancashire Cup Final. Barrow dominated the match, defeating Oldham 12–2 at Station Road, Swinton.

Willie and international scrum-half Ted Toohey bring home the Lancashire Cup.

Barrow before the 1955 Challenge Cup semi-final against Hunslet at Central Park, Wigan. Back: Frank Hill (trainer), Frank Barton, Jimmy Lewthwaite, Les Belshaw, Reg Parker, Phil Jackson, Vince McKeating, Dennis Goodwin and Walter Bouyer (assistant coach). Front: Jack Grundy, Frank Castle, Willie Horne (captain and coach), Ted Toohey, Clive Best and Bill Healey.

Jimmy Lewthwaite scores the match-winning try in the 1955 Challenge Cup semi-final when Barrow defeated Hunslet 9–6. The woman in the light coat and dark hat, overcome with emotion, ran on the pitch and hugged the Barrow wingman.

CHAPTER NINETEEN

THE DRESSING ROOM

WE WERE all terribly nervous. I roomed with Dennis Goodwin and I can remember him saying to me the night before the cup final: "Don't talk to me about rugby, Reg. Anything but rugby." Each player knew he might never get another chance to play at Wembley.

Yet somehow Willie calmed everyone down. Just by being there. I've come across many top players but there'll never be another like Willie Horne. He was a complete footballer, a man who could do anything. When he said something we all listened. It was like that in the dressing room before the kick-off.

Personally I remember thinking that we had the greatest stand-off half the game has ever seen as our captain. He would inspire us as he always did. So what could possibly go wrong? I know the rest of the Barrow team felt the same way. He had complete command of us all. A legend in his own lifetime. Our idol.

REG PARKER
Barrow RLFC second-row forward, 1955 Challenge Cup Final

TENSION stains the air. They have been told to get ready but most of the Barrow players still wander aimlessly around the dressing room praying for time to pass more quickly, not sure what to do. Sound ebbs and flows inexplicably. One moment a hubbub of chatter, the next an eerie silence so it seems inappropriate to talk, the crowd's cheers filter through the stone walls. And all the while a dripping tap echoes in the background.

Red shirts hang forlornly from rows of pegs above folded shorts and socks, neat and regimented, accentuating the unsettling knowledge that today's game is different from any other – that it's special, unique – the final of the Challenge Cup. They don't come any bigger. Scrum-half Ted Toohey is the first to change, as he always is. He lies on a bench in the middle of the room, eyes closed while reserve Danny Leatherbarrow rubs his leg muscles expertly like an old baker kneading dough, the flesh turning red from the increased circulation.

"Half-an-hour to go," someone shouts. The room is full now, players, directors and coaching staff mixing together, making it appear confined and cramped. No one says much. But they're thinking plenty. Every now and then someone might pat a player on the back without speaking or reach down to shake a trembling hand before moving on, mumbling a familiar phrase . . . "good luck" or "let's give 'em Hell," depending on the personality of the man in question, the mood drifting irrevocably towards confrontation.

Occasionally someone enters the room and the noise sweeps in with him, the patriotic notes of the Grenadier Guards marching on the soft grass a hundred yards away, the tune easy to follow so that in different circumstances one might consider whistling along. But not today. Then the door closes and the song is muted and unrecognisable as if the volume has been turned down on a transistor radio.

Everyone is putting on playing kit now, taking turns for a rub down while trainer Wally Bowyer straps ankles and wrists, but not out of medical necessity. The reason is more simple. Strapping makes some players feel good. It gives them confidence.

"Ten minutes lads," an anonymous voice warns as forwards Jack Grundy and Bill Healey circulate, encouraging, cajoling as if the fear of failure has passed them by, as in fact it has, while in a corner Ted Toohey slumps unaffected by the enormity of the challenge before him . . . asleep. Yes, he's flat out. But no one gives him a second glance. Ted often dozes off before a big match. They have seen it all before, yet today of all days, they had not expected it. Not now. How could he? But there he is, dead to the world, while they sit shaking, apprehension gnawing at their souls.

Everyone is changed when Barrow chairman John Atkinson begins addressing the players. He speaks softly, suggesting they enjoy themselves, that all that matters is trying their best. He adds how well they have done to reach the final, that win or lose he is proud of them. But no one's thinking about losing. It is an obligatory speech voiced without emotion and it is noticeable in that cauldron of excitement that he seems subdued and preoccupied in the manner of a man who's just remembered he's left his car lights on. No matter. When he's finished the babble restarts, many players taking a quick peep in Willie's direction hoping they might be infected by his confidence and apparent detachment. They respect him obediently, without question, so much so that it is inconceivable to them that the occasion could erode his skills and his capacity for inspiration.

Inside Willie is as nervous as everyone else. But watching him, it is impossible to detect apprehension. Yes, Willie has seen it all before, the cup finals, the internationals, the Test matches. But today means more to him than anything that has gone before. Barrow is his town. And outside are his family, his friends and his supporters, the people who matter. He wants to win so badly it almost hurts inside him. And it's going to be tough. Willie knows that. His defence is still faultless and his passing still outrageously accurate but he is no longer a young man. Time was when a second-row forward made a break and looked around for a halfback Willie would always be there. But now. Well, he might not make it.

Across a corridor, separated by 20 feet and two walls of concrete, Workington's preparations are almost complete. Coach Jim Brough is talking, trying to pacify shattered nerves and manufacture controlled expectation. Some sit in silence while others intermittently bark out empty cliches such as "we can do it" or "come on Town." But no one's listening.

Bill Wookey is in a corner, face drained, arms hanging by his side. He's the Workington stand-off half. He's 18. And he's from Barrow. So marking the master carries more deep-rooted mental pressures than performing with distinction under pressure with 70,000 people watching your every move. Bill has always looked up to Willie. Now he is expected to subdue his contribution, to shadow his genius. You might as well ask me to walk on the moon, he thinks.

"What's up marra?" asks 18-year-old scrum-half Sol Roper. "You're not nervous are you?" There's a mischievous impudence about him common to all great half backs. Sol laughs a lot. He has a child's face, the look of a boy scout, and you are left thinking growing old would be unsuitable for him.

"I'm bloody terrified," Bill says, perspiring with consternation.

"What for, man? Horne and Toohey are old men. We've got nowt to worry about. It's going to be easy."

Bill smiles politely. But he remains unconvinced. Captain Bill Ivison is talking now, the customary routine they've heard a hundred times before – basics such as keeping onside and moving up a line. Still, they listen courteously, in silence, bar a solitary interruption when a forward bellows "come on, come on," and bangs a table so violently a pile of folded towels falls to the floor.

"Five minutes," someone says back in the Barrow dressing room. Nothing much to do now but wait. Willie kneels by Bill Healey, who is still cocky, still calm, while all around them big men are stricken with self-doubt, anxiety fermenting like a virus.

"Right Bill," he says, his legs glistening with liniment. "I want you to watch Bill Ivison and don't take any dummies. Every time he has the ball tackle him, and tackle him hard."

"OK Willie," he answers. "I'll do my best." Willie nods as he walks to the centre of the room comforted by the unshakeable belief that his request will be granted, that the job will get done. He has asked him to mark men before and Bill has never failed him. He's watched over great back row forwards like Vince Karalius, Ken Traill and Les White and they have all been rendered impotent and ineffective. So Willie knows he's asked the right man.

"I want everyone to watch Bill Ivison," he repeats to the rest of the team, silence immediate and obedient. "All Workington's attacks come from him. You all know we're here to win so let's get out there and do it. Keep it tight early and let's get on top right away."

His team begin shouting their approval, shaking hands and wishing each other well as a bell rings out, the kind you hear when you walk into a grocer's shop, two long rings, a moment's silence before more shouting and backslapping, Willie is already at the door holding a ball. It is time. And they are ready.

★ ★ ★

Out into the corridor they march, alongside the Workington players, next to them, so close that shoulders brush as they line up behind their captains, two rows of men. They are standing on a slight incline waiting for the signal to walk onto the field that no one can see. Not yet. Up ahead groundsmen and officials mill about as the band marches off, still playing. The delay is only slight, just a few seconds. Some jog lightly on the spot, arms hanging limply while others stand still as statues staring ahead, desperate for the match to start but knowing the kick-off is still ten minutes away. The time is slow and painful, the tension rising tangibly as if you could reach out and touch it. No one is talking. But they are all thinking, some good, some bad. Everyone is jumpy, fear penetrating reason, infiltrating the subconscious and all the time there's the crowd, hopeful and expectant, chanting and cheering, heightening the pressure of anticipation, the fear of failure. Ahead, Willie and Bill talk quietly.

"Good luck Willie," Bill says and if you could hear him you would know he means it, that the words are spoken sincerely, that they are much more than the empty obligation of a courteous man.

"Thanks Bill. Let's hope it's a good, clean game."

They're old friends, you see. They've played together for England. Bill and Willie like each other. The chat is carefree and casual as a housewife might speak to a neighbour hanging out washing, the breeze rustling through her hair as she reaches forward, a long line of clothes stretching out behind her, 'good drying day,' she'd say, pegs in her mouth.

They're moving now, out into the sun, the sky blue and cloudless, the air still, Workington to the left, Barrow to the right, each man walking slowly. Willie looks solemn. Bill smiles. He's wearing number 14 instead of the customary 13, unwilling to chance bad luck. Not today. At the halfway line, two columns of men, the odd arm thrown up acknowledging where a player believes a loved one sits, proud but nervous. The two captains are a similar height but Bill is 30 pounds heavier, hands like shovels, thick shoulders like a Canadian lumberjack.

The players turn to face each other a few yards apart, staring but seeing nothing, as the band plays God Save the Queen, eyes filling, the crowd tuneless but enthusiastic. The Duke of Edinburgh shakes hands with each player, first Barrow then Workington, small talk, "good luck," he says, "enjoy the game." But no one's interested. The referee blows his whistle and the players break away rapidly, picking up balls, passing, warming up, loosening muscles, everyone keen to start.

Bill Ivison wins the toss, signalling to his side with a wave of his hand to change ends. The crowd settles, briefly subdued, before a piercing roar greets the kick-off, the ball booted deep into the Workington half towards international winger Ike Southward.

In fewer than 90 minutes it will be all over. There will be a winner. And there will be a loser. Barrow are ready. Every man. And they don't want to lose.

CHAPTER TWENTY

WE WON THE CUP

I REMEMBER something happening in the cup final that left me shaking my head not believing what I had seen. There was a scrum in Barrow's half early on. Willie got the ball and someone charged his kick down and we nearly scored. A couple of minutes later there was another scrum in the same place but this time Willie kicked deep, more than 60 yards before the ball bounced a couple of times and went into touch. He did that regularly throughout the final.

The first mistake could have cost Barrow the match but it didn't bother Willie. Anyone else would have been shaken, but not him. I've never met anyone so self-confident.

Of course I couldn't mark him. No one could. He was never there to mark. Even from a scrum there was no telling where he'd be or what he was going to do. And there were so many things he was capable of. Willie was very quick over 25 yards or he might kick or put out a long pass or there might be a move on. Playing with Willie must have been marvellous. Everyone will have known something special was going to happen, that with him in the team it was just a matter of time.

It was Willie's Wembley. There's no doubt about that.

BILL WOOKEY
Workington Town stand-off half and 1958 British Lion

THE FIRST half was direct, unspectacular and tough – forty minutes' hostile confrontation between two teams more accustomed to enterprising football. But this was Wembley. Traditionally the Challenge Cup Final stifles flair and subdues creativity, the terrible fear of defeat overwhelming participants so utterly they oppose risk. They resist responsibility. They don't take chances.

Territorially at least Barrow had been dominant. But they could not turn pressure into points. Town defended with courage, repelling the red shirts with the same admirable conviction that had seen them defeat Leeds, St Helens and Featherstone Rovers in similar circumstances on their way to the final. There was one significant difference that would ultimately prove crucial. They did not get the ball.

In 1955 rugby league was not like today. Players obeyed the laws of the game or they were sent off. And that meant a scrum-half caught by an observant referee feeding his own hooker gave away a free kick. In 1955 there were no differential penalties. The innocent team were given, and more often than not took, the opportunity of kicking a goal and scoring two points. So a scrum-half who did not throw the ball in straight did not remain in the team long, even if he tackled like a terrier and scored tries with clockwork regularity. Possession was that important.

There were more scrums in those days too, often as many as 70 in a game, almost one a minute. Hookers, above all else, were hookers. It was a specific skill you acquired as a small boy watching older, experienced players as one might learn to become an accomplished pianist. You picked up the subtleties of how to strike first, the signals of your scrum-half and the essential relationship that needs to be developed with an open-side prop forward. Generally it was a gift that can only be marginally developed by training. Good hookers were born, not made.

A professional hooker will be workmanlike and reliable in the loose. Nothing more is expected from him. But he must get the ball. If he has not won 50 per cent of the scrums he will consider the match a personal failure even if he scored the winning try or made a host of wonderful tackles.

Your side might be a point ahead with time running out as the referee signals a scrimmage close to your own tryline. You do not have the benefit of the feed or the head and only the most optimistic supporter will believe you can win the ball. But if you are successful and the pack clears the line, until the game has ended you will be a hero. The captain will congratulate you and other players will pat you on the back. And they will be right to do so. To win the ball at such a stage of the match, against all odds, would be a contribution to the team equivalent to, say, a winger scoring a try from his own 25 or a second-row forward completing 35 tackles.

There were 28 scrums in the first half of the cup final. Barrow, or rather Vince McKeating, won 21 of them, a remarkable achievement by a man who, ironically, had assisted Workington Town to lift the cup three years earlier. He was a man of indeterminate age. It was said he was close to 40. Perhaps. Perhaps not. Looking at him, his grey hair and his lived-in face, it was an opinion not without foundation. But Vince could hook that ball. And now a player Barrow bought from Dewsbury for £75 was all but destroying Workington's hopes of victory by his monotonous domination of the scrimmages.

But you can have too much of the ball. Barrow squandered chances, dropping passes, wandering offside and mistiming runs. They tried everything, Willie taking the ball at first receiver as he had for more than 12 years, testing Town's defences, left then right, a long pass, a kick or a run down the blind like a chess grand master probing for a weakness, searching, testing. But they could not find a way through. Town held firm. At half-time the sides were locked 2-2 with a penalty by Australian centre threequarter Tony Paskins cancelled by Willie's goal ten minutes later.

The Grenadier Guards marched on the field, drums beating, instruments blaring, as the players shuffled off for a short rest, to regroup, to treat injuries, and consider if pre-match plans were in need of alteration. Barrow were not overly concerned. And Willie said so. When you have six internationals in your back line, possession usually means points. It's just a matter of time. Be patient, Willie told them. Don't worry, Barrow are on top, and likely to remain so.

Workington had an unlikely diversion to distract them from contemplation of their inability to win possession. A telegram was waiting for centre threequarter Eppie Gibson. "**CONGRATULATIONS. YOU HAVE A DAUGHTER HELEN KAY, 6LBS 8OZS, SISTER FOR SUSAN. – LOVE MARIE.**"

A few handshakes and good wishes before coach Jim Brough began trying to stimulate the enthusiasm of his troops. They were tiring. He could see that. Tackling for more than 25 minutes is exhausting work, especially for big forwards. In every scrum you are required to push hard, to strain with all the power you can muster, to try to give your hooker an advantage. Your heels dig in the soft turf, thighs straining, five, ten, 15 seconds, then the ball is lost and you scatter quickly to take your place in the defensive line, feeling as if you've been working in the garden all day digging deep trenches. Now it's all sharp sprinting, up then back, but the red shirts keep pouring forward, driving into you. And there's no respite. They keep on coming. Another scrum. When will they stop? And still you can't win the ball.

The Workington pack were wearing the glazed expressions that afflict all men in the early stages of fatigue. Some sat panting, snatching quick breaths to placate tired lungs, others stood, drinking, talking nervously, the way you do when awaiting important news and you fear something bad is about to happen. In a few moments they would have to go out and start again, more of the same, repelling the Barrow forwards, so fit, so strong and relentless, chasing the backs, jinking, weaving, running quickly and all the time that man Horne patrolling behind his team, ordering, organising, pointing, telling his players what he expects from them. The bell rang. Jim Brough continued his monologue of encouragement as they walked to the door looking disinterested as if they had been listening to a weather forecast. Barrow were on top. And there wasn't much they could do about it.

★ ★ ★

The first half had been unpleasant and frustrating for Workington supporters. Of course, they took some solace from the level scoreline but the pertinent question was how long they could hold out. The crowd did not have long to wait before Willie provided the answer. After six minutes he kicked a penalty goal from an angle you would not wish to attempt if your life depended on the outcome. Two minutes later he dropped a goal, the ball in his hands momentarily before sailing between the uprights, Willie already trotting to the halfway line knowing the attempt was successful. Drop goals always came easily to him – even at Wembley.

Barrow were four points ahead. Again they pushed forward, threatening. And again Workington responded, tackling fiercely, tired men lurching from one side to another, like small boats in a violent sea. Town were beginning to buckle. There was a desperate look about them, the crowd yelling impatiently. Barrow had to score. How could Town resist such an onslaught? They could not keep it up. Surely. Yet they did. Somehow.

Captain Bill Ivison was everywhere, covering, urging, leading from the front, a tackle here, a tackle there, up and down, courage and defiance emanating from his presence. You watched the white shirts and marvelled at their unshakeable spirit. But fate was about to deliver a blow that would terminate any dwindling hopes of a comeback. Scrum-half Sol Roper tore a shoulder muscle and was stretchered off, briefly unconscious. To his credit he returned a few minutes later to shuffle up and down the right wing, intermittently standing in the way of Barrow runners mercilessly exploiting the weakness. He was brave but as acutely ineffective as you would expect from someone without the use of an arm.

Vince McKeating continued to churn out the ball from the scrums, but in the 62nd minute he made what was, for him, an unlikely contribution. He scored a try. It was not like him. He had played 58 times for Barrow and managed only five tries, so scoring was unfamiliar to him. Hardly surprising when you consider his captain's standing orders.

"Keep out of the way," Willie had told him, orders Vince willingly obeyed. But for once he was in the right place at the right time, the ball flashing across the threequarters to the left wing, faster than a fit man can run, where Vince was standing, having a rest, as if he was not part of the action, but an observer, as one might look over the shoulder of a card player in a bridge tournament. He was actually standing *outside* Frank Castle. No one ever stands outside a winger. It is taboo, a place no professional rugby league player would think of being. Never. But there he was, catching a pass and diving over the tryline with just a hint of offside, while the Town players exchanged bemused looks, as if they were asking each other: "What the hell was he doing there?"

A couple of minutes later Dennis Goodwin scored Barrow's second try, another linking move, full of fast hands and excellent support play, Willie's team searching for gaps, openings that suddenly appear when exhausted men who have given everything, and much, much more, realise they have nothing left to give. Willie converted both tries to give his side a 16-2 lead. After 55 years they were going to win the cup. That was now beyond doubt.

But Workington were not ready to give up. Knowing time was slipping away they began throwing the ball around without regard to risk, admirable tactics that produced a daring try by Ken Faulder. Then Barrow came back, the game exploding into a thrilling finale that no one fortunate enough to witness would ever forget.

Bill Healey, the loose forward who had made a colossal contribution to his team's cause, burst through Workington's uneven defensive line, a row of fatigued men, who had begun so straight and united but had now disintegrated into an incoherent mess. He fed Jack Grundy who in turn passed to Castle, the winger falling over the tryline with Sol Roper holding on hopelessly with his good arm. Again Willie converted, his sixth successful kick, equalling the Challenge Cup Final record set by Huddersfield captain Len Bowkett in 1933. Workington rallied once more with Eppie Gibson dummying his way through for an outstanding individual try. But it mattered not.

Soon after the restart Willie got the ball and ambled towards Bill Wookey who tackled him carefully, almost affectionately as a father might tuck a small daughter in bed on a cold, winter night. Then it was over. Referee Ron Gelder blew his whistle as the two half backs embraced, emotion flooding between them, one soaking in the ecstasy of victory the other overcome by the wretched pain of defeat. Later Bill was to recall that final tackle was the only time he had caught Willie in the entire 80 minutes.

Barrow supporters looked on, drinking in the euphoria of success, admiration and gratitude floating down from the terraces of the old stadium. And there in the centre of the field, among the mingling mass of players was Willie. Above all else there was Willie. His work-rate, as always, had been tireless. He had tackled enthusiastically, kicked accurately in the loose as well as those six successful conversions and drop goals achieved under the most intense pressure. He had made all these contributions and much, much more. And now it was time to receive the Challenge Cup for which his town had been praying for decades.

Willie walked up the steps in front of his team, each man dodging hands stretching to pat backs and rub heads. He seemed almost embarrassed by the adulation as the Duke of Edinburgh handed over the cup, Willie's hair dishevelled, his hands shaking with anticipation.

"Congratulations," the Duke said. "My goodness, rugby league's a hard game." It was a polite understatement that did not require an answer. Willie was away now, moving down the steps, through more outstretched arms, searching to touch the cup and experience a personal piece of history, something to tell their grandchildren: "I was at Wembley when Barrow beat Workington Town. And I touched the cup. Honestly, I actually touched the cup."

Out on to the field, the cheers turned briefly from celebration and gratitude to respect and sympathy as the Workington players received losers' medals, gracious, dignified and respectful, before leaving the field to begin the awful task of coming to terms with failure. Willie was carried off the pitch by Vince McKeating and Frank Barton, the rest of his team surrounding them as he held the cup up high, the cup many said he would never win. He was too small, too weak, too quiet, too honest, too sincere. But they were wrong. And here he was savouring the moment, all the more agreeable for their misgiving.

Back in the dressing room the Barrow players were immersed in celebration, enjoying the unfamiliar sound of popping champagne corks and the clink of glasses toasting a great triumph, planning what they were going to do with their £45 winning money. They left Wembley stadium for an evening of subdued satisfaction that comes to all sportsmen who have stared adversity in the face and won a famous victory. What they really wanted was to get home where those who had been unable to make the trip to London were enjoying a more boisterous and traditional Saturday night preparing to welcome their heroes.

The party travelled to Ulverston on Monday but the threat of a rail strike had caused confusion over plans to parade the Challenge Cup through the streets in the traditional manner. To make matters worse, Rugby League authorities had insisted Barrow play their final match of the season at home to Leigh that night. They arrived at Ulverston station at 4.55pm where an open-topped bus took players and directors around the town centre, the shops bedecked in bunting, everyone cheering, waving, a huge sign outside the Coronation Hall proclaiming "Good Old Willie."

Onward to Lindal, through more huge crowds, through Dalton, Tudor Square, around the castle to Abbey Road, time getting short as thousands made for Craven Park. Past the Strawberry Hotel, the White House, the Coliseum, the Evening Mail offices and on to Ramsden Square, a bulging throng of humanity clapping spontaneously, engulfed in admiration and gratitude, until finally they reached the ground. And there at the main entrance the first person to welcome them was Willie's mother, overcome with emotion, a kiss for her son, more cheers, and then they were gone.

Ten minutes later, at 6.25pm, Willie ran on the pitch through a human tunnel formed by the Leigh players smiling, paying their respects to a great side led by a great man. More than 15,000 fans crammed into the ground to watch a thrilling match which Barrow lost 21-15. But no one cared. A final lap of honour, one more chance to see the cup, before the party slipped away for a "quiet" celebration at the Washington Hotel, where a crowd of more than 500 was waiting.

On Thursday, players and officials attended a civic reception at the Town Hall where the Mayor, Alderman T. A. Tyson made an emotional speech of appreciation. "I have been following Barrow RL since 1910," he said. "Now you have won the Challenge Cup and made this the greatest year of my life."

Willie answered on behalf of his team. "We have played every round away but in every game we felt we were at home through the cheers of our own supporters," he said. "This is the best side I have captained and I am proud to have led such a grand set of lads."

It took some time for Furness to return to normal. The general consensus was that Barrow had won primarily because of their wonderful team spirit and the outstanding contribution of back row forwards Reg Parker, Bill Healey and Jack Grundy who was awarded the Lance Todd Trophy. But after a week no one was talking about them. They were talking about Willie.

Barrow supporters recalled the four goals he made to knock out Dewsbury in the first round. Then there was that spark of genius to create

Jimmy Lewthwaite's winning try in the semi-final, not forgetting his touchline conversion. And those six kicks at Wembley that ripped the heart out of Workington. But most of all they spoke graciously of what he had done for Barrow since he signed in 1943 – 357 matches ago.

Willie Horne was an ordinary man who had achieved extraordinary things. Yet talking to him you would think he was a competent turner, or a carpenter, or a coppersmith or a bus conductor, that he was no different from anyone else. You could search forever and a day and you would not find a solitary person who did not like him.

Greatness is all the more appropriate when it touches ordinary, decent people. So, in Barrow at least, the 1955 Challenge Cup Final will always be remembered as Willie's finest hour, the day fate paid its dues and handed him and his team the greatest prize in rugby league. The pride and contentment did not diminish throughout that summer. When supporters looked forward to the next season many asked: how can we top that, the Lancashire Cup and the Challenge Cup in one season. As for Willie, he was just taking one game at a time, just as he always had.

He wasn't ready for retirement. Not yet.

CHAPTER TWENTY ONE

THE FINAL WHISTLE

EVERYONE has marvelled at the play of Barrow stand-off half Willie Horne but selectors seem to have forgotten to tell coaches that up-and-coming youngsters should model themselves on this great star.

Besides having an astute rugby brain, he had clever hands and feet to match that clever head. I have been associated with rugby league for 38 years and to my mind Willie Horne was as much the complete player as we have ever seen.

CYRIL BRIGGS
Rugby League journalist, Saturday, January 31, 1959

WHAT a pass . . . perfection. Mind you, it had to be. The gap remained open for less than two seconds, a blink of the eye, a moment so brief if you looked at your watch and back at the field the opportunity would have disappeared along with Barrow's last chance of a spectacular comeback.

Barrow were losing the 1957 Challenge Cup Final against Leeds nine points to seven. Time was up. They had been awarded a free kick so close to their own line Willie could have turned around and touched the goal posts. So Barrow had 100 yards to cover and less than a minute in which to do so. A pretty tall order.

The safe option, the one most stand-off halves would have chosen, was a kick to touch followed by a couple of predictable plods by exhausted forwards, who, like as not, would have been thrown to the ground by the Leeds pack, already anticipating a euphoric walk up the Wembley steps a few moments later. The situation was grave but Barrow supporters had not abandoned hope. They had been watching Willie snatch unlikely victories in similarly dire circumstances for many years. As long as he was on the field, remote though it seemed, there was still a chance.

Willie took a short tap, turned left and made that pass, the ball twisting through the air, a yard over the heads of three forwards who knew better than reach up to try to catch it. Ten yards in front, the Leeds defence were in no hurry to organise a straight line. The match had been a tough one; the Yorkshiremen had given as much as any man could give. They were exhausted.

Johnny Rea, Barrow's 20-year-old centre threequarter, had moved forward, concentrating, like all good players, never taking his eyes off Willie, just in case. The ball arrived a yard in front of him, begging to be caught. Then he was away, between startled Leeds defenders, who responded quickly, closing the gap, momentarily as wide as a garage door. But too late. Johnny was gone. And Leeds knew they were in trouble. You could see alarm in their faces, grim expressions of fear as they turned to give chase, backs and forwards stampeding together in a confused blur of blue, white and amber.

The pass had been so accurate, an overweight, middle-aged man could have ambled 20 or 30 yards before being caught. But Johnny Rea was no geriatric. He was a professional centre threequarter with a reputation, a justifiable one, for scoring tries and running round people at considerable speed. The pass was worthy of the occasion, deserving to be converted into the winning try. But there was still much to be done.

The crowd were surprisingly quiet and subdued, as if they dare not cheer lest they somehow debilitated Rea's dramatic run. The centre was still hurtling down the field, followed on the outside, by Frank Castle, the Barrow winger – without doubt the fastest man on the pitch, probably on any pitch in the world for that matter.

Getting to the halfway line had been the easy part for a man who could run as quickly as Johnny. Now he was tiring. Things began happening quickly. In such circumstances you make decisions by instinct rather than calculating risk and probability as a poker player might analyse a promising hand. There's no time. Up ahead, Leeds full back Pat Quinn was ready, shuffling across, arms extended, preparing to shepherd Rea to safety. Of course, Quinn had all the advantages. He had run no more than 30 yards, slowly, jogging into position to await the imminent arrival of the Barrow player, while Rea had covered 70 yards, flat out, at the sort of pace you would hope to employ if a wild animal was chasing you.

Almost on top of Quinn now, Rea turned to his left expecting to see the comforting sight of Castle on his shoulder, those large hands pleading for the pass he would be delighted to provide. Castle should have been there. But he was not. And Rea did not know where he was. There was no shout, you see. Or if there was Rea did not hear him.

Professional rugby league players know all about communication. It is second nature, an integral part of the game, no less important than correct tackling technique or persistent support play. Rea had expected that shout and not hearing it was a crippling blow.

If you ever watch a game close to, leaning on the wall surrounding the pitch, you will be amazed at the amount and volume of yelling undertaken by the players. Shouting is expected from them. So the unknown position of Castle left Rea with two choices, each with an unpredictable outcome. He could try to run around Quinn, a former England rugby union international renowned as a dependable defender. Such an attempt probably carried no more than a one in ten chance of being successful. Or he could kick ahead on the theoretical assumption that Castle must be somewhere in the vicinity. Understandably he chose the second. What he did not know was that Castle had inexplicably moved to Rea's inside, towards the Leeds cover, chasing desperately like a pack of hounds cornering a tired fox.

As he made that kick Johnny could hear the pounding steps and heavy breathing of frantic men behind him, close to, reaching out. Who were they? Friend or foe? Away it went. The kick was a good one too, the ball bouncing wildly towards the tryline, empty and inviting, five men chasing, three from Leeds, two from Barrow. Quinn threw Rea to the ground. Thirty yards ahead of them the cup final hung in the balance, resting on luck, 77,000 fans holding their breath, many looking away, unwilling to witness the outcome.

Winning meant everything. Barrow's right winger Jimmy Lewthwaite was almost there now, a spectacular achievement considering he had been furthest from Rea when he had made his break a few seconds before. It was typical of him, always trying, never giving up when all appeared lost. So near. Too late. Leeds number two George Broughton dived on the ball pulling it towards him as a drowning man might grab a lifebelt. The referee blew his whistle. "Hard luck Johnny," Willie said, patting the youngster on the shoulder. "You made a great attempt."

"Thanks Willie," Johnny answered, suddenly feeling better.

It was over. Barrow had lost.

★ ★ ★

Barrow, Dalton and Ulverston were communities engulfed in celebration following the 1955 Challenge Cup final. That was natural and only to be expected. But the club drew loyal support from all over the north of England. Followers came from Broughton, Coniston, Kendal, Lancaster, Carnforth, Grange-over-Sands and Millom – especially from Millom. The mining town, all black smoke and tall chimneys, had a strong amateur tradition, one that ensured a steady supply of talented players, each man gifted with equal portions of passion and commitment.

Several hundred supporters travelled to Craven Park for Barrow's home matches, special trains tooting across the Duddon Valley, laden with enthusiastic fans whose affection was not diluted by their geographical isolation.

So when someone suggested it might be an honourable gesture to take the Challenge Cup to Millom, Willie was happy to help out. His team had enjoyed watching a thousand faces light up at their presence as they toured the hospitals and old people's homes dotted around Furness. Now it was Millom's turn.

The Barrow players dutifully shook hands, had their pictures taken and waved cheerfully to their Cumberland supporters. But if they were truthful, they would admit to feeling rather weary. The day after the trip Willie clocked on at 6am at Barrow Steelworks where he found a worrying note waiting for him. See the works foreman, it demanded abruptly, suggesting the meeting was likely to be an unpleasant one. General Manager Mr T. G. Marple wanted to know why Willie had taken Tuesday off work. It seems there had been some sort of misunderstanding. Five minutes later Willie walked out of the factory, unable to stomach the questioning, the bureaucracy and the implication that he had somehow behaved unreasonably.

The following week he began selling insurance for Royal Liver from their offices in Duke Street. Getting inside customers' houses was simple. It's not every day a former Great Britain international knocks on your door. So he drank lots of tea, ate plenty of biscuits . . . and left empty-handed. He was not very good at suggesting that perhaps it might be wise to put a few shillings life insurance aside each week for Aunt May or that an accrued policy would be financially prudent.

After three months he resigned, relieved to escape a persuasive world where success was calculated by his ability to encourage poor people to part with money. The next day he was helping Bessie in their sports shop which had, by now, become something of a success. That's another story recounted later.

Back on the rugby field it was business as usual. In 1956 Willie played 39 times for Barrow, helping the club climb to seventh in the league. There was big disappointment when they were beaten in the Challenge Cup semi-final by St Helens. The first match, at Station Road, Swinton, ended a 5-5 draw in front of a 38,897 crowd. Four days later Barrow lost 10-5 in a replay at Central Park, Wigan, a dramatic game watched by 44,731 fans.

Next season Willie again made 39 appearances as Barrow finished third in the league, the highest position in the club's long history. They earned a trip to Wembley after defeating Leigh in an epic semi-final requiring another replay, the two ties watched by more than 63,000 people. As we have seen, Barrow lost the final to Leeds in dramatic style. Now Johnny Rea, who signed from local amateurs Holker Pioneers for £200, was being tipped as a future international.

In 1958 Willie was appointed player coach of the 'A' team but intermittently he was called into the first 13 where his presence usually produced a healthy reversal of fortunes as the young side responded to his encouragement. Yes, he was a shade slower, but his inspirational qualities were, if anything, heightened by his physical decline. After all, he was 36. Then there were the injuries . . . the sprained ankles, the pulled muscles, the calf strains and the terrible stiffness of aching joints. But everyone still looked up to him and welcomed his selection.

In August Tom Smith, a young forward who went on to play for Warrington, came to Barrow on trial. "Will I be playing with Willie Horne?" he asked on his first appearance at Craven Park.

BARROW 51 BATLEY 16

When Willie Horne led Barrow onto the pitch he was doing more than just making a personal comeback after a lay-off of more than four months. He brought confidence to the young Barrow side who so far this season had appeared leaderless. Horne's presence was worth seven tries to Barrow. His understanding with "Dinks" Harris and his way of pivoting play towards speed-men Lowther and Castle made Barrow's biggest victory seem in the bag right from the kick-off.

NORTH WEST EVENING MAIL, September 29, 1958

BARROW 26 CASTLEFORD 0

The Horne magic solved Barrow's number one problem: how to get the moves they learn in training to work on the field. His experience and prompting in the middle, welded Barrow into the powerful, attacking machine they ought to be.

NORTH WEST EVENING MAIL, February 9, 1959

The Horne dynasty had ended. His team had grown old. The game was changing. Willie's career had mirrored a golden age of rugby league with record crowds and widespread interest in the sport. Throughout the Forties and Fifties Craven Park attendances had averaged more than 10,000 but spectators were starting to lose interest. Mass ownership of TV sets was just around the corner. In 1959 the average gate had plummeted to barely 5,000, two years later it would be fewer than 3,000.

Jimmy Lewthwaite retired, though not before setting a new club record when he scored 50 tries in his final season, beating the previous best held by Frank Castle. Vince McKeating had gone too. Others had been transferred – Bill Healey to Blackpool, Reg Parker to Wakefield Trinity (£800) and Ted Toohey to Leigh (£400).

On March 16, 1958, Willie played his final game of rugby league, helping Barrow defeat Swinton at Craven Park 10-5. There was no announcement. No fanfare. Willie had never liked fuss. And it was fitting that the Evening Mail, which had charted his rise to greatness with accuracy, pride and sincerity, should pay tribute with this simple paragraph in the match report: *"Willie Horne was again a guiding hand for Barrow, steadying a youthful back division."*

Willie had made 462 appearances for Barrow, scoring 112 tries and kicking 741 goals. He played 14 times for Lancashire, 14 for England and 16 for Great Britain, plus a further eight full Test matches, amassing more than 2,000 points. Statistically his record compared with the best players the game had produced since that historic split from rugby union in a Huddersfield hotel 64 years before. But his genius was multi-faceted, diverse in ways that could not be measured in the same way one might compare opening batsmen or Olympic sprinters. He had a limitless supply of courage, vision and inspiration, imparting confidence and faith around him. But how good was he?

Was Willie Horne really the best ever?

Willie and Workington skipper Bill Ivison lead out the teams for the 1955 Challenge Cup Final. "Good luck, Willie," Bill said, as they prepared for the kick-off.

His Royal Highness the Duke of Edinburgh meets Barrow hooker Vince McKeating. The Cumberland forward, who was signed from Dewsbury for £75, won 21 out of 28 first half scrums.

Barrow second-row Reg Parker tackles Workington Town's 18-year-old forward Brian Edgar watched by international winger Ike Southward.

Lance Todd trophy winner Jack Grundy makes a break through the Workington defence.

Bill Wookey, the 18-year-old Workington stand-off half who was born in Barrow. "It was Willie's final," he said. "There's no doubt about that."

Barrow centre three-quarter Dennis Goodwin pushes off Workington's Australian Tony Paskins.

Town scrum-half Sol Roper is about to be tackled by Barrow's giant second-row forward Reg Parker. Eighteen-year-old Roper was stretchered off in the first half with a torn shoulder muscle but he returned later despite being in severe pain.

The Duke of Edinburgh presents the Challenge Cup to Willie. "My goodness," said Prince Philip. "Rugby League's a tough game."

Down the famous Wembley steps where so many sporting heroes had gone before. At 33, Willie had finally fulfilled his dream and won the trophy a town had craved for.

Off the open-topped coach at Craven Park, the first person to greet Willie was his mother, proud and emotional.

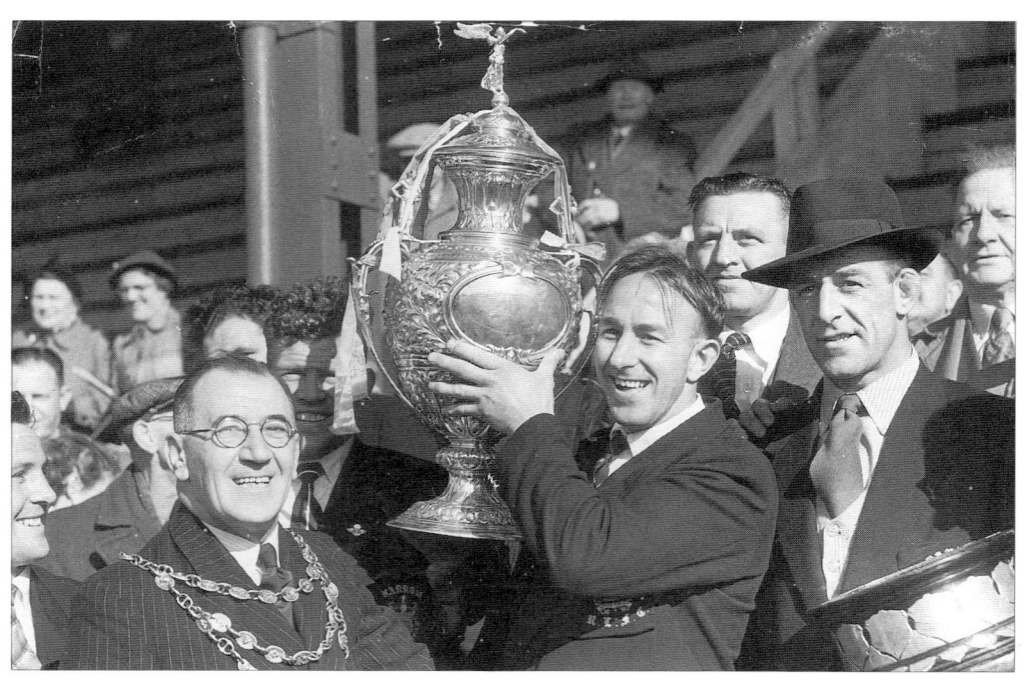

Willie and his vice-captain Jack Grundy show off the Challenge Cup to Barrow mayor Alderman T. A. Tyson who said, "This is the greatest year of my life."

Leigh players clap the Barrow team on the field following their Challenge Cup victory. Barrow lost a thrilling match 21–15 in front of 15,000 fans.

Huge crowds greet the Barrow Wembley party at the town hall before a civic reception. Willie told the dignitaries, "This is the best side I have captained. I am proud to lead such a grand set of lads."

At the end of the 1955 season Barrow RLFC held a dinner at the Imperial Hotel where they paraded the Lancashire Cup and the Challenge Cup. In the picture with Willie and Barrow chairman John Atkinson are Warrington skipper Albert Naughton and chairman Mr Davies with the Rugby League Championship Cup and the Lancashire League Trophy. The message on the back of the photograph from Lancashire official Wilf Brown says simply.. "To Willie Horne, the best ever!"

Barrow defeated Leigh in the 1957 Challenge Cup semi-final after a replay. Here Jimmy Lewthwaite slips by former Barrow halfback Ted Toohey on his way to the matchwinning try. Barrow won 15-10 at Station Road, Swinton. The attendance was 28,431.

Willie and Leeds captain Keith McLellan lead out the teams for the 1957 Challenge Cup final.

Leeds' first try by full back Pat Quinn was disputed by the Barrow players but the referee ruled it legitimate.

International second-row forward Don Robinson scores Leeds' third try breaking through the tackles of Don Wilson and Joe Ball.

Barrow troop off the Wembley pitch after their 9–7 defeat by Leeds who celebrate in the background. Johnny Rea, to the right in the foreground, came desperately close to snatching victory in the final minute.

Johnny Rea, Barrow centre-threequarter, scores a try against Oldham at Craven Park. In the background is a large advertisement for Willie's shop in Paxton Terrace.

Barrow's veteran winger Jimmy Lewthwaite broke the club's try-scoring record in 1957 with 50 touchdowns. Here Jimmy scores against Hull despite the efforts of Colin Hutton and Bill Drake.

CHAPTER TWENTY TWO

THE LEGEND

> WILLIE HORNE studied the opposition, directed team tactics in the dressing room, and led Barrow to the field where he proceeded to direct the play, take the penalties, make the breaks to score the tries, kick the goals with that unorthodox run-up and was fearless in his split-second timing in tackling even the biggest forwards.
>
> Willie's extra touches such as uncanny interceptions, his vital drop goals, his mastery of the long pass, his terrible hand-and-foot tackles (as testified by the toughest players in the game), and his ability to make the closest-marking opposition go the wrong way were always a joy to the Barrow fan and to any neutral observer.
>
> DAILY HERALD, Saturday, January 14, 1956

IN THE mid-Fifties the Daily Herald ran a competition inviting readers to vote for the best stand-off half in the history of rugby league. Willie Horne won by what the national newspaper referred to as a healthy margin. Vic Hey of Leeds and Australia was second with Kiwi Cec Mountford third. Next were Leslie Fairclough (St Helens) and Emlyn Jenkins (Salford).

Seven years later the Daily Express asked readers to nominate "the greatest players who have contributed to the increased popularity of rugby league." Willie Horne was runner-up, a handful of votes behind Warrington's Australian winger Brian Bevan, the most prolific try scorer in the game's history with 834 touchdowns. They were followed by Lewis Jones, Gus Risman and Tom Van Vollenhoven.

To describe anyone as the greatest ever at anything is, of course, subjective and personal whether you're talking about rugby players, marathon runners, ballroom dancers or landscape gardeners. All anyone can do is be the best in their own fleeting era.

The next chapter is devoted to tributes to Willie Horne from those who saw his genius first hand – players and referees, friends and rivals. I have interviewed more than 200 people — reporters, statisticians, Australians, Welshmen, forwards and backs and one 89-year-old Barrow man who began watching rugby league way back in 1914.

When I spoke to these people I did not prepare a list of questions as I normally would. My lack of preparation was by design. I wanted replies to be sincere and spontaneous, free from cliche-ridden answers. I wanted the truth. One by one they said the same thing in different ways, using anecdotes to illustrate their admiration. They'd never seen anyone better, they said.

They recounted colourful stories with a disarming honesty, each one saying Willie was a great man with as much conviction as they said he was a great player. They were eager to help, as if there were considerable frustration at their previous lack of opportunity to put on record their thoughts about this remarkable man.

Memory is selective. Dropped passes, missed tackles and mediocre performances are conveniently forgotten, consigned to the mind's refuse tip, so that in time all that is left are the wonderful games, the match-winning tries and the emotion and drama of exciting comebacks. It's the same in any sport. But it is especially true of Willie, who is revered with almost religious fervour by the people of Barrow.

To be successful, an international stand-off half needs many skills. To excel in all aspects of the position is as unlikely as, say, a concert pianist making a century break at snooker or a Test batsman having a scratch handicap at golf.

Above all, he must have super-courage. I say super because all rugby league players have courage. You need to be brave to walk onto the field even if your performance is incompetent. It's a hard game played by hard men who get hurt often – and, sooner or later, seriously.

In 1958 Great Britain played Australia in the Second Test at Brisbane. The Tourists were struggling to hold onto the Ashes after the Kangaroos had won the First Test 25–8 at Sydney. Prop forward Alan Prescott broke his arm after only three minutes but he dismissed pleas to leave the field, and carried the ball into the unyielding wall of green and gold shirts repeatedly and with such valour that his team were inspired to a sensational 25–18 win. The fairytale had a happy ending when Great Britain won the Third Test at Sydney Cricket Ground. Prescott will forever be remembered with particular affection for his gallantry and refusal to give in.

Willie had courage like that. He was not a big man, yet he welcomed the physical side of the game as if he was feeding off those who doubted he had the fortitude to withstand the challenge of such a violent sport.

In one match against Wigan, Willie was elbowed in the face. "You'll have to come off," he was told by the Barrow trainer. "You've fractured your cheekbone." Like Prescott he stayed on, ignoring the pain with such fortitude that the Wigan players were unaware how badly he was hurt. The following week he played again, his face still bruised and swollen.

A stand-off half also needs speed, especially off the mark. He does not have to run the length of the field. Wingers and centres are usually more capable sprinters. Willie was quick over a short distance and he could swerve and side-step both ways, making gaps for supporting players who, once Willie had the ball, followed obediently, knowing he would rather make a try for somebody else than score himself.

Then there is footballing skill, the ability to pass both ways, flat and fast with split-second timing when a narrow gap appears. St Helens international centre threequarter Duggie Greenall told me he went on the 1954 tour because his winger scored four tries in an England international against Other Nationalities at Central Park, Wigan. Duggie got the credit and a seat on the plane to Australia but, he said, it was Willie's passing that set up his personal triumph.

When players talk of Willie's vision and distribution they speak with respect, tinged with a hint of awe as though he was so accurate all they had to do was loiter in approximately the right place and the ball would arrive as if by magic, the defensive line parting like the Red Sea as they ambled towards the tryline unopposed.

It can't have been that easy. But the wonderment and sincerity with which they recall such stories is infectious and overwhelming, leaving me with no choice but to conclude Willie Horne was born with a rare and entertaining gift for throwing a rugby ball.

And there's more. Willie did something no one else could, and still can't. Other great halfbacks, notably Australian Wally Lewis, could throw a long pass that missed out two players, perhaps on occasion three. But Willie's long passes spiralled through the air sometimes as far as 35 yards into the welcoming hands of speedy wingers. He held the point of the ball in the palm of his hand using a casual, lazy swing of his arm to propel the leather such immense distances.

He used this unpredictable ploy rarely, but often enough to render opposing backs fearful of the disastrous consequences of drifting out of position. I am told wingers playing against Barrow would be so worried about the threat of the long pass that they spent most of the match watching Willie closely through troubled eyes like a schoolboy waiting for a firework to explode.

And a stand-off half, if he is to be considered great, not just good, should also be able to kick. He must have the ability to ignore the approaching shadows of muscular men with painful plans of terminal collision to boot the ball up the field accurately so it bounces into touch gaining the team valuable yards. Willie did that, I am told, better than anyone else. And he could kick goals too.

Billy Ivison, the Workington Town international loose forward told me how he spent most of his pre-match team talks trying to work out ways to stop Willie kicking drop goals. They tried one man, then another, then three. They never stopped him. Billy rates Willie as the greatest drop-kicker he ever saw. He was simply unstoppable, the ball caught and over the bar in less time than it takes to clap your hands.

There are many players who have enjoyed successful careers, won cup finals, played test matches and toured Australia who are remembered for their skills and statistical achievements. But although their records may compare with others they are not considered great if they had a nasty, vicious streak. If they played dirty.

The laws of libel prevent me naming an international who had a marvellous career yet when his name is mentioned it is with begrudging respect as his memory evokes the day he kicked, spat, gouged or bit his contemporaries. When players describe him the words are spoken impatiently as one might talk of a traffic accident, toothache, poverty, racism or the day your grandmother died. Even now he may not be troubled by remorse but it's a sad waste for a fine player to be remembered in such an unpleasant way.

Willie was never like that. Everyone liked and respected him, not just for the inspirational way he played, but because he did so with such honesty and sportsmanship. Barrow second-row forward Reg Parker told me he has visited Australia and New Zealand five times since the Fifties and everywhere he went he was asked how Willie was. That's how fondly they think of him Down Under.

A stand-off half must also be able to tackle, not just opposing halfbacks and lightweight threequarters. He should cover and step into the defensive line where necessary, halting prop forwards instinctively, without thinking.

Ken Gee, Wigan's great international was once asked who was the toughest player he ever came up against. The story goes that he sat back in his chair deep in thought, no doubt recalling monster Australian forwards, before leaning forward and saying confidently: "Willie Horne. He was the toughest. His hand and foot tackle was terrible."

Today many stand-off halves don't tackle as if it is not expected of them, as though it is somehow inappropriate. Willie brought big men down easily with a natural, graceful rhythm unlike any other halfback.

Picture the scene: Barrow are defending on their own 25-yard line, backs to the wall, holding on to a slender lead with time running out. You keep glancing at your watch willing the seconds to tick by as the opponents creep nearer and nearer to the tryline. A Barrow forward, puffing with fatigue, jogs back into line more slowly than those around him. He's blowing hard, the effort of the last few minutes showing on his red face, sweating, lines of concentration etched on his brow.

Things happen quickly now. Willie motions to the blind side. The forward nods in agreement and moves slowly from centre stage, anonymous among the backs, where he can recover. Willie is in the middle of the defensive line, next to the play-the-ball. He moves up quickly but not so fast as to leave behind the larger, slower men around him. The ball is thrown to a halfback and on to a prop barging forward confidently, encouraged by the sight of a smaller man before him, someone he can run over to set up the winning try.

He runs quickly, flat out, his knees lifting up and down powerfully and for a moment you'll shudder thinking of the awful injury those pumping legs can inflict as you recall the black afternoon someone was stretchered off and the story you read in the next day's papers saying his jaw is broken and he might never play again. Images will flash before you . . . the black suits of the

St. John Ambulance Brigade, the crowd's sporting applause, the anxious wife making soup and small talk, the stricken player receiving visitors with a trembling wave, unable to answer, his face frozen by steel wire wrapped around his teeth.

The forward is on top of Willie now. Still moving quickly he pushes his arm towards Willie's face as he prepares to burst through looking first to one side then the other, searching for supporting players. Then a blur of activity, the arm pushed aside, a spindly leg stuck out, the forward hurled in the air before crashing to the ground, his progress stopped in an instant as a small sparrow might fly into french windows on a hot, spring afternoon.

And if you're near enough you'll see his face, his staring eyes, his bewilderment as he gasps for air. His momentum has shaken the ball clear where it is eagerly accepted by a Barrow player. A minute later the referee blows his whistle to end the game. Another thrilling match, another Barrow victory, another Willie Horne story — the legend goes on.

CHAPTER TWENTY THREE

THE TRIBUTES

ARTHUR CLUES
Second row forward
Wests, New South Wales, Leeds, Hunslet and Australia
1943 to 1957

In 1946 I played against Great Britain five times, twice for New South Wales and in all three Tests. I thought I could play a bit. Then I saw the tourists and I realised I knew nothing about the game. Ken Gee, Joe Egan and Willie Horne could make the ball talk.

The first time I saw Willie play I realised what a mighty footballer he was. All the Australians rated him highly. I didn't believe them, but at the end of that tour it was obvious he was even better than they had said.

He was the first round-the-corner kicker. Now everyone does it. When we saw him we thought: "This Pommie has no chance of kicking any goals. He doesn't look like he knows where the goal posts are." He didn't miss many. In all my time in the game he was one of the greatest players I ever saw. Willie was a complete footballer. He could read a game, kick tactically or high over the top. He had plenty of pace and he knew how to draw a man and when to pass.

In rugby you sometimes get players who won't work in defence. Willie was never like that. He was always in the thick of things, among the forwards, knocking everyone down, round the legs, never dirty or malicious.

I'll never forget his hand and foot tackle. He used to send me six feet in the air and when I came down I didn't know where I was. He did that to all the big lads. You got plenty of stick when you played against Willie. Nowadays rugby league is a different game. It's all about brute force and fitness. The skill's all gone. You can't compare past with present but the only stand-off today who comes even close to Willie is Warrington halfback and former Wales rugby union captain Jonathan Davies.

In my time Willie had so much skill everyone admired him. When I played for Other Nationalities that great Kiwi halfback Cec Mountford was in the team. He was always saying what a wonderful player Willie was. After we both retired I got to know Willie pretty well. He was just how I imagined he would be – a super fellow, one of nature's gentlemen. There's never been a better person play rugby league. He is one of the nicest, kindest men I have ever met and he deserves all the success he had.

The town of Barrow should worship Willie Horne.

ALAN DAVIES
Centre threequarter
Oldham, Wigan, Wakefield Trinity, Salford
Lancashire, England and Great Britain
1950 to 1965

My father was a respected stand-off half for Leigh before the War. When I was growing up, each time Barrow played Leigh he made a point of taking me to the game. "Watch Willie Horne closely son," he'd say. "That's how a stand-off half should play." So Willie was always a hero of mine.

He was the captain when I played my first international against Wales. I'll never forget what happened. I was the centre and I was struggling to get the ball to my winger who was a big name, an experienced player. At half-time I was feeling really dejected when I felt Willie's arm around me. "Don't you worry, Alan," he said. "You know how quick you are. Ignore the winger and have a go yourself." So I did and I managed to score two tries. To think a player of his standing should take the time to talk to someone like me. It was a special moment.

At Oldham we had a brilliant half-back signed from Salford called Frank Stirrup. He was a wonderful player, a great thinker and tactician who was the linchpin of the side. We were playing at Barrow and for once Oldham were well on top. Barrow were defending deep in their own half when there was a scrum. I was looking around working out how we might score when I heard a booming voice call out. "Watch Horne," Frank screamed. "You never know what he's going to do next. Mark him tight. Don't take your eyes off him." There can be no better tribute than that. Frank only respected the very best and that day he was actually panicking.

Willie rates alongside any stand-off half I've ever seen. He had a lazy style, strolling about unconcerned, making everything look so easy. It was quite amazing really.

Marking Willie was like marking a ghost. One moment you had him covered, the next he was gone.

JOE EGAN
Hooker
Wigan, Leigh, Lancashire, England and Great Britain
1938 to 1955

As time slips by great players are gradually forgotten. I'm sure this book will tell the Willie Horne story and remind everyone what a special talent he had.

There have been many outstanding stars, men who have left their mark on the history of the game. Willie was more than a great player. He was a leader with the rare gift of inspiring those around him.

At Central Park we thought of Willie as one of our own. Everyone rated him and those of us fortunate enough to play representative matches in the same team always looked forward to meeting him. He was a great character who mixed well and enjoyed a laugh.

My old colleague Ken Gee, that great prop forward, greeted Willie the same way every time he saw him. "Ey Horney, tha's cost me some money in thee time," he'd laugh in his broad Wigan accent, referring to matches when Willie led Barrow to victory over us. He had particularly painful memories of a third round cup-tie in 1949 when Wigan took a seven point lead before Barrow eventually won 8-7, thanks to a last-minute penalty goal from Willie.

When we went on the 1946 Australian tour together, we travelled on an aircraft carrier called the Indomitable. To pass the time someone ran a hockey tournament. Of course Willie played for our team, the Wigan Wallopers, another example of how we looked on him as one of us.

I always smile when I think of an incident on a boat trip around an Australian harbour when the captain took the players to the engine room and explained how powerful it was. Someone shouted: "If you don't stop, Willie Horne will buy it." He bought that many presents we all joked he was taking something home for every person who lived in Barrow.

When I played against Willie the first thing I did after the final whistle was run to him to shake his hand. Now when I look back I realise how many happy memories I have of our time together both on and off the field.

He is truly one of the greats.

TREVOR FOSTER
Second row forward
Bradford Northern, Wales and Great Britain
1938 to 1955

I treasure my memories of Willie Horne. We went on the 1946 Lions tour to Australia together and one of the main reasons for us remaining unbeaten in the three tests was Willie's great relationship with scrum-half Tommy McCue and loose forward Ike Owens. They tore the Aussies to ribbons with their tricks around the scrums. Willie had a great tour, always showing up with his classy attacking play, probing for openings, tactical running and kicking.

Back home he was a major figure in the game for many seasons, leading a fine Barrow side from the front. Willie always had to contend with close marking because we all knew what he was capable of doing with the ball. Willie was born with a natural ability but it was his quick brain that made him stand out. While everyone was thinking about what he was going to do he'd already done it.

Whenever Bradford Northern played Barrow it was always the same in our dressing room before the match. All we talked about was how we were going to stop him. In those days rugby league was more about science and thinking than today. It didn't matter where Willie was on the field. He could always open up play for others to score tries from anywhere. He was an artist. It was like watching poetry in motion.

Willie had a big heart; he never knew when he was beaten. He had such determination to win yet he was a great sport. You could tell Willie loved the game. He never had a bad thought in his head on the field. He just wanted to play rugby. I was attacked many times but I never thought of retaliating. I would just have been lowering my own standards. Willie was like that. He always had a smile on his face. My Bradford colleagues Willie Davies and Ernest Ward thought the world of Willie. That's how I feel. He's one of the best stand-off halves I've seen.

It was an honour to know and play with him. The great Willie Horne.

PETER FOX
Loose forward
Featherstone Rovers, Batley, Hull Kingston Rovers and Wakefield Trinity
1953 to 1966

First team coach of Bradford Northern

I'll never forget the first time I went to Wembley to watch the Challenge Cup final in 1951. Wigan beat Barrow and their stand-off half Cec Mountford was voted man of the match. But for me, Willie was the best player on the field. I was only a young fellow and he made a great impression on me. Willie was just a wisp of a man and he took my eye immediately, playing behind a beaten pack but never giving in, taking responsibility, trying to make play.

A couple of years later, in one of my first games for Featherstone, I played at Barrow. Before the game our captain Eric Batten told me how good Willie was and that as loose forward it was my responsibility to get out of the scrum quickly and tackle him. That wasn't easy, I can tell you. I think Frank Castle got three tries and Jimmy Lewthwaite two and they were all down to Willie's running and passing. After that he was the first name I looked for.

The true test of greatness is how long you play at the highest level. Willie played at the top for a long, long time. Technically he was head and shoulders above everyone of that era. Willie was one of the most constructive stand-off halves I have ever seen. He had all the skills and he could tackle anyone. He was deceptively strong, a tough man.

When forwards saw him they thought they could knock him out of the way, no trouble. But he'd bundle them up easily and they'd end up on their back every time. Willie was unassuming off the field but when he talked rugby he made sense, he encouraged people by example.

I had many favourite players of that time, men like Harry Street, Ike Williams, Des Clarkson, Billy Blan and Bill Ivison. But Willie Horne was my hero.

RON GELDER
First grade referee – 1946-1964
In charge of four Challenge Cup finals
1954, 1955, 1956 and 1958

Willie was a unique player and a unique person. I could write a Jeffrey Archer novel on the times we met on the field. There were league, county semi-finals and finals, internationals and perhaps the greatest of all the Wembley cup finals.

I don't believe there's a stand-off half in the game today who could live with Willie. They say Leeds and Great Britain player Garry Schofield is the best in the world now. Over 80 minutes he couldn't compare with Willie.

Willie and Cec Mountford, that great New Zealand halfback, are the two best number sixes I've seen. They were so special they stood out, and in the Forties and Fifties there were many wonderful players. When Cec was missing from the Wigan team they seemed ordinary. Barrow were like that without Willie. And don't forget the Barrow side then was packed with internationals.

And what a great skipper he was. On the field we never had a cross word. Like everyone, sometimes I made mistakes. When that happened I'd apologise to Willie and he'd just smile and get on with the game. Team-mates did what he wanted because, like everyone else in the game, they respected him so much.

Many times I'd call Willie and one of his players to one side to warn the player in question to behave. They always did. Willie made sure of that. That's how much everyone thought of him.

Many years after my retirement from the game I visited Barrow on business. I'll never forget meeting Willie in his sports shop, surrounded by loaves of bread and eggs waiting to be fried, with the kettle boiling away in the background. It was one of the greatest hours of my life.

Barrow should be proud of Willie. What an example he is to children. He has a heart of gold. If anyone deserves a gold medal from Esther Rantzen it's Willie Horne.

EPPIE GIBSON
Centre threequarter
Workington, Whitehaven, Cumberland and England
1947 to 1961

I played against Willie many times. I had always known he was a great stand-off half but it wasn't until we played together that I realised how special he was.

I remember a match for England against Other Nationalities in 1953. They had a great side, many said better than the Australian tourists with stars such as Brian Bevan, Lionel Cooper, Arthur Clues, Pat Devery and Tony Paskins.

Willie was skipper and I remember him telling me and Duggie Greenall, the other centre, what he wanted from us. The threequarters scored six tries that day, and every one was down to Willie. His great asset was his wonderful timing of a pass, that split second you wanted the ball to put you in the clear. Breaks were always on whenever Willie played.

I'm often asked who is the greatest player I ever saw. Willie has to be there right near the top of the tree. He was that good.

DUGGIE GREENALL
Centre-threequarter
St Helens, Wigan, Bradford Northern,
Lancashire, England and Great Britain
1946 to 1960

When you play in the backs you hope, one day, you'll be lucky enough to play with a stand-off half like Willie Horne. He was a centre's dream.

In 1952 Great Britain played Australia at Swinton with the Ashes at stake. I managed to score two tries but the second was easy. Willie gave me a beautiful back pass that tore the Aussies' defence to ribbons leaving me to walk over and put the ball down under the posts.

Then there was an international in 1953 when my winger was Peter Norburn from Swinton – a second-row forward, yet he scored four tries. I got the credit but it was Willie's wonderful passing that made it easy for me. I went on that tour to Australia and I know I've got Willie to thank. He should have gone too. There isn't a stand-off half in the game today who's a patch on Willie. He had so much class.What people don't realise is that Barrow were good but not great, even with Willie in the team. If he'd have played with one of the wealthy clubs such as Leeds or Wigan I can't imagine what he would have achieved. As it is he's as good a stand-off as I've ever seen.

EMLYN HUGHES
Born Barrow-in-Furness on August 28, 1947
Midfield and central defender
Blackpool, Liverpool, Wolverhampton Wanderers and Rotherham United
62 England caps including 23 as captain
1963 to 1983

My father played for Barrow RL with Willie Horne. They went on the 1946 Tour together. He always told me Willie was the best. He said he was a genius who was that good he could make the ball talk.

When I was growing up in Barrow, Willie was sport to everyone. It didn't matter if you wanted a soccer ball, a rugby ball or a cricket bat, you never thought of going anywhere else. He always knocked a few bob off and gave a packet of sweets to the kids. And if you were too young to go on your own he had a cup of tea waiting for your mam. He looked after everyone and you knew you were getting a good deal.

When I first started playing for Liverpool I often popped in to see Willie in the summer. It was nice to have a chat and a cuppa at the back of the shop. I enjoyed talking to Willie. It was a help because as an ex-pro he understood the sort of pressure you are under.

I have never called him Willie, always Mr Horne. I wouldn't be that cheeky and anyway if I had I would have got a belt off my father. Even when I was an England international it still had to be Mr Horne.

Whenever I meet people from rugby league they always talk of Willie with deep respect. He was a great player but there's more to it than that. He's such a super person.

BILLY IVISON
Loose forward
Workington, Cumberland and England
1945 to 1959

Workington won the Challenge Cup at Wembley in 1952. It was a great feeling getting the cup and bringing it home. When we played Barrow in 1955 I wanted to win badly. We all did. But Barrow were too good for us.

I can remember walking off the field, watching Willie lead his team up the steps to get the cup. I can honestly say I was proud of him. No one deserved it more and that made me feel better.

We played together for England and ever since he has been my friend. Everyone thought the world of Willie, especially his team. Anyone could see that. No one in rugby league anywhere had a bad word to say about him. Everyone respected Willie for the way he handled himself on and off the field.

Willie was very frustrating to play against, especially the way he could drop goals. You knew when he was going to do it but no matter how hard you tried to stop him you couldn't. There's never been a better drop-goaler than Willie.

PHIL JACKSON
Centre threequarter
Barrow, Lancashire, England and Great Britain
1950 to 1959

I'm still closely involved in rugby league and I am often asked who is the greatest rugby league footballer I have ever seen. When I was a kid playing for Risedale School in Barrow I thought it was Willie Horne. Then when I signed on and played with him I knew without the slightest doubt he was the best.

Willie wasn't a big man so he needed to have all the skills. He did, in abundance. He is the originator of many of the plays that have come into the Australian game in recent years, skills such as the long cut-out pass. Willie was especially good at that. The Australians call it a "face ball."

His whole game was based on out-thinking the opposition, whereas now the winners are the biggest and fittest after 80 minutes of wearing each other down. Willie had the lot – speed off the mark, wonderful long kicking and the ability to pick gaps in defences when there appeared to be no way through.

When you understand what a complete attacking player Willie was, you could be excused for thinking he didn't have much in defence. On the contrary, he was a defender of the highest order. As I said, he was not a big man and as such many massive forwards straightened up and ran at Willie flat out, much to their regret. Willie was the best exponent of the hand and foot tackle I have ever seen. Add to that his wonderful low tackling and you had a great defender.

What always surprised me was how few notoriously "dirty" players put the dirt on Willie. He seemed to command respect from everyone and I can honestly say I never saw Willie commit a single dirty act in all our times together.

I spent most of my career with Willie and I learned a vast amount from him, particularly the finer points of individual skills. Unfortunately we see so few players with these skills now and as a result the game has suffered as a spectacle.

As a man Willie is the most humble person I have met. Nothing in his demeanour suggests he was such a great sportsman. Willie never swore and very seldom raised his voice above a moderate level even when he gave us a "roasting" for indifferent play at half-time. Instead, he would frequently pull off an act of genius in the second half and that would motivate us to better things.

It is obvious I am a great Willie Horne fan but I think you will find anyone who saw him play or played with or against him will share my opinion.

To me he will always be the GREAT Willie Horne. The best player I have ever seen.

JIMMY LEWTHWAITE
Wing threequarter
Barrow, Cumberland and England
1943 to 1957

There were lots of things Willie Horne could do better than anyone else, but for me it was the way he moved off both feet, either way, so quickly, that made him special. Time and again he beat his marker to set up tries for the rest of the team.

Willie was a natural footballer, a brainy player who always thought quicker than anyone else. We were playing Leeds at Odsal in the semi-final of the Challenge Cup in 1951. Barrow were behind, and running out of time, when we were awarded a free kick in front of the sticks. The Leeds players walked to the tryline expecting a kick at goal, like everyone else in the ground. But Willie took a tap and passed the ball to me for a try that got us back in the match. We eventually drew and won the replay to make our first appearance at Wembley.

I could never understand those who said Willie wasn't big enough. They can't have seen him stripped off. He was all muscle, a strong man. That was how he could tackle 18-stone forwards, without fear every time.

Like all great players Willie was a marked man. Often opposing players would chase him around trying to give him a belt, hoping to lessen his influence on a game. I can hardly remember anyone ever catching him. Willie was too quick.

When we went on the 1946 Tour to Australia, a lot of folk were saying Willie Davies, from Bradford Northern, would play at stand-off half in the Test matches. He was a good player but I knew once we got out there and everyone saw what Willie Horne could do that he would be the man. And he was. He had a great Tour.

Willie was the greatest stand-off half I've ever seen, a complete footballer who could do anything. It was an honour and a privilege to play together and to know him as a friend.

IKE OWENS
Loose forward
Leeds, Castleford, Huddersfield, York, Wales and Great Britain
1943 to 1954

Every single one of the Leeds players knew Willie Horne was a great player. In the dressing room before we played Barrow everyone wanted to know how we were going to mark him. Sometimes it took three of us, covering all over the field yet somehow each time he found a way to have an outstanding game.

There have been a lot of good stand-off halves but Willie stood out because he was so reliable. In all my career I never saw him have a bad game, not once. He was a shrewd tactician who never wasted a pass. And in defence he was just as good.

I had the honour of playing with Willie for Great Britain in the 1946 Australian Tour. Willie Davies of Bradford Northern was a very good player, yet Willie Horne played in all the Test matches. That was the right decision. He had an excellent Tour and there's no doubt he was a key factor in the Lions holding on to the Ashes.

Watching Willie play was amazing. He was so placid, a real gentleman, yet on the field he had a special gift to mesmerise everyone.

TED PARKE
Risedale Old Boys Games Master
1928 to 1939

I can remember the first time I saw Willie Horne play rugby. He was only 11 yet right away I wanted to pick him for Risedale's first team. He was a natural.

It was a bad time for me when I took Willie for trials for Lancashire and he wasn't picked. He should have been, yet perhaps I didn't push the selectors enough. The two teachers who had the most to say were rooting for their own men. Neither of them was a patch on Willie. When they announced the team we were both brokenhearted.

As a pupil or a player Willie was never any trouble. He had good manners, a real credit to his parents. Everyone liked him. Even now when we bump into each other he still calls me sir.

When he went on to captain Barrow, Lancashire and Great Britain, it didn't surprise me. I always knew he was that good. I've been watching rugby for more than 60 years and in my opinion he's the best stand-off who has ever played the game. It didn't matter to Willie how big his opponents were.

I felt so proud when he achieved so many great things. He's a lovely person, one of the nicest men I've ever met. When he came back from one tour of Australia he brought me a lovely memento. To think after all that time he still remembered me. That's the sort of man he is.

GEORGE PHILPOTT
First Grade Referee
1951-1968

Willie is one of the outstanding stars and personalities of rugby league. Together with Trevor Foster and Gus Risman, he forms a trio of sportsmen who attained the highest standards, both on and off the field, our game has ever produced.

I remember refereeing a game at Warrington once and a Barrow forward complained about one of my decisions. I turned to take him to task but I was too late. Willie was quietly but forcefully reprimanding him. He turned to me and said, "Sorry about that sir. It won't happen again." And it didn't.

My one regret as a referee was not being able to officiate in matches between Barrow and Leeds, Hunslet or Bramley because I was born in Leeds. I would have loved to have been in the middle when Willie played for Barrow and the Leeds stand-off half was Vic Hey, that great Australian international.

I knew Vic very well and he once told me Willie was the best five-eighth he ever played against. "Time and again, I thought I had Willie in my sights and at the last second he just disappeared," Vic would say. A great tribute to Willie's skill.

During my career I came to Barrow many times. My wife and I had friends at Delhi Street on Walney Island. I'd either play golf at Furness or bowls at Vickerstown Institute. It didn't matter where we went in the town, the name of Willie Horne was always mentioned with great pride by everyone, a fitting tribute to a man who was, and for me still is, "the daddy of them all."

ALAN PRESCOTT
Prop forward and captain
Halifax, St. Helens
Lancashire, England and Great Britain.
1958 Tour Captain
1943 to 1960

Willie Horne was a fantastic player who played in a great team. My old coach at St Helens, Jim Sullivan, rated the Barrow side in the Fifties very highly. When you look at the team that's hardly surprising. Barrow had internationals such as Phil Jackson, Frank Castle, Joe Jones, Jimmy Lewthwaite, Jack Grundy and Ted Toohey. Yet Willie was the leader.

He was a very astute skipper. I took over the captaincy of Great Britain from Willie and he taught me so much in every aspect of the game, both on and off the field.

All the top sides enjoyed playing against Barrow. You knew you would be in for a great game. Barrow had a reputation as the cleanest side in the league. A lot of credit must go to Willie. His presence on the field was a big incentive to his men.

I was proud to play with or against Willie. What a player and what a man.

MARTIN RYAN
Full back
Wigan, Leigh, Lancashire,
England and Great Britain
1940 to 1955

If I was picking my all-time team Willie would be the stand-off half. In fact he'd be the first name down. I've never seen anyone better in any position. He was superior to everyone in everyway. Willie could do things with the ball no one else could. Wigan winger Martin Offiah cost £440,000 yet if Willie was playing against him, Martin wouldn't make a yard. You couldn't put a price on Willie today.

He could read the game like nobody else. Everyone looked up to him. At Wigan we all respected him. Every match you played against Barrow was tough. It didn't matter what the score was, Willie was always in the thick of the action, tackling his heart out, with a smile on his face.

I can still see him now, calling the Great Britain team together in a big match, everyone listening, Willie telling us what he wanted. We all learned so much from him. There was never any monkey business from Willie, but he could tackle anyone, the bigger the better. Willie was every inch a gentleman. I've never heard him swear, not once. Everyone liked him.

Actually, we all loved him.

ARTHUR SPENCER
Barrow Boys scrum-half 1936
Barrow RL scrum-half and centre
1947 to 1953

I played with Willie for Barrow Schools against Salford in the semi-final of the Lancashire Cup. He was a quiet captain but very effective. He dictated our matches the same way he did as a professional. Some said he was too small, yet he was made of much sterner stuff than they realised. Willie was very strong and giant forwards didn't matter to him. He could handle them with no bother.

Once Barrow RL were at Salford and they had a giant Canadian prop forward called Day. He must have been 18 stones. Willie hand and footed him so high he was squealing when he hit the ground. He was furious and for the next few minutes all we could hear him saying was: "Where's Horne. Let me get him."

Willie never even looked at him and when Day got the ball again he ran straight at Willie flat out. The same thing happened, a perfect hand and foot that sent him up into the air. After that we never saw Day again. He might as well have not been on the field.

I remember an Easter match at Huddersfield. It was a sunny day and we had to walk around a cricket pitch. Just outside the dressing room Harry Sunderland, a well-known writer at that time, shouted to Willie that Barrow would be struggling – they had just signed some new players I think. Willie whispered to me under his breath: "They've only got 13 players, the same as us."

He was always like that, never willing to play underdog to anyone. He got thumped often, though he never showed any emotion. It was as though he was saying to himself that it had happened and he couldn't do anything about it. He never complained. He just got on with the job.

Willie Horne was the best defensive stand-off I have ever seen. He was the best forward in the team as well as the best back. And he was a great creative player. Everything he did was done with such perfect timing it always looked easy, his instinct was so good.

FRANK STIRRUP
Scrum-half–Leigh, Salford, Oldham and Lancashire
1946 to 1960

Willie was the best stand-off half I've ever seen. He was a thinking footballer who had to be watched all the time. I remember one game when Oldham played at Barrow. Willie was about to take a kick at goal. I kept on telling our forwards to concentrate on what he was doing. You never knew what he was up to. They didn't listen and as they stood under the posts Willie tapped it to himself and scored a try. That was typical of him. He was a very, very clever player.

I once saw David Bolton play against Willie. He was a real flyer, one of the fastest players in the game, but he never got past Willie. Everything he did he made look easy, yet off the field he was so unassuming, a real genuine lad who never shirked anything.

Barrow were known throughout the league as a good footballing side and that was all down to Willie. Every time there was a scrum they were trying something different. I picked up so much from watching him. Whenever I could I went to see Barrow play so I could learn from the things Willie did, the things no one else even thought of. In a minor sort of way I tried to model myself on him.

To me Willie Horne will always be the king.

KEN TRAILL
Loose forward
Hunslet, Bradford Northern, Halifax, Wakefield Trinity,
Yorkshire, England and Great Britain
1944 to 1958

There are good players, great players and then there's Willie Horne. He was on another planet to everyone else. He was that good. I had the privilege of playing with Willie many times and you knew whenever he was on the field that something special was likely to happen. He had such class.

When I think of all the brilliant stand-offs of that era, Willie Horne is one of the greatest. What made him such an effective captain was that it didn't matter what he asked the team to do, everyone knew Willie could do it better than them.

I played with a good number six at Wakefield, Harold Poynton. He was like Willie in many ways. Harold was unassuming and never big-headed. And he made play and scored tries. Yet even he wasn't as good as Willie. Harold wasn't quite as brainy. But then neither was anyone else.

Along with Jimmy Lewthwaite, the Barrow winger, Willie sets a great example for others to follow. Everyone liked him. A perfect gentleman.

DICKIE WILLIAMS
Stand-off half
Leeds, Hunslet, Wales and Great Britain
1946 to 1957

I don't know where the expression "they gave me the willies" came from but I know what it meant to me . . . trying to cope with the outstanding talent of Willie Horne and usually failing miserably. And I know I wasn't on my own.

I was delighted to be selected for the 1950 Tour along with Willie, who was still creating his magic with Barrow. Unfortunately he suffered a serious injury and spent most of the Tour on the touchline. The loss of such a major talent was a devastating blow to our team and could well have been the main reason we lost the Ashes.

Willie put paid to any ideas I had for a second trip to Wembley. In 1951 Barrow beat Leeds in the Challenge Cup semi-final and four years later they repeated the process when I was playing with Hunslet. Needless to say Willie was the brains behind those Barrow successes and he received a just reward when he captained his team to victory over Workington Town in 1955.

I remember Willie as a modest, popular and unassuming young man. Barrow-in-Furness can be justly proud of Willie Horne, in fact they should idolise him.

Belle Vue players Tom Kenny and Ray Price are unable to stop Willie slipping by on the blindside at Craven Park.

Huddersfield's Australian stand-off half Pat Devery, Willie and Jimmy Lewthwaite in action during a Challenge Cup tie at Fartown. "Willie Horne is the greatest player I have ever seen," says Jimmy.

Willie supports a break by Jimmy Lewthwaite in a league match against Swinton at Craven Park.

The England team who were defeated by Other Nationalities at Borough Park, Workington on Spetember 19, 1949. Back: Danny Naughton, Jimmy Hayton, Jimmy Featherstone, Charlie Armitt, Ernie Ashcroft, Geoff Clark and Willie Horne. Front: Billy Ivison, Ted Kerwick, Johnny Lawrenson, Jimmy Ledgard, Joe Egan (captain) and Tommy Bradshaw.

EPPIE GIBSON – Centre threequarter, Workington, Cumberland and England: "I had always known Willie was a great stand-off half but it wasn't until I played with him I realised how special he was. Breaks were always on when Willie was playing."

ARTHUR CLUES – Second-row forward, Leeds, Hunslet and Australia: "Willie was a mighty footballer. All the Australians rated him highly. He could make the ball talk. Willie Horne is one of rugby league's greatest players."

MARTIN RYAN – Full back, Wigan, Lancashire, England and Great Britain: "If I was picking my all-time team Willie would be the first name down. I've never seen anyone better in any position. Everyone liked him. In fact, we all loved him."

JOE EGAN – Hooker, Wigan, Lancashire, England and Great Britain: "At Wigan we all thought of Willie as one of our own. He was more than a great player, he was a leader with the rare gift of inspiring others. He is truly one of the greats."

ALAN PRESCOTT – Prop forward, St Helens, Lancashire, England and Great Britain: "*Willie taught me so much about every aspect of rugby league, both on and off the field. I was proud to play with or against him. What a player and what a man.*"

TREVOR FOSTER – Second-row forward, Bradford Northern, Wales and Great Britain: "I treasure my memories of Willie Horne. He was born with a natural ability but it was his quick brain that made him stand out. He was an artist. It was like watching poetry in motion."

KEN GEE – Prop forward, Wigan, Lancashire, England and Great Britain. "Willie was the toughest opponent I ever played against. That hand and foot tackle was terrible."

Willie in his Paxton Terrace shop shortly after he retired from rugby league in 1959. The photograph was found at the back of an old scrapbook. The caption read simply, "Willie Horne, the one and only."

Willie practises in the nets at Vickers Sports Club, Hawcoat Lane, as a 17-year-old junior. In September, 1939 he scored his first North Lancashire League century, 101 not out at Millom.

Millom's triumphant Higson Cup team of 1947. Herbert Grayson (chairman), Alf Horne, Willie Horne, Wilf Thomas (12th man), Jack Dinsdale, Ken Richards, Jimmy Proctor, Alf Mackereth (scorer). Front: Alan Robinson, Tommy Peters, Ken Sneesby, Tommy Foster, George Sharp, Billy Rook, Tommy Shovelton.

A North Lancashire and District Representative XI at Furness Park, in the late 1940s. Back: J. Paterson, B. Boynes, H. Nutton, A. Paterson, J. McDougall, D. McIntosh, J. C. Dickinson, W. Horne, W. Gaskell and T. Slee. Front: B. Knowelden, H. Gibbon, F. H. Moore (captain), F. French and F. Conlin.

Ulverston CC in 1948, the year Willie topped the averages for the second time. Back: John Gifford, Frank Simm, Willie Horne, James Walker and Bill Dixon. Front: Alf Horne, John McKeown, Bob Cathey, Eddie Miller, Ted Jackson and Ken Ireland.

Furness CC's winning Higson Cup team from 1949. Back: Alan Waite, Billy Allcock, Jimmy Bawden, Len Wilkinson, Ken Bennett, Willie Horne. Front: Albert Williams, John Hardy, Sid Redhead, Billy Ormandy and Howard Tickle.

Willie won the Higson Cup for the third time with three different clubs when he helped Vickerstown win the trophy in 1958. Back: Philip Dunn, Billy Morgan, Fred Roskell, Paddy Deallott, Leo Woods, Ernie Ottley (captain), Willie Horne, Joe Bateman, Arthur Proctor, Alf Horne and Tommy Woods.

Fred Roskell and Willie walk out to open the batting for Vickerstown at Workington. "Willie is the best thing that ever happened to our club," says Fred.

Willie does not like making public appearances but in 1991 he was persuaded to open Barrow's new Leisure Centre. The road leading to the entrance is named the Willie Horne Way.

CHAPTER TWENTY FOUR

THE SHOP

I STARTED three youth teams for Barrow Wanderers in 1979. Willie gave us all three strips for nothing and threw in track suits and balls as well, hundreds of pounds worth of gear. In fact I can't recall buying a ball in the 25 years I dealt with Willie and his wife Bessie.

Before that I started a team called Lisco Sun and I can remember going to see Willie with a plastic bag full of copper and silver we had collected. He sold me a full strip for a fiver. I don't know how he ever stayed in business. But that was the sort of man he was. He took everyone at face value and I'm sure he would have given me the keys to the shop if I had asked him.

Another time I started refereeing and I couldn't afford a kit. I needn't have worried. Willie gave me everything free, including a stop watch. Sometimes we got kit cheap because of the colours. I ran the Bluebird Club and Willie once gave us a strip of red and yellow shirts and black shorts. Everyone called us the deckchairs.

In my opinion the Sunday League and Barrow Wanderers wouldn't have existed without Willie's shop. He gave unlimited credit to just about every team. He did that with everyone. He was a Godsend.

As a person I can't think of anyone to compare him with. There's only ever been one Willie Horne. That's what I think of him. To me he's a saint. There's no praise high enough. He deserves an award for what he has done for the footballing community in Furness.

CLLR. JEFF WADSWORTH
Manager of Furness football clubs for 30 years

I COULD TELL straight away he was a nice man. There was a sincerity about him. He had a soft, friendly face so it was easy to picture him laughing courteously at some late-night party. He reminded me of a teacher I once had at South Walney Junior School and even now I can still see her wiping flooding tears from a child who had fallen or sticking a plaster on a grazed knee. We all liked her, and, if I was any judge of character, I was sure he would be similarly popular with his pupils.

"Hello Willie," he said warmly, though it was obvious they had never met before. He was hoping to start a school team, soccer I think he said. The children had raised £15 and he wondered if he might buy some pairs of socks, you know, to make them see they were getting somewhere and encourage further fundraising.

"Go on in and take a seat," said Willie. "We'll soon sort you out. What colour would you like?"

"Green please," he answered.

Willie was already away, running up the stairs to the third floor. We heard the muffled noise of steps and containers being moved before he returned much quicker than I had expected. He was holding two large boxes, one under each arm. A few minutes later Willie was back again with two further identical boxes, placing them carefully on top of the others. One final trip, this time returning with a huge plastic bag, the kind you see women carrying to the local launderette on a Saturday morning bursting with a week's washing.

I watched the teacher's reaction to all this mysterious manoeuvring. For a moment his lips parted slightly and I sensed he was debating if it would be wise to inquire after the contents of those boxes. Then his mouth snapped shut in an instant as if he had thought better of it.

Willie began washing cups, filling a battered kettle with water while we indulged in pleasant small talk . . . the merits of Barrow's latest signing, if it was likely to rain and what was on TV that night.

"Well I'd better be off," the teacher said, putting on his coat and glancing at his watch uneasily before looking in Willie's direction, unsure what to do next.

"I'll give you a hand," Willie said picking up two boxes easily although in fact they looked quite heavy. He was still a strong man, capable of making a strenuous physical act appear effortless with a certain grace and natural rhythm prevalent among all great sportsmen.

"But what's in the boxes?" the teacher asked rather shyly, answering his own question, lifting a lid and peering inside, his eyes sparkling widely like a small child opening a present on Christmas Day. The boxes contained a full kit – 13 pairs of socks, 13 shorts and 13 shirts. And there were two track suits in the plastic bag.

"I can't take all this, Willie," he said, but his voice lacked assurance, as though he knew protesting would be hopeless. He tried anyway. But Willie had made his mind up and further argument, although understandable, would evidently prove futile.

"I don't want any money," said Willie, gesturing the teacher to leave. "It's old stock." I'd heard that one before. "Oh, and you'll be needing this," he went on, placing a soccer ball on top of the box and pointing to the stairs with just a hint of impatience. The teacher left, bewildered but contented as one might act following a telephone call relating good news that had been unexpected, a pools win, perhaps.

I know this story is true. I saw it happen . . . everything. And I have witnessed enough similar cases to enable me to conclude this was likely to be the small tip of an extremely large iceberg. Willie's generosity and selflessness were well-known, but I never grew weary of watching people's response, which was nearly always identical to the teacher's – a red-faced mixture of embarrassment and gratitude. Yes, he gave things away all right. But there was much more to Willie's shop than the uncontrolled benevolence of a kind man.

★ ★ ★

In 1968, town centre redevelopment forced Willie and Bessie to move the shop from Paxton Terrace, 150 yards along William Street to Cavendish Street. The three storey premises had been a crockery shop called Dowlings, before that Paiges, a clothes store specialising in Scout and Guide uniforms and camping equipment. It was a change they had not wanted. Willie and Bessie were happy where they were but in time they came to recognise the compulsory relocation carried many benefits, not least lots of extra space for stock and display.

Willie remained upstairs, away from customers, where, it was hoped, his fondness for charity would be less of a threat to the shop's profitability. That was the plan anyway. He was certainly kept busy, sending boots and the like down a wooden chute specially constructed for the purpose by fellow Barrow RL player Derek Cockin. Willie had his own room, the size of an average lounge. There was an electric cooker in one corner, by a window through which a sizeable number of scraggy pigeons slipped in each day cooing contentedly as Willie fed them pieces of stale bread. A small table was positioned against the wall, surrounded by six or seven chairs, though you considered yourself fortunate should you manage to acquire one.

It was a mecca, a meeting place, a sanctuary for sportsmen – footballers, cricketers, rugby players, darters, bowlers and many, many more. Then there were the lunchtimes. There were two shifts, early and late.

First in were Stan Halesworth, Terry Morris, Pablo Millardship and Dave Knowles. They arrived at precisely 12.08. You could set your watch by them and not worry about missing that important meeting. Other regulars would hear the works buzzer and leave certain seats vacant respectfully.

Giving way to the incoming diners always put me in mind of a similar arrangement at the Harbour Hotel, a pub on the Strand where I had been drinking for many years. There was a regular called Bill Bailey, a charming man with a round face and a thick mop of black hair. He was a touch overweight but Bill was still a handsome man who talked quickly, interspersing his words and staccato sentences with a nervous whistle as though he was constantly anxious to finish what he had to say as quickly as possible, lest he was interrupted.

Bill sat on a stool at the end of the bar, next to the dartboard. No one ever sat on that stool. I had always imagined it would be a particularly unpleasant experience, that the other regulars would respond by scowling and whispering indiscreetly making you feel as if you had walked across a grave or told a dirty joke in mixed company. Yet I cannot recall Bill's ownership of the stool ever being mentioned or discussed. We all knew it was his stool, knowledge that, looking back, seemed to have been circulated by some sort of mental telepathy. It was like that in Willie's shop at lunchtime. Seats were made available for specific people at specific times, something we were all aware of instinctively as one knows how to catch a ball or write your name.

I was in the late shift along with Ken Benson and Peter Leach. We arrived at the shop around 12.45, all chaos and jokes, Willie washing pots and peeling potatoes, steam from a boiling kettle hanging in the air, everyone talking, the witty banter and lively argument you're always likely to hear among good friends at ease in each other's company.

I guess there were around 30 who you could call regulars, friends who dropped in on Willie three or four times a week. But there were many others whose visits were unpredictable, so that when you heard footsteps coming up the stairs you could never be certain who they belonged to. It was more like a busy railway station than a sports shop.

I remember one young man walking into Willie's room looking embarrassed as if he felt he ought not be there. He was small with the innocent face of a child that appeared at odds with his oily hands and the blue overalls of Vickers shipyard.

"You wanted to see me Willie?" he asked and on closer inspection I saw he had wide shoulders and strong arms suggesting he was likely to be a good sportsman, probably very good.

"Yes," Willie answered. "Pop upstairs and pick yourself two pairs of boots. Any you want."

The stranger returned ten minutes later with two boxes that Willie took from him, placing them in a plastic bag and ordering him to leave, muttering something about good luck and for him to take care. The man stopped and thought about offering some money but he knew in the circumstances it would be inappropriate so he left uneasily, mumbling over and over, "Thanks Willie." Three times I think he said it.

The next day there was another visitor we had not seem before. He was a much bigger man who responded to Willie's generosity with similar bewilderment. I found out later they were David Cairns and Steve Kirkby, 18-year-old rugby league players from Askam who had recently been selected for the 1979 British Amateur Rugby League tour to Australia. Soon after that trip they turned professional, enjoying lengthy and successful careers. David, a scrum half, became a Great Britain international who served Barrow and Salford, while Steve, a fearless and respected second-row forward, played with some distinction for Barrow, Whitehaven and Carlisle. I am told Willie made similar contributions to many other Furness sportsmen and women who had shown promise. Yet it was something you did not hear of. And he preferred it that way.

Being allowed into Willie's shop, becoming part of his family, was an honour we did not accept lightly. There was an aura of goodness about the place. We felt a sort of bonding, a oneness. Favours were granted, houses rewired, cars mended and sinks fitted. No one ever asked for money. That would have been considered bad form, almost an insult. And all the time Willie was at the heart of things, running up and down the stairs between brews.

He had never been what you might call an extrovert. But here, among his friends, he spoke often, contributing to the conversation with sensitivity, knowledge and understanding. No one argued. Not seriously. But when there was disagreement, each party would plead their case while Willie listened, concentrating, before giving his own measured opinion. And when that opinion matched your own you felt an inner satisfaction as though you had been right all the time and Willie's support was sufficient confirmation to prove your case.

He would never be so forward as to offer advice without invitation. But if you needed counselling on, say, a recurring injury, a problem at work or if it would be wise to apply for that post in Glasgow, Willie was always there, talking sensibly with an unusual gift of simplifying what had previously appeared complex and puzzling. He was a special friend to all of us, someone we were fond of, someone many of us, literally, loved. And it was a rare event for his guidance ever to prove unwise.

Take the case of a Barrow-born rugby union player in turmoil over the temptations of turning professional. Ken Moss was his name. I think it was a Saturday morning when he came to the shop. He was one of the biggest men I had ever seen – tall, muscular, menacing, though it quickly became apparent that Ken was charming, likeable and friendly. He had a narrow waist, that of a dancer, but his shoulders were huge, so wide his jacket seemed too small for him. His hair was long, black and curly, his face dominated by a flat nose and though at first I took Ken to be around 30 I soon realised he was much younger, only 20 perhaps. He began telling us of his dilemma, quickly falling at ease. Willie had that effect on people.

"I don't know what to do Willie," he said, shaking his head in frustration. He exuded confidence, though he was not arrogant, and I was left thinking Ken was the kind of man you would want as a friend if a drunk was pushing you in a pub or a dance. "Widnes want me to sign," he went on, "but I'd rather wait and try to get my England union cap first."

We knew all about Ken. He was a wonderful flanker for Broughton Park and a regular choice for Lancashire. I had watched him on television the week before and heard the grating voice of Nigel Starmer-Smith droning on about how Ken had dominated the line-outs and that he was a formidable, adventurous forward. And now the national papers were full of extravagant speculation about his imminent defection to rugby league. Some reports were accompanied by a photograph of Ken sitting in the Widnes dug-out looking pensive while coach Doug Laughton puffed away on a cigarette.

So when Ken told us he had been offered £40,000 we believed him. What should he do? He had an opportunity for financial security, a chance to receive the sort of money one associated with Hollywood actors, best-selling authors and Manchester United footballers. Yet we could see that England cap meant so much to him.

"Take it," Willie said directly. "You'll still be an international at rugby league. You might break your leg tomorrow." I felt for Ken. It was a big decision that required careful thought. We did not see much of him after that. But he did not join Widnes. They had grown impatient and signed somebody else. Ken went to London to play for Wasps, hoping to improve his reputation and further his claims for that England cap. Then he was badly injured, a dodgy knee if memory serves. Now I don't know where he is or what became of him. But I bet he wished he'd taken Willie's advice.

I have to confess that knowing Willie, as I did, him being Great Britain captain and all, was always a source of pride to me. I bragged about our friendship to my own rugby league team, Corporation Combine. We were coached by Tony Bailiff and Gordon Christie and though we enjoyed great team spirit primarily based on our collective capacity to consume vast quantities of beer on a Saturday night, our performances were, at best, moderate.

Once I dislocated my thumb and it became a sort of ritual to drop into Willie's shop each Saturday lunchtime so he could strap it for me, something he did expertly in just a few seconds. Soon Alan Roper joined me, then Alan Park, Ian Gerrish and Frank Cassidy and another and another until the whole damn team were queuing at the foot of the stairs, holding rolls of white tape and pairs of scissors. We left the shop infected with an unshakeable belief that Willie had imparted a drop of his genius into each one of us.

So Willie and his shop meant many things to many people. But of all the things I saw there, it was his generosity and warm personality that I look back on with the deepest affection. Most of us had never seen him play rugby league though we knew he was brave, inspirational, adventurous and unique. Our fathers had told us. But that had nothing to do with the frequency of our visits.

We went there because, well, we loved him.

CHAPTER TWENTY FIVE

BAT AND BALL

WILLIE Horne was the best thing that ever happened to Vickerstown Cricket Club. He was popular and settled in perfectly with the lads. I opened the batting with Willie and he was a dream to play with. All I had to do was hold my end up and watch him do all the scoring. Once we were playing at Carlisle and we scored 70 runs in the first five overs, with Willie hitting 50 of them. Every now and then I see Albert Cracknell, Carlisle's great batsman of that time, and he always pulls my leg about it.

I suppose to some people Willie was unorthodox. It was all off the cuff. I don't think he knew what he was going to do next. He was just as likely to hit the first ball of the match for four. He did that quite often.

When he was batting there was always something going on. Cricket was never boring with him in the team. Willie had all the shots so there was no way to set a field to stop him scoring. There's a standing joke at Vickerstown even now after all these years. When Willie's name is mentioned we all stand up and bow as a mark of respect. That's how highly we think of him.

Over the years I've watched a lot of players but Willie was out of this world. For natural ability he's the best local cricketer I've ever seen.

FRED ROSKELL
Opening batsman, Vickerstown CC – 1939-1967

THERE'S a story that's been doing the rounds for close on 60 years now. They say there was a sports teacher at Risedale school called Ted Parke. He was a useful batsman who understood technique, the wisdom of using a straight bat and getting to the pitch of the ball.

Mr Parke, if you believe the story, was a popular man who enjoyed coaching children, a kindly teacher who did not consider it unreasonable to stay behind after school to pass on his knowledge. Anyway, according to the story, Mr Parke had an engaging trick he employed at the end of a coaching session. He replaced the bails with pennies and invited children to bowl him out, a formidable task, one they found difficult to perform. Occasionally he let a ball through and pretended to be surprised as his stumps fell and eager children picked up the pennies and headed for the corner shop. In 1934 a penny bought you a bagful of sweets so the trick was a useful incentive that taught the children to concentrate and bowl a good line and length. Mr Parke, it seems, was a good man.

The story goes that when Willie Horne started at Risedale and joined in these coaching sessions Mr Parke found himself and his wickets in some disarray. They say Willie's bowling was accurate and persistent, enabling him to hit the wickets so frequently that one night poor Mr Parke actually ran out of money. The following evening his generous invitation to bowl him out was withdrawn. They say he reintroduced it the day Willie left the school. You have to agree it's a good story but perhaps a bit farfetched. However, I know it is true. Ted Parke told me.

★ ★ ★

When Willie walked out to bat he did so with a certain urgency and impatience. People took notice. Children stopped playing, bars emptied and old women sitting in deck chairs put down bundles of knitting. There was that mood of expectation you feel before the start of a cup final or when the curtain is about to go up on a particularly fine play. Willie was an entertainer who enjoyed scoring runs with a flair and unorthodox technique that appeared perilous viewed from the pavilion. He took chances.

If ever he played poker he would probably lose all his money quickly. He would gamble with promising hands by bluffing and taking outrageous risks on the turn of a card. That was the way he was. He played cricket in the same cavalier manner as he played rugby league. So he was known as a crowd pleaser.

Watching him construct a lengthy innings revealed much about his temperament. Willie radiated optimism and energy, prowling about the crease, restless when he did not have the strike, concentrating sharply when he did. He was an artist and as befits all sportsmen touched with genius he was unpredictable, so it would be fair to call him a "streak" player. When Willie was on form, bowlers found him bewildering and impossible to pin down. He could play all the shots in the coaching manual and one or two others besides. His adventurous style encouraged bowlers to believe they might tempt him into a mistake, that if they were lucky he might attack a straight ball once too often. But there was more method in his technique than seemed apparent from the boundary. Willie had a considerable calmness of temperament, though he was not, by nature, a cautious man. And it is worth recording that many of his greatest innings came in the face of seemingly overwhelming odds.

It is possible to be a successful batsman if you have only a moderate amount of courage. You can push, deflect, poke, cut and drive all day and the odds are pretty high that you will not injure yourself. But if you pull and hook often you need to be a very brave man. If you are facing a fast bowler and mistime the stroke, the ball is liable to knock you out as effectively as if a strong man had whacked you on the head with a hammer.

Willie pulled all short-pitched balls with an innocent disregard for what might happen if he made a mistake. He could do this through his great gift for calculating angles and reacting instantly. He had so much time. A batsman who pulls and hooks will score lots of runs. The strokes do not require power because you are merely deflecting a ball already travelling at considerable speed. You guide it, help it on its way as one might push a rowing boat down a steep slipway. Then there were the quick singles.

An international stand-off half needs to be able to run 20 yards faster than any man on the pitch. The average cover fielder was not familiar with Willie's sprinting and response to opportunity. So quick singles were frequent. And the fact that they were expected did not diminish their effectiveness. Quite the opposite. The quick single was a weapon of intimidation as well as a useful and reliable method of accumulating runs. Fielders were nervous, you understand, worried that they had fewer than four seconds in which to pick up the ball and throw it at the stumps, a target narrower than a loaf of bread. When Willie was in partnership with his brother Alf, which was often, the constant threat of quick singles reduced fielders to something approaching panic.

Willie did not hit many sixes. When you bash the ball over the ropes it is in the air and usually that means it is only a matter of time before you are caught. He preferred to collect his runs by persistent stroke play and delicate deflections, sweeping the ball between fielders, along the ground, something he did often and with great accuracy. He could bowl a bit too. Willie employed a short run-up and though he was no more than gentle medium pace he was accurate and repetitive, frustrating batsmen who did not enjoy the worrying knowledge that the penalty for missing the ball was likely to be three stumps knocked out of the ground followed by a lonely walk back to the pavilion.

Willie fielded throughout his career at first slip, which is surprising considering how fast he could run. You would have thought he might be better employed in the covers, stopping runs and getting batsmen out. Not so. All the captains he played under knew Willie was such a wonderful catcher that he had to be in the slips. So he could bat, he could bowl and he could field. But it would be remiss not to mention his great sportsmanship.

Cricket can be a cruel game that tests the resolve of the strongest character. Consider, if you will, the annoyance of a bad decision. You are up at 7am to prepare for the long journey to Carlisle, a tortuous three-hour trip along meandering lanes, the coach brushing overhanging branches as it slowly negotiates the A6, climbing to the summit of Shap before dropping sharply into the city. Carlisle bat first and put on a big score and you have fielded on the boundary, hardly touching the ball. It's a good wicket and you know there are runs to be had if you concentrate and execute shots correctly.

The first ball you receive clips your pads on the way to the wicketkeeper who jumps up in the air appealing for a catch, supported by the bowler and close-in fielders, everyone staring at the umpire, pleading for the decision. He looks down the wicket, pausing for a moment, before you see the awful sight of his arm stretching forward, finger pointing to the sky. You are out and there's nothing you can do about it. Bad decisions are part of the game but they are never easy things to deal with. More emotional batsmen are prone to argument and throwing bats at dressing room walls. But not Willie. He accepted them with good grace and a shake of his head.

Let's examine his career more closely.

Willie began playing organised cricket for Risedale School when he was 12. Their home ground was on Barrow Park with the wicket occupying the approximate position taken today by the deep end of the swimming pool in the town's Leisure Centre. The pitch was also used for football matches, so come the cricket season the bounce was, to say the least, variable. But Willie's remarkable eye for a ball was so pronounced he did not find the pitch enough of a handicap to limit his capacity to score runs.

When he was 15 Willie joined Vickers Sports Club in Hawcoat Lane where the runs continued to flow unabated. He played in the Under-18 team, batting at number four, benefiting from frequent advice from club professional Haydn Nutton, a Yorkshireman who had led the league's batsmen in 1937 averaging 88 and hitting a record 880 runs. He encouraged Willie to temper his attacking instincts and improve his defensive technique, which would, he warned, be put under great strain when the quality of bowling improved.

Soon he was promoted to the 'A' team where he made a host of big scores that persuaded selectors it was time for a call-up into the first eleven. He joined older men such as Sid Redhead, Bryn Knowelden (who was destined to become a rugby league international), Ken Postlethwaite, Frank Carradus and brother Alf Horne, who was the wicketkeeper. In September, 1939, Willie scored 101 not out at Millom but soon after, the league was forced to abandon fixtures as the German Wehrmacht marched across Europe. Four years later the Furness War League was formed, with Willie topping the averages, his wonderful season including centuries against Vickerstown and Millom. He had begun bowling regularly too, returning impressive figures that earned him a justifiable reputation as a fine all-rounder.

Towards the end of the season, Millom secretary Jack Dinsdale invited Willie to guest for the Cumberland side in a friendly weekend fixture against a Services XI. Again he scored an unbeaten century.

"Willie and I hit it off right away," recalls Jack. "So after talking to the committee it was unanimously decided to invite him to be our professional the following season. We were delighted when he agreed."

Alf joined Willie, the two brothers travelling to Millom on Willie's BSA motorbike. His wages were 30 shillings (£1-50) a match.

"Normally a professional didn't get paid if the game was rained off," says Jack. "But with Willie we always made sure he got his money. Everyone was so pleased with him. He was an extremely good athlete, a brilliant fielder, a good bowler and a nice lad. Getting him to Millom proved to be an inspirational decision."

Willie hit 90 not out in his first game for Millom at neighbouring Haverigg. It was a faultless innings, all the more remarkable given the state of the outfield; the grass was so long it resembled a field of wheat waiting to be harvested.

"Rationing meant there was no petrol for the mower to cut the outfield," says Jack. "It was no one's fault but the grass was very, very long. I think Willie only hit one four, so it shows what a great knock it was."

Willie topped the averages in his first season at Millom with 48.18, more than eight runs ahead of his nearest rival, Haydn Nutton, his former mentor at Vickers. Millom unexpectedly won a Higson Cup semi-final against Vickers, thanks to Willie's match-winning half century, but they lost the final to Furness despite another 54 from Willie.

News of his powerful, dominating performances drifted down to Manchester so no one was surprised when Lancashire County Cricket Club invited him to play in a three-day match against Warwickshire at Edgbaston. He scored six and 20 not out, impressing officials sufficiently for them to inquire if he might consider leaving the shipyard and becoming a full-time cricketer. But, they said, that would mean retiring from rugby. Naturally he said no.

Millom retained Willie for the following season, but his selection for the British Lions tour to Australia meant he spent the summer 12,000 miles away helping his country retain the Ashes. Alf took over as Millom's professional. In 1947 it was business as usual with Millom winning the Higson Cup 21 years after their last success. Often big cricket matches are won by the team whose professional comes on top, gets a few runs or takes the most wickets. Willie bowled Kendal pro Peter Greenwood for just three runs, going on to finish with 6-47. Greenwood joined Lancashire the following season. Millom knocked off the 102 runs for five wickets with Willie hitting a rapid 28. His season included 6-18 at Netherfield and 97 not out in Millom's Higson Cup semi-final victory over Ulverston.

In 1948 Willie moved to Ulverston as professional where he joined Eddie Miller, a magnificent, text-book batsman who was destined to be the leading amateur six times, top the averages five times and hit most runs six times.

"Bob Cathay, our skipper who worked at Vickers, persuaded Willie to come to Ulverston," says Eddie who was the Carnforth professional for six years. "Willie batted first wicket down. I was next. I would often say to him, 'Is the ball doing much?' He would reply, 'No, nothing at all.' Then, when I started batting, I realised it was moving appreciably. I don't know if he didn't see such things or if he ignored them.

"Willie was an entertainer, a crowd-puller. Everyone loved to see him play. He had his own following. The thing with Willie was his instinct for doing the right thing at the right time. Maybe he wasn't as stylish as some but he was very effective. Willie was so fast on his feet you had to bowl a perfect line and length. No one could pin him down.

"He was quick to drive or hook, a natural artist capable of doing whatever was required to enable his team to win. And, of course, he was a useful bowler and a brilliant slip fielder who could turn a game with his catching. Willie was a great friend and team-mate who played the game how it should be played. He tried his best but if he lost, he always congratulated the winners. And he never questioned any umpire's decisions."

Willie topped the averages again, hitting 397 runs including a wonderful knock of 129 not out at Haverigg. Against Workington he scored an unbeaten 50 in a century second wicket stand with Alf who made 66. At the end of the season Willie received an unexpected visit from Furness chairman Bill Gaitskell. "Come and play for us as an amateur," he asked. "We'll give you £40."

So he left Tarn Close for Furness Park where he continued his relentless pursuit of big scores. Furness won the Higson Cup after a century stand between Willie and Ken Bennett, who each made 58 out of a total of 149. The next highest score was from former Lancashire pro Lenny Wilkinson who managed just five runs. Ulverston collapsed with Willie chipping in with two wickets for 20 runs in 14 overs. In a league match at Ernest Pass, Barrow, Willie hit an unbeaten century in only 80 minutes with the Evening Mail drooling: "This was a magnificent knock full of blazing strokes and devil-may-care batting." The following Monday he scored 124 against Vickerstown.

In 1950 Willie was again in Australia with the Great Britain rugby league team and he missed the next two years as well, unable to get time off his job in the Wireworks. In 1953 he joined Vickerstown, his last club, after a special request from opening batsman Fred Roskell who persuaded Willie's boss to allow him to finish on Saturday lunchtimes.

The first year at Rainey Park, Willie was runner-up in the averages, amassing 532 runs for an average of 59. His season included knocks of 85 not out against Whitehaven, 93 not out at Dalton and 92 against Barrow. The Evening Mail's comment on that score ran like this: "It was a typical Horne innings, always bright and refreshing. If anything he is a better bat than ever because he now plays down the line and in this knock at least he did not go across once."

For the next few seasons the runs kept coming and in 1958 he won the averages for the fourth time in his career. He hit 99 at Haverigg before being caught on the boundary, 81 not out against Barrow and 94 not out from a total of 157 for 1 declared at Workington. At Carlisle, Willie and Fred Roskell put on an opening partnership of 175 in less than two hours. In 1961 Willie hit another unbeaten century, reported enthusiastically by the Evening Mail: "Swashbuckling Willie Horne was the Vickerstown hero. He carried his bat to an unbeaten 100 out of a total of 171." Vickerstown finished league champions, six points ahead of Workington.

Willie's final season was 1962 when his sports shop became so hectic he could not justify missing the busiest day of the week. He still made big scores, however, including 70 at Carnforth, 50 at Dalton, 59 at Workington and 72 not out against Millom.

So Willie finally bowed out of the North Lancashire and District Cricket League, behind him more than 20 centuries, 8,000 runs and dozens of wickets and catches.

"Willie Horne was a one off," says Eddie Miller. "To me he was the Denis Compton of local cricket. There can be no higher tribute than that."

CHAPTER TWENTY SIX

HOME IS THE HERO

I'M NO DIFFERENT to anyone else. I was born with a bit of a gift, that's all. I owe everything to my family, the support I got from my mother and father and, of course, my brothers Alf and George. Then there were all the great players I was fortunate to play with. They made me. Without them I'd have been nothing. When I look back I know I've been very, very lucky.

WILLIE HORNE
February 17, 1994

THE BUNGALOW is in a quiet part of town. A long row of terraced, sandstone houses stands opposite, red bricks seeping nostalgia, a link to a forgotten era when Cornish miners travelled north, full of optimism, to dig iron ore hundreds of feet below the Furness countryside. Double-glazed windows look down on rows of cars, bumper to bumper, Escorts, Cavaliers and the odd Volvo Estate. The garden is neat. Conifer bushes dwarf scattered annuals, pretty and colourful, small beds surrounded by Lakeland slate. Everything is practical, designed with an eye for convenience, so much so that it is safe to assume the owners have more important matters to attend to than pruning roses and spraying hungry greenfly.

The entrance is off a long concrete drive through sliding glass doors, a sharp left and you're in the lounge. The room is tidy and decorated with a certain charm and style. In one corner, a large television set gazes out above a VCR and a satellite receiver, red lights flickering, the presence of small children suggested by a large pile of videos – Tom and Jerry cartoons and Disney films. Lakeland landscapes fill the walls, oil paintings of Hawkshead's narrow streets, Victorian shoppers in tall hats mingling against a background of desolate, snow-capped mountains. Tucked away in another corner, a dated record player, the kind usually owned by older people with a fondness for Glenn Miller and Vera Lynn.

There isn't much else on view that might reveal the identity of the bungalow's occupants. It is typical of 1,000 other South Cumbria homes, the type humble, decent people aspire to own after a lifetime of posting letters, driving buses or welding pipes in the claustrophobic darkness deep inside a nuclear submarine.

What makes it remarkable are the things that are missing rather than the things you can see. There are no photographs. No trophies. No medals. No posters. You could search all day and you would not find a solitary symbol of sporting excellence. Yet this is the home of someone special, who, if he had a mind to, could fill a warehouse with images of greatness. It is the home of a private, simple man who pulled on a blue and white shirt every Saturday afternoon for more than 16 years, who captained his town, his county and his country, a unique man who did everything with skill and courage, oh, so much courage.

Willie Horne and his wife Bessie live here. And yes, he has many trophies. Only you can't see them. They're buried in black bags in the loft, along with old lamps and dusty boxes of books. Willie prefers it that way, kept out of view, away from inquisitive eyes. He's special all right, partly through the wonderful things he could do on a rugby field and partly through his response to adulation. He is modest in the extreme, dismissing praise with an embarrassed wave of the hand. If you did not know him you might be forgiven for thinking his response was in some way improper. That perhaps his family and friends, occasionally at least, might become a shade irritated. Not so. That's the way he is. And that's one of the reasons we all love him so much.

Willie is the sort of man who makes friends easily. He likes people. You feel at ease in his company, safe in the knowledge that he could never be anything other than placid and respectful. If Willie were to go on holiday it is likely he would be on first name terms with waiters by the end of the week, that the man in the paper shop would remember him. Each morning they would exchange courteous conversation so the man would know Willie came from Barrow, that he enjoyed a game of golf and watching football on the television. But he would not be aware that the morning visitor with the flat cap and the warm smile is one of the greatest rugby league players the world has ever seen. Willie never speaks of his achievements.

Occasionally I try to imagine what Willie might have become had he been born in Southampton, Glasgow or Sunderland, away from rugby league, where his sporting excellence would have remained hidden and untapped. It's easy to picture him at the head of a classroom, pointing towards a blackboard, his long fingers white with chalk. He would be talking quietly but with a certain authority, while rows of pupils sat alert and attentive. He would have been good at that. Yes, Willie would have made an excellent teacher.

Rugby league players, thankfully, still make a pleasant contrast to the appalling standards of behaviour displayed on our television sets each week by adolescent soccer stars. Football is all hostility and confrontation. No one smiles anymore. Players snarl, bicker petulantly with referees, everyone's pushing, talking, arguing, grimacing, shouting – brave men without a soul. Winning is everything. A capacity to loathe the opposition is considered an attribute. You need to hate to perform well. Without aggression you are weak, you lack spirit, you're a nobody. If a soccer player is known as a good loser who shakes hands graciously with opponents at the conclusion of a tough match, win or lose, in some circles his character would be open to question.

We are justly proud of how professional rugby league players behave. Everyone plays to win but there is something uplifting in the way our heroes embrace at the final whistle and head for the dressing room, arm in arm, through clapping supporters wearing different colours, chatting respectfully about the match. But we must take care. There's too much talk of intensity and visualisation, tackle counts and percentage football. Defence dominates and rugby league is a worse game for it. Artists such as Willie Horne are disappearing. More recently we marvelled at free spirits such as Wally Lewis, Peter Sterling, Steve Norton, Tony Myler and Andy Gregory. Where are they now?

Rugby league is often compared to a battlefield. Always has been. And any journalist will tell you, describing a Test match without some reference to warfare is a tough proposition. We slip into comfortable cliches, and though they are things we all recognise and try to avoid, they creep in like an unseen virus. You will not have to search very long to find meaningless phrases scattered throughout this book. Fighting spirit, deafening roars and brave troops sneak up on you. Of course, many of the things we associate with war are present on a rugby field. Teams attempt to gain ground, there is pain, there is unity, there is leadership and there is bravery. Above all else, there is bravery. How would someone like Willie fit in with the "modern" game, mentally? His pre-match talks did not include bashing lockers and shouting: "Kill, kill, kill." He is devoid of belligerence. Off the field he is a gentle man, incapable of an unpleasant thought. He'd give you the shirt off his back.

"There's no one today who even compares to Willie Horne," former Great Britain scrum half Alex Murphy says in the introduction to this book. "If he was playing now he'd be like a Penny Black . . . priceless." That's the charm of Willie Horne. Off the rugby field, a mild man, on it a giant among giants. The best ever.

Most sporting biographies include a chapter in which the player names his favourite team, describing in some detail the qualities of each selection. It's what newspaper reporters refer to as "good copy." Such a chapter does not require research and can be written in the first person, usually very quickly. I had planned to include one in this book. When I asked Willie to think about the great players he had seen, he went silent, closing his eyes, concentrating, before leaning forward and talking quickly, as if he had just met an old friend and couldn't wait to tell me about it.

"Well there's Phil Jackson, Ken Gee, Gus Risman and Tommy Bradshaw," he said, the names gushing out without pause. I probed him further and together we went on a magical journey, Willie describing the biggest, the fastest, the strongest, the toughest – men like Brian Bevan, Arthur Clues, Ike Owens, Ted Toohey, Trevor Foster, Jimmy Lewthwaite and

Martin Ryan. I felt humble and honoured yet, sadly, I am not permitted to share my knowledge with you.

"I've been thinking, Mike," Willie told me nervously the next time we met. "I'd rather not pick my best team if you don't mind. There have been so many good players and I'm too old to fall out with anyone." He was apologetic and a little upset as though he felt he had let me down. I know if I had pushed he would have reconsidered. But I didn't. I never could.

Watching rugby league with Willie is an education but one that demands a certain skill you can only acquire in time, over many months. You need to be able to translate his comments because he does not indulge in what the rest of us might call criticism. If, for example, he says a certain player had a quiet game, he means his work-rate was poor, usually in defence. The player is lazy. And if he describes a forward as "flash," the player in question, like as not, does his running in the centre, away from the hostility of big men. That's another charming thing about him – a complete absence of unpleasant characteristics that afflict the rest of us in varying degrees. He is devoid of badness.

So what became of him when he left Craven Park in 1959 after conquering the world? Well, for a start, he played golf, reducing his handicap to eight in less than a year, a considerable achievement, comparable with, say, an opening batsman scoring a century in his maiden Test match. Willie has an unorthodox swing. He has a bad grip, a bad stance, a bad set-up, so if he ever had a lesson, which he hasn't, a professional would probably recommend major changes . . . until he saw him hit the ball. He's good, you see, and a few years ago he was very good. He plays quickly too. Willie puts the ball on a tee peg, step backs and hits it, just like he kicked all those goals at Craven Park, at Headingley, at Station Road, in Sydney, and at Wembley Stadium. He has a simple swing, with a wonderful rhythm that is powerful and repetitive, his mind uncluttered with doubts and anxieties about a straight left arm, an aesthetic follow-through and a high finish. Now he plays a tidy game off 18.

Willie played bowls for a while with the police and the United Club but he stopped in 1974. Today he laughs and says it's a game for old men and that he might play again in 10 or 15 years. He probably will. For a while he ran a table tennis team called Horne's Hornets with Stan Houldsworth, Jimmy Lewthwaite, Neil Honeyman and Jack Yates. They operated from the sports shop in Cavendish Street. He was a tough opponent, I'm told, with quick reflexes.

Willie and Bessie retired from the shop in 1988. It was a decision they did not plan in advance. Willie had been admitted to hospital amid unpleasant rumours, heart trouble and the like. That first night, when no one knew the extent of his illness, I was anxious and frightened. I felt how I had always imagined one might feel living on the Florida coast and hearing a hurricane warning on the radio – fear of the unknown, not daring to think what might happen. Thankfully it was a small ulcer that responded to treatment and he was out in a couple of days. Soon afterwards he told us he was leaving the shop. It was as if he had suddenly realised time had become precious.

At first, he missed his friends but many of us still see him regularly. Frank Jones, Stan Halesworth, Jimmy Capstick, Kevin Proctor, Les Baynes, Peter McDonald, Bill Wookey, Ron Nelson, Ged Woods, George Kelly, Des Johnson and Joe Bateman all pop down for a chat, a cup of tea, half a loaf of bread and the crackers and the biscuits and the cakes.

I don't know why, but I have always thought of Willie as being indestructible. He has been a close friend for more than 20 years but he has not grown old. Willie never changes. He's the same person now as he was all those years ago, wearing the red, white and blue of Great Britain, tackling huge Australians with a courage and determination that often inspired those around him to great, historic victories. Willie has no envy, no greed, he is generous with money and praise, he never talks badly of anyone, he is loyal, he is honest, he thinks of others, never himself, he trusts people without cause, always, no matter how many times they let him down, he has an illogical faith in goodness, he's the nicest person I've ever met.

★ ★ ★

If I was a better writer this book would have had everything in it. I would have told you about the day Willie hand and footed that great Australian forward Arthur Clues, 16 stones of intimidation, and how Arthur chased Willie all over the field before catching him and that Willie ended up in hospital with concussion. I would have written about the day Risedale school cricket team were a man short and Willie made the numbers up and won the match hitting 99 not out at Vickerstown Cricket Club when he was just 13; and that the real reason he was one of the first rugby league players in history to kick side-foot was because he couldn't afford boots and it hurt less that way; and how his father played centre threequarter for Idle; and how Willie gets upset when he talks of his mother and father but it is something he thinks I do not notice. But I do.

This book should tell you of the time I asked Willie about a photograph I had come across in which he was receiving a large cup from an old man with white hair and that he disappeared and returned a few minutes later, from the garage I think, and showed me the cup, saying it was "a little something I won in 1955" and how I discovered later that rugby league supporters had voted him the best player in the world. And I wanted, if I was a better writer, to tell you about the time Willie gave an Australian shirt worn by Pat Devery in the Third Test in 1946 to an overweight customer who called in his shop upset because he could not find a shirt big enough to fit him; and how when Willie umpired cricket matches he gave all the fielders liquorice torpedoes.

I should have told you of a cold day in the middle of winter when I watched Willie score a hole in one with a driver at the tenth hole at Furness

Golf Club and how he just said it was a fluke and walked to the next tee as if it was a simple act like shaking your hand; and that if you lose a ball in his company, which in my case is fairly often, Willie puts those huge hands of his into his bag and throws over a new one, everytime; and how I ripped my waterproof jacket and Willie gave me his entire Gortex suit worth £160; and that he came back from the 1950 Australian Tour and had to borrow money from Rugby League secretary Bill Fallowfield because he had spent so much on presents; and how he was advised by many experienced observers not to tackle as much and to back up more, you know, look more flash, but he ignored them and defended in every game as though his life depended on the outcome; and that he never swears; and that local soccer player Dave Knowles once told me he looks up to Willie like a father.

There is nothing in this book about when I was on holiday with Willie in St Andrews and an attractive lady stopped him in the street and said he was the greatest player she had ever seen and that a similar thing happened in Llandudno and again in a Wigan golf club when an old man was reduced to tears, saying over and over again: "I've seen Willie Horne, THE Willie Horne," as if he thought he was having a dream and might wake up any moment. If I were more of a writer I would have told you about the amount of food Willie went through in a week, feeding friends in his sports shop . . . six dozen eggs, 24 loaves and a hundred weight of potatoes.

Then there was a man I interviewed who grew up with Willie, whose memory wasn't too good but he could remember as if it were yesterday "Willie side-stepping off the wall" and how certain he was his memory was accurate. Yet it is an act, try as I can, I cannot imagine, but somehow I believed him; and that Reg Parker, Barrow's giant second-row forward, was once asked by Jim Sullivan to sign for Wigan and Reg told the legendary Welshman: "I might, if you sign Willie Horne;" and I must not forget a special day I spent at Great Clifton with the family of Billy Little and how they made my father and me so welcome and that Billy's nephew Bobby, who was a brave, reliable loose forward with Salford, recalled the day he came home from school and his father told him: "Tha's finished with learning, son" and took him down the pit that night, into the inky darkness, among the noise, the heat, the pain, the horror, deep below the Cumberland countryside, and he was barely 12 years old.

There ought also to be the story of Ted Toohey, Barrow's international scrum-half, who, when possession was important, would throw the ball, laces up, into the face of the opposing hooker. One day at St Helens, he stood too near the scrum and a prop forward kicked him in the face and knocked out most of his teeth but he refused to leave the field, blood soaking his shirt. Ted was like that. And there ought to be something about the time I phoned Harry Edgar, editor of Open Rugby, asking if he might help publicise this book, and he answered: "It will be a pleasure. Willie Horne was my father's favourite player." And he did, too. There ought to be something about how I met Willie's brother George and he promised to lend me a photograph of his family, the one reproduced at the front of this book, and that he walked to the Evening Mail office the next day in the middle of a dreadful rainstorm and gave it to me to keep, saying how proud he was of Willie and that he hoped everything would turn out well.

There should have been something about the time Willie opened Holker Pioneers Rugby League Club's newly-built dressing rooms and the man on the gate didn't recognise him and charged the admission price of £1 and Willie just smiled politely and paid anyway. There should have been the story of how Willie was knocked out playing stick, roger, dodger when he was seven and an ambulanceman in Middle Field called Mr Tait realised it was serious and took him to North Lonsdale Hospital on a corporation tram and that when he got there the doctors lanced the swelling with great speed and concern, saying if he had been five minutes longer he would have died.

If I had been a better writer this book would have told you of the nights I spent interviewing Alf Horne in his Marsh Street home, his dog barking at passers-by nervously, flames from a coal fire dancing up the chimney, while he talked with accuracy and great detail of his family and Willie's childhood. And I wanted to tell you of the great social evenings I had with Alf, my father, Bill Wookey, Peter Leach, Billy Little, Peter McDonald and Jackie Spooner, a former team-mate of Willie's, a funny man who told us many stories such as how, when Barrow were ahead and defending at Craven Park, Willie would pass him the ball shouting: "kick it in the blinkin' Ambrose."

And, finally if I was a better writer, I would have told you of Labour councillor Les Burns's proposal to make Willie a Freeman of the Borough and how the town prepared with some anticipation to join in the celebrations, no one thinking for one moment it was any more than he deserved. And I would have told you that the Conservatives voted against the motion with some shameful excuse about "precedents."

People who know about such matters tell me Tory leader Councillor Ted Smith is a decent, honourable man, a man of integrity who entered politics to help make a better, more just society. If I were more of a writer, Councillor Smith might read this book and discover the things Willie has done and the honour he brought to his family, his sport and, most of all to Barrow, the town where he was born 72 years ago, the town where he has always lived, the town that loves him.

If only Willie could, after all, be made Freeman of the Borough. Now wouldn't that be something.

On Wednesday, July 20, 1994, Barrow Council held an extraordinary meeting with a solitary item on the agenda. Labour Councillor Les Burns proposed Willie Horne should be made Freeman of the Borough.

"Everyone in Barrow knows Willie was a supreme rugby player, probably the best in the world," he said. "He was a great sportsman and everyone is proud of him."

The proposal was accepted unanimously.

Jimmy Linn, Barrow's lifelong supporter, shows off the 1946 Tour cap he was given by Willie last year. "Willie Horne was a genius," says Jim. "And I'll tell you something else too. He's the nicest person I've ever met."

POSTSCRIPT

I COULD tell instantly I was in the presence of a remarkable man. Jimmy Linn, I was told, has a memory for rugby league history like a human IBM computer. He's interesting and talkative and he's known Willie Horne for a long, long time. So off I went, notebook in hand, not knowing much else apart from an understandable assumption that he must be quite old.

Jimmy has lived in Cote Ley Crescent on Walney Island for 30 years. He doesn't like change. The door was open so I knocked loudly before walking in. He was sitting in a comfortable chair next to a small bed, the size you might expect to find in a teenager's room. I was surprised at his appearance. He was much younger than I had imagined and though he was bald he had a pleasant face, the kind that smiles easily, giving off an aura of sincerity and friendship. It was obvious he liked people, making friends, talking.

On the mantlepiece were a dozen trophies with golden figures of bowlers delivering the ball above silver signs inscribed with words too small for me to read. Above, several pictures, including a water colour of the Lake District, grey mountains peaking through wispy clouds at serene lakes while a tall fisherman cast his line over the tranquil waters. To the right, in pride of place, a large framed photograph of a handsome young man and his wife on their wedding day, arm in arm, grinning with pride.

"That's me and May when we were married in 1926," Jimmy says reading the inquisitive look in my eyes. Arithmetic was never my favourite subject but a hasty mental sum told me he was in fact a very old man.

A couple of opening questions and he relaxed and began reeling off dates and recounting big matches, never stuttering or struggling to find the words. Back he went to 1914, the first rugby match he had seen. Barrow beat Wakefield Trinity at Little Park, Roose. Jimmy's good on dates, yet I found myself doubting the accuracy of his memory. It was all so long ago. How could he remember? I felt guilty about doubting him, as if I was misplacing his trust and honesty. But journalists are trained to check and double check. So I did. When I got back to work and dusted off the old files I discovered each time he was right, the correct result, the correct scorers. Somehow I knew I would. It was uncanny.

He spoke of many players – brave, mysterious men who exist only in fading photographs, old programmes and the memory of admiring, elderly men such as Jimmy. Harry Gifford, Bill Burgess and Charlie Carr – the names tripped off his tongue and he began to smile and talk quickly describing a try here, a tackle there, confident his memory was not playing tricks and could never fail him.

It gave me a nice feeling inside, seeing Jimmy enjoying himself so much, heartened by our nostalgic journey. I wondered how old he was. So I asked him.

"I'm 89 Mike," he said, matter-of-factly, as though he was telling me the time. Then the telephone rang and I saw the only visible sign of his great age as he moved around the room, shuffling, taking short, unsure steps, the way I had expected from someone born in 1905. Back in his seat he regained the persona of a middle-aged man and I instantly forgot his age and its brief intrusion into our talk.

He had a quality about him, a sincerity, a charm. I had the impression Jimmy felt life had been pretty good to him. Afterwards I found out how May had been seriously ill and how he had to nurse her for more than 30 years. And I was told he'd been out of work during the Depression and, like everyone else, how he sometimes didn't get enough to eat. Then there was his weak heart – angina, he said. Yet these traumas had passed him by without leaving their mark on his character. Besides, he wanted to talk about rugby, not himself.

He was off again, another game at Little Park.

"I remember one match when there had been a lot of heavy snow," he said, leaning forward out of his chair to get closer to me. "Hunslet came but they didn't want to play. The weather was that bad.

"We all huddled together in the old Ship Hotel, then when the referee said the game was on we moved the snow off the pitch so the players could see the lines. It was terrible." I closed my eyes. His descriptions were so believable, so colourful I could feel the icy wind chilling my ears, the snow blasting into my face.

"Barrow lost the toss and played into the blizzard and somehow Ted Thornbarrow scored a try to put us three points up at half-time. Hunslet refused to come out for the second half, but we won the replay."

Jimmy was born in Govan, Glasgow. He moved to Barrow when he was eight. Now there isn't a trace of Scotland in his accent. He's pure Barrovian.

"I was out of work in 1931," he continued. "So I helped build Craven Park. I'll never forget the following year when a season ticket cost 13/6 (67p) yet I couldn't afford it. Nobody could."

Suddenly he stopped talking and shuffled out of the room, returning a moment later carrying a brown parcel carefully, with respect, as an archbishop might hold a 14th crucifix."

What do you think of that, Mike?" he asked.

Inside was a cap, maroon with yellow braid. There was a badge on the front, hand stitched, depicting a lion, a daffodil, a thistle, a rose and what looked like a piece of clover. It was soft and beautiful and though I wasn't sure what it was I could tell it was very old.

"Look inside," he said. There was a size sewn into the silk lining – 6 $7/8$, and under the numbers a name and date, printed neatly: **WILLIE HORNE 1946.**" I found out later it was a tourist cap, worth several hundred pounds.

"He gave it to me last month when I was feeling a bit low. It didn't half make me feel better. Willie sees me regular. He always brings me a bag of shopping, you know, tea, milk, potatoes that sort of thing. Willie is a grand lad. Do you know Mike I've watched all the top players, brilliant men like Jim Sullivan, Gus Risman, Tommy Bradshaw and Alex Murphy. Yet Willie Horne is the greatest rugby league player I've ever seen. There's no one to touch him. He was a genius.

"And I'll tell you something else too," Jimmy says, pausing for greater emphasis. "He's the nicest person I've ever met. I love Willie Horne."

"We all do, Jim," I said, closing my notebook. "We all do."

ACKNOWLEDGEMENTS

THERE have been so many people who helped me complete this book it's difficult to know where to start. Firstly there are the 200 people I interviewed who spoke sincerely and openly, revealing so many things that would have stayed secret forever. When I mentioned Willie's name, doors opened, telephones were answered, everyone wanted to help. Thank you. I hope I have honoured the trust you placed in me.

Thank you to Willie himself for all the wonderful nights we spent together looking back at his career, thank you for being my best friend, thank you for being Godfather to my son John, thank you for allowing me to tell your story when I know you would have preferred to remain anonymous. Thank you to the North West Evening Mail for support and allowing me to complete my research in their offices and also for the use of copyrighted photographs without payment. Thank you to Keith Sutton, Donald Martin and Lyndsay Aspin.

Thanks to Alen and Anne McFadzean of Red Earth Publications for advice and guidance, to Peter Leach and Jeremy Harris for help on computers, to Frank Baker, Billy Tucker, Gordon Duff and countless others for the loan of scrapbooks and programmes, to Harry Edgar of Open Rugby for support and publicity, to Brenda Davies and Barbara Robbins, John Huxley, Peter and Avril McDonald, to Micron Video and Dave Makin for film of Barrow RL in the Fifties, Martin Hebbert and the VSEL Press Office, Julia Johnson, Alice Leach, Bryn Trescatheric, Arthur Evans, Peter Simpson, Barrow Library, particularly Ron Smith and Lisa Colclough, Phil Heath of Heath's Bookshop, and Mr Cathcart of the Book Corner, Barrow, to Keith Nutter, Tom Welsh, Frank McKeever, Paddy McAteer, Frank Cassidy, Glyn Powell, Don Pettingale and to Vic Higham for the details on Freddie Cotton.

Thank you to Cheryl Draper for secretarial work. Then there are the photographs.

Thank you to the photographic department of the Evening Mail, to Eddie Tweedie, Jennifer Caine, Ronnie Kershaw, Ian Duncan and Ian Kershaw, to Marie Senior, Billy Little's family, Paul Milburn for the picture of Great Clifton, Jimmy Lewthwaite, The Dock Museum, Hulton-Deutsch for the photographs of the 1952 Tests, to Ian Collis for sending the photograph of Greg Hawick from Australia, to Furness Cricket Club, Alf and Sylvia Horne, George Horne, Fred Roskell, Frank Simm, Kate Prodhan, Tom Bromley's family, Eddie Worrall, Rodney Bradshaw, Mr Kissack, Jill Hughes, Stan and Les Morgan and Raymond Sankey.

Thank you to the Kirkby Trust for financial assistance, to everyone at Dixon Printers especially Howard Duff and Mary Ridings. Thank you to Paul Creber for editing the manuscript with patience and skill and to Nick

Helliwell for the final proof-read. Thank you to Simon Gray for the design of the front cover, to Stuart Smith for the superb paintings and to Alex Murphy for taking the time to provide such a moving introduction.

I must give a special mention to Robert Gate, a stranger who became a close friend. Robert, Rugby League's official historian, provided all the statistics, many photographs and checked my copy for accuracy. Thank you Robert, I'll never forget all you have done for me.

Finally there's my family. I had read acknowledgements in other books and considered them something of an obligation. Not now. My mother and father have always been there, supporting and encouraging as has my mother-in-law Kath. Then there's my wife Lesley and our sons John and David, putting up with me disappearing for hours most nights for the past two years. Words don't seem enough. All I can do is say no one could ever ask for a better family.

APPENDIX I
Willie Horne's Playing Career

OLDHAM

Debut on December 25, 1942 v Leeds, away, lost 5-36

	App	Tries	Goals	Points
1942 – 43	2	0	1	2

BARROW

Debut on March 13, 1943 v St Helens, away, Challenge Cup, first round, first leg, lost 2–13.

	App	Tries	Goals	Points
1942 – 43	1	0	0	0
1943 – 44	24	10	58	146
1944 – 45	28	6	35	88
1945 – 46	21	15	51	147
1946 – 47	28	6	47	112
1947 – 48	17	0	24	48
1948 – 49	37	7	23	67
1949 – 50	31	2	19	44
1950 – 51	28	5	40	95
1951 – 52	43	12	131	298
1952 – 53	28	11	60	153
1953 – 54	34	5	27	69
1954 – 55	37	11	86	205
1955 – 56	37	11	113	259
1956 – 57	39	7	19	59
1957 – 58	17	3	1	11
1958 – 59	12	1	7	17
Totals	462	112	741	1818

Final game on March 14, 1959 v Swinton, at home, won 10–5.

TEST MATCHES

Date	Opponents	Venue	Result	Score		Att
17–6–1946	Australia	Sydney	Drew	8–8	Try	64,527
6–7–1946	Australia	Brisbane	Won	14–5		40,500
20–7–1946	Australia	Sydney	Won	20–7		35,294
20–12–1947	New Zealand	Odsal	Won	25–9	Goal	42,685
9–10–1948	Australia	Leeds	Won	23–21		36,529
4–10–1952	Australia	Leeds	Won	19–6	5 goals	Capt. 34,505
8–11–1952	Australia	Swinton	Won	21–5	Goal	Capt. 32,421
13–12–1952	Australia	Odsal	Lost	7–27	Try	Capt. 30,509

ENGLAND

Date	Opponents	Venue	Result	Score		Att
10–3–1945	Wales	Wigan	Won	18–8	Try	23,500
24–11–1945	Wales	Swansea	Lost	3–11		30,000
23–2–1946	France	Swinton	Won	16–6	2 goals	20,500
12–10–1946	Wales	Swinton	Lost	10–13		20,213
16–11–1946	Wales	Swansea	Won	19–5		25,000
8–12–1946	France	Bordeaux	Won	3–0		24,100
17–5–1947	France	Leeds	Won	5–2		21,000
6–12–1947	Wales	Swansea	Won	18–7	2 goals	10,000
19–9–1949	Other Nats	Workington	Won	13–7		17,576
23–4–1952	Other Nats	Wigan	Won	31–18	Try, 3 goals	19,785
17–9–1952	Wales	Wigan	Won	19–8		Capt. 13,503
11–4–1953	France	Paris	Won	15–13	3 goals	Capt. 25,000
16–9–1953	Wales	St Helens	Won	24–5	Try	Capt. 19,357
28–11–1953	Other Nats.	Wigan	Won	30–22	3 goals	Capt. 19,012

7–10–1944 RL XIII 27 Northern Command 23 at Fartown, one try, two goals. Att. 3,500
24–2–1954 Whites 17 Reds 17, Tour trial at Leeds, one goal. Att. 11,752.
24–5–1953 Great Britain 17, France 28, International at Lyons. Captain.

LANCASHIRE

Date	Opponents	Venue	Result	Score		Att
10–11–1945	Yorkshire	Swinton	Won	17–6		11,059
26–1–1946	Cumberland	Workington	Won	18–3	Try, 3 goals	10,026
9–11–1946	Yorkshire	Hunslet	Lost	10–13	Try	5,000
4–1–1947	Cumberland	Barrow	Drew	0–0		8,148
20–4–1949	Cumberland	Salford	Lost	9–15	3 goals	6,000
12–10–1949	Cumberland	Workington	Lost	11–22		10,000
14–5–1951	Cumberland	Barrow	Won	13–12	2 goals	Capt. 11,452
10–10–1951	Yorkshire	Leigh	Lost	5–15	Goal	Capt. 11,573
12–5–1952	Cumberland	Whitehaven	Won	19–11	2 goals	Capt. 8,500
8–10–1952	Cumberland	St Helens	Won	41–14	Try, 7 goals	Capt. 12,000
19–11–1952	Australia	Warrington	Lost	11–36	Try	Capt. 5,845
21–9–1953	Cumberland	Whitehaven	Lost	5–15	Goal	Capt. 6,000
15–9–1954	Cumberland	Wigan	Won	24–7		Capt.
6–10–1954	Yorkshire	Odsal	Lost	10–20		8,500

1946 TOUR (excluding Test matches)

Date	Opponents	Venue	Result	Score		Att
May 22	Southem Division	Junee	Won	36–4	2 tries	6,135
June 1	New South Wales	Sydney	Won	14–10		51,364
June 2	South Coast Division	Wollongong	Lost	12–15	3 goals	13,352
June 12	Western Division	Orange	Won	33–2		8,318
June 25	Wide Bay	Bundaberg	Won	16–12	Try	6,356
June 30	North Queensland	Townsville	Won	55–16	2 tries, 2 goals	7,567
July 11	Ipswich	Ipswich	Won	29–12	2 tries, goal	5,237
July 13	Toowoomba	Toowoomba	Won	34–5	Try	9,863
July 29	West Coast	Greymouth	Lost	8–17		4,000
August 3	Auckland	Auckland	Won	9–7		20,000
August 12	Auckland	Auckland	Won	22–9		12,400

1950 TOUR (excluding Test matches)

Date	Opponents	Venue	Result	Score		Att
May 24	Monaro	Canberra	Won	37–10		4,000
May 31	Riverina	Cootamundra	Won	23–13	4 goals	8,000
June 14	North Coast	Kempsy	Won	37–7		7,000
June 17	Queensland	Brisbane	Lost	14–15		22,148
June 25	Cent. Queensland	Rockhampton	Won	88–0	2 tries, 9 goals	7,000

CAREER TOTALS

	App	Tries	Goals	Points
Barrow	462	112	741	1818
Oldham	2	0	1	2
Lancashire	14	4	19	50
Tests	8	2	7	20
England	14	3	13	35
Great Britain (non–Test)	1	0	0	0
Tour Trial 1954	1	0	1	2
Representative	1	1	2	7
1946 Tour (excluding Tests)	11	8	6	36
1950 Tour (excluding Tests)	5	2	13	32
Totals	519	132	803	2002

1946 GREAT BRITAIN TOUR OF AUSTRALIA AND NEW ZEALAND

	App	Tries	Goals	Points
A. J. Risman (Salford) Captain	14	3	31	71
A. Bassett (Halifax)	11	18	0	54
E. Batten (Bradford Northern)	13	17	0	51
G. Curran (Salford)	16	2	0	6
W. H. T. Davies (Bradford Northern)	14	5	0	15
J. Egan (Wigan)	17	6	0	18
T. J. F. Foster (Bradford Northern)	10	1	0	3
K. Gee (Wigan)	18	1	0	3
W. HORNE (Barrow)	14	9	6	39
F. Hughes (Workington Town)	13	4	0	12
D. Jenkins (Leeds)	11	1	0	3
A. E. Johnson (Warrington)	17	15	3	51
J. Jones (Barrow)	11	2	1	8
J. Kitching (Bradford Northern)	12	17	0	51
B. Knowelden (Barrow)	13	16	0	48
J. Lewthwaite (Barrow)	15	25	0	75
T. McCue (Widnes)	15	0	0	0
H. Murphy (Wakefield Trinity)	1	1	0	3
R. Nicholson (Huddersfield)	11	5	0	15
I. A. Owens (Leeds)	18	11	4	41
D. Phillips (Oldham)	18	3	0	9
M. Ryan (Wigan)	4	1	0	3
E. Ward (Bradford Northern)	16	4	43	98
E. H. Ward (Wigan)	12	5	32	79
F. W. Whitcombe (Bradford Northern)	19	3	0	9
L. White (York)	18	6	0	18

Managers: W. Popplewell (Bramley) and W. M. Gabbatt (Barrow).

TOUR SUMMARY

					For			Against		
IN AUSTRALIA	P	W	D	L	Tries	Goals	Pts	Tries	Goals	Pts
Tests	3	2	1	0	10	6	42	4	4	20
Other games	17	14	0	3	136	94	596	32	41	178
Total	20	16	1	3	146	100	638	36	45	198
IN NEW ZEALAND										
Test	1	0	0	1	2	1	8	1	5	13
Other games	6	5	0	1	33	19	137	11	16	65
Total	7	5	0	2	35	20	145	12	21	78
TOUR TOTAL	27	21	1	5	181	120	783	48	66	276

1950 GREAT BRITAIN TOUR OF AUSTRALIA AND NEW ZEALAND

	App	Tries	Goals	Points
E. Ward (Bradford Northern) Captain	15	7	52	125
E.J. Ashcroft (Wigan)	11	5	0	15
T. Bradshaw (Wigan)	15	1	0	3
J. Cunliffe (Wigan)	17	14	8	58
T. Danby (Salford)	18	34	0	102
A. H. Daniels (Halifax)	5	5	0	15
J. Egan (Wigan)	15	3	0	9
J. J. Featherstone (Warrington)	14	10	0	30
K. Gee (Wigan)	14	1	9	21
E. Gwyther (Belle Vue Rangers)	15	2	0	6
F. Higgins (Widnes)	14	4	0	12
J. Hilton (Wigan)	12	22	0	66
W. HORNE (Barrow)	5	2	13	32
J. A. Ledgard (Leigh)	12	2	37	80
H. Murphy (Wakefield Trinity)	13	2	1	8
D. Naughton (Widnes)	8	2	0	6
F. Osmond (Swinton)	10	4	0	12
A. J. Pepperell (Workington Town)	11	7	0	21
D. V. Phillips (Belle Vue Rangers)	12	7	0	21
R. Pollard (Dewsbury)	9	5	6	27
W. G. Ratcliffe (Wigan)	11	6	0	18
M. Ryan (Wigan)	12	4	1	14
R. Ryan (Warrington)	12	5	0	15
H. Street (Dewsbury)	15	2	0	6
K. Traill (Bradford Northern)	15	7	0	21
R. Williams (Leeds)	15	7	0	21

Business manager: G. Oldroyd (Dewsbury). Team manager: T. Spedding (Belle Vue Rangers).

TOUR SUMMARY

					For			Against		
IN AUSTRALIA	P	W	D	L	Tries	Goals	Pts	Tries	Goals	Pts
Tests	3	1	0	2	3	1	11	4	6	24
Other games	16	14	0	2	130	101	592	18	50	154
Total	19	15	0	4	133	102	603	22	56	178
IN NEW ZEALAND										
Tests	2	0	0	2	5	4	23	6	9	36
Other games	4	4	0	0	32	21	138	10	11	52
Total	6	4	0	2	37	25	161	16	20	88
TOUR TOTAL	25	19	0	6	170	127	764	38	76	266

APPENDIX 2
North Lancashire and District Cricket League Batting Averages

1945

	Inn	Not out	High	Total	Average
W. HORNE (Millom)	14	3	90	530	48.18
S. Redhead (VSC)	13	3	97	401	40.10
A. Graves (Whitehaven)	13	4	93*	331	36.77
A. Horne (VSC)	13	2	56*	294	26.72
H. Gibbon (Furness)	13	1	82	293	24.40
H. Penhallurick (Dalton)	13	1	46	277	23.08
F. Harrison (Vickerstown)	13	2	40*	214	19.45
A. Sutcliffe (Whitehaven)	13	1	64	214	17.83
R. Birk (Millom)	13	1	61*	195	16.25
I. Smith (Millom)	14	3	38	177	16.09

1947

	Inn	Not out	High	Total	Average
E. W. Whitefield (Whitehaven)	18	7	73*	442	40.18
H. Nutton (VSC)	19	4	84	519	34.60
W. HORNE (Millom)	14	3	97*	424	35.30
E. Ottley (Vickerstown)	18	2	108	482	30.12
J. E. Wilson (Haverigg)	18	5	55*	384	29.50
F. Harrison (Netherfield)	19	2	54*	475	27.94
J. C. B. McDougall (Barrow)	12	1	51	296	26.90
S. Redhead (Vicker SC)	17	2	97	387	25.80
W. Harrison (Kendal)	15	3	53	304	25.50
H. Gibbon (Furness)	19	1	65	328	23.42

1948

	Inn	Not out	High	Total	Average
W. HORNE (Ulverston)	14	3	129*	397	36.09
R. J. Newall (Whitehaven)	18	2	83*	572	35.70
S. Redhead (Furness)	16	2	141	498	35.57
C. S. Clarkson (Barrow)	12	2	54	376	34.18
R. J. McIntosh (Barrow)	14	2	106*	397	33.08
L. Wilkinson (Furness)	18	2	114*	525	32.81
E. Miller (Ulverston)	13	2	57	357	32.45
J. E. Gibson (Dalton)	18	1	96	548	32.23
F. T. Long (Kendal)	13	6	43*	223	31.85
E. Leeming (Kendal)	19	2	111*	486	28.58

1949

	Inn	Not out	High	Total	Average
R. S. Ellwood (Kendal)	18	6	106*	610	50.83
H. Nutton (Vickers SC)	19	5	104*	680	48.57
E. Miller (Ulverston)	13	4	100*	391	43.44
W. A. Talbot (Workington)	20	3	79	461	27.11
W. HORNE (Furness)	15	2	105	352	27.07
R. J. Newall (Whitehaven)	18	2	45	431	26.93
J. Stabler (Carlisle)	16	4	51	305	25.41
E. Hoskin (Haverigg)	15	1	82*	338	24.14
J Farren (Haverigg)	19	3	52*	377	23.56
J. Newman (Vickers SC)	18	3	60*	346	23.06

1953

	Inn	Not out	High	Total	Average
N. Emery (Whitehaven)	12	7	73*	298	59.60
W. HORNE (Vickerstown)	13	4	100*	532	59.10
C. Tomkin (Barrow)	14	3	67	440	40.00
A. Burrows (Vickerstown)	15	2	81*	512	39.40
H. Dalzell (Netherfield)	15	4	61	399	36.30
R. Beard (Whitehaven)	19	1	92	623	34.60
K. Brothwood (Netherfield)	19	3	113*	512	32.00
S. K. Girdhari (Millom)	17	1	113	502	31.40
R. English (Workington)	14	2	68*	360	30.00
D. J. Hair (Carlisle)	14	2	69	353	29.60

1961

	Inn	Not out	High	Total	Average
G. A. Edrich (Workington)	17	6	87	638	58.00
S. Mohammed (Haverigg)	18	3	122*	665	44.33
R. Kenny (Penrith)	16	1	79	580	38.67
W. HORNE (Vickerstown)	13	1	100*	436	36.33
E. Miller (Ulverston)	17	4	65*	466	35.84
E. Ottley (Vickerstown)	17	4	77	456	35.08
H. Meageen (Workington)	16	4	83	418	34.83
D. T. Wilson (Carnforth)	17	1	75	530	33.12
H. Stretch (Lindal)	15	3	74	387	32.25
A. J. Pemberton (Dalton)	18	4	75*	437	31.21

*Not out

Willie Horne topped the averages in 1944 and again in 1958 but those statistics are unavailable.

Higson Cup

The Higson Cup is the the most important trophy in the North Lancashire and District Cricket League. Willie Horne played in four Higson Cup finals, winning the trophy three times with three different clubs.

1945 HIGSON CUP FINAL

MILLOM

T. Shovelton	c Moore b French	0
W. Rooke	b Martin	7
W. Horne	b Ormandy	53
H. Billing	b Martin	4
F. Lees	b Davies	21
I. Smith	b Ormandy	7
N. Grimshaw	b Ormandy	2
K. R. Sneesby	b Davies	1
E. Fallows	b Ormandy	0
E. Whitehead	not out	3
E. Ellwood	run out	1
	Extras	12
	Total	111

Bowling: F. French 8–1–27–1; A. Martin 8–1–39–2; W. H. Davies 6–1–20–2; W. Ommandy 5–1–12–4.

FURNESS

F. H. Moore	c Fallows b Lees	18
A. E. Williams	c and b Lees	24
B. Knowelden	b Billing	4
F. French	b Lees	3
G. Southam	b Billing	6
P. Martin	b Billing	6
D. Ellis	lbw Shovelton	0
W. Allcock	not out	2
	Extras	10
	Total (for 7)	139

Bowling: F. Lees 14–1–63–3; H. Billing 11–2–19–3; T. Shovelton 3–0–23–1.

FURNESS WON BY 28 RUNS.

1947 HIGSON CUP FINAL

KENDAL

W. Harrison	b Horne	52
A. Leggatt	b Horne	7
H. Morgan	b Horne	4
P. Greenwood	b Horne	0
R. S. Ellwood	b Proctor	3
B. Reed	lbw Proctor	14
H. Dalzell	c W Horne b Proctor	5
A. Johnson	b Proctor	0
J. May	b Horne	5
F. T. Long	not out	4
G. Sibley	b Horne	0
	Extras	8
	Total	102

Bowling: W. Horne 16.4–3–47–6; J. Proctor 16–1–47–4.

MILLOM

T. Foster	c Morgan b Ellwood	1
W. Rook	b Greenwood	6
W. Horne	c Reed b Dalzell	28
A. Horne	b Dalzell	16
J. Proctor	b Dalzell	30
T. A. H. Peter	not out	6
	Extras	6
	Total (for 5)	103

Bowling: P. Greenwood 9–0–41–1; R. S. Ellwood 10–0–37–1; H. Dalzell 7–0–19–3.

MILLOM WON BY SEVEN WICKETS.

1949 HIGSON CUP FINAL

FURNESS

S. Redhead	c G. Rutter b Gifford	3
A. Williams	run out	1
L. Wilkinson	c G. Rutter b McEwan	5
W. Horne	b Anderson	58
K. Bennett	b Anderson	58
J. Bawden	b Anderson	3
A. Waite	b Gifford	1
J. S. Hardy	not out	1
W. Allcock	b Anderson	1
H. Tickle	not out	0
	Extras	18
	Total (for 8)	149

Bowling: McEwan 15–3–47–1; Gifford 16–3–43–2; Anderson 10-1-25-4; Burton 4-1-16-0.

ULVERSTON

F. W. Anderson	b Wilkinson	3
K. J. Ireland	run out	18
E. Miller	run out	16
R. Cathey	b Bennett	3
G. Rutter	b Wilkinson	15
J. McEwan	b Horne	1
W. E. Burton	run out	4
J. Gifford	b Horne	31
E. Jackson	run out	1
F. Simm	not out	5
E. Rutter	not out	4
	Extras	5
	Total (for 9)	106

Bowling: Wilkinson 23-3-60-2; Bennett 8–1–21–1; Horne 14–4–20–2.

FURNESS WON BY 43 RUNS.

1958 HIGSON CUP FINAL

VICKERSTOWN

F. Roskell	c Halliday b Purdon	22
W. Horne	c Millership b Landells	10
L. Woods	b Purdon	0
P. Dunn	run out	8
E. Ottley	c Millership b Purdon	19
A. Procter	b Thompson	0
J. Bateman	run out	2
P. Deallott	st Millership b Thompson	31
A. Horne	not out	3
T. Wood	b Purdon	0
	Extras	5
	Total	118

Bowling: Purdon 18–3–35–4; Landells 14–1–46–1; Thompson 10–4–18–3; Meageen 1–0–4–0.

WORKINGTON

H. Halliday	b Procter	4
R. J. English	lbw b Procter	10
H. Meageen	c A. Horne b Wood	7
E. Purdon	lbw b Procter	0
R. J. Faville	b Wood	0
S. Millership	lbw b Wood	1
T. Thompson	c Roskell b Wood	7
N. Dixon	c Bateman b Deallott	23
T. Palmer	c W. Horne b Deallott	14
A. Robinson	b Wood	1
H. Landells	not out	7
	Extras	1
	Total	75

Bowling: Procter 15–2–25–3; Wood 19–8–28–5; Deallott 6.5–1–17–2; Morgan 1–0–4–0.

VICKERSTOWN WON BY 43 RUNS.

APPENDIX 3
Billy Little's Playing Career

BARROW

Debut on March 12, 1932 v Wakefield Trinity, home, lost 8–12, one try.

	App	Tries	Goals	Points
1931 – 32	6	1	0	3
1932 – 33	40	5	0	15
1933 – 34	37	9	0	27
1934 – 35	37	5	2	19
1935 – 36	38	4	17	46
1936 – 37	38	5	15	45
1937 – 38	42	2	4	14
1938 – 39	41	2	3	12
1939 – 40	26	5	0	15
1942 – 43	2	0	0	0
1943 – 44	29	1	0	3
1944 – 45	31	1	0	3
1945 – 46	35	4	1	14
1946 – 47	21	2	2	10
1947 – 48	2	1	0	3
Totals	425	47	44	229

Final game on September 10, 1947 v Belle Vue Rangers, away, Lancashire Cup, first round, second leg, lost 2–37.

ENGLAND

Date	Opponents	Venue	Result	Score		Att
30–3–1933	Other Nats	Workington	Won	34–27		11,000
13–1–1934	Australia	Gateshead	Won	19–14	Try	15,576
15–4–1934	France	Paris	Won	32–21	Try	22,000

28–4–1935 RL XIII 32 French XIII 12 at Paris, one try. Att. 10,000.
12–2–1936 Whites 19 Stripes 0 at Leeds, tour trial. Att. 5,000.
23–3–1940 Lancs XIII 10 Yorks XIII 13 at Barrow. Att. 8,683.

CUMBERLAND

Date	Opponents	Venue	Result	Score		Att
1–10–1932	Yorkshire	Whitehaven	Won	39–10	Try	5,900
15–10–1932	Lancashire	Barrow	Won	9–3		12,689
28–10–1933	Lancashire	Workington	Won	10–0		6,400
6–12–1933	Yorkshire	Dewsbury	Won	15–11		2,000
9–12–1933	Australians	Whitehaven	Won	17–16		5,800
21–9–1935	Lancashire	Whitehaven	Lost	4–7		5,000
23–10–1935	Yorkshire	Bradford	Won	19–15		4,000
10–10–1936	Yorkshire	Workington	Won	16–10		10,600
31–10–1936	Lancashire	St. Helens	Drew	10–10		
18–9–1937	Lancashire	Workington	Lost	17–23		10,200
10–11–1937	Yorkshire	Hunslet	Drew	7–7		1,100
14–9–1938	Lancashire	Wigan	Lost	7–8		5,000
1–10–1938	Yorkshire	Workington	Won	16–6		7,240
26–1–1946	Lancashire	Workington	Lost	3–18		10,026
26–9–1946	Yorkshire	Workington	Lost	9–11		11,300

CAREER TOTALS

	App	Tries	Goals	Points
Barrow	425	47	44	229
England	3	2	0	6
Cumberland	15	1	0	3
Tour trial 1936	1	0	0	0
Representative	2	1	0	3
Totals	446	51	44	241

SUBSCRIBERS

THANK YOU to the following list of subscribers who helped make this book possible.

Bill Abernethy, Brisbane, Australia
Tony Ackroyd, Halifax
David Alexander, Askam-in-Furness
George Allen, Barrow-in-Furness
John Allen, Barrow-in-Furness
W. D. Ambrose, Ormskirk
R. Anderson, Barrow-in-Furness
George Appleton, Ulverston
Frank Armer, Barrow-in-Furness
C. G. Armistead, Poole, Dorset
Alvan Armstrong, Barrow-in-Furness
George Armstrong, Millom
Gordon R. Armstrong, Barrow-in-Furness
Jean, Alan & Alison Armstrong, Barrow-in-Furness
Patricia Arthur, Birkenhead
A. Aspin, Barrow-in-Furness
Michael Athersmith, Barrow-in-Furness
Harold Atkinson, Swarthmoor
R. B. Austin, Knaresborough
T. Ayres, Barrow-in-Furness
Brian Backhouse, Dalton-in-Furness
John Backhouse, Barrow-in-Furness
Brian Bagot, Barrow-in-Furness
Derek Baker, Barrow-in-Furness
Dr Mark Baker, Barrow-in-Furness
Mark Barrow, Coniston
Tony Bayliff, Barrow-in-Furness
Barbara Beattie, Manchester
Anthony Bell, Barrow-in-Furness
Austin I. L. & Angela Bell, Dalton-in-Furness
David Bell, Barrow-in-Furness
Ernie Benn, Ulverston
Anne Benson, Barrow-in-Furness
Ian Benson, Ambleside
Stuart Berry, Halifax
Richard Best, Barrow-in-Furness
Les Bettinson, Stockport
Kathleen Bissett, Barrow-in-Furness
Joseph Alan Blackburn, Dalton-in-Furness
Alan Blackwood, Barrow-in-Furness
Frank Blake, Barrow-in-Furness
Patrick Blake, Barrow-in-Furness
Tricia Blake, Barrow-in-Furness
George Blanshard, Barrow-in-Furness
Jimmy Blanshard, Barrow-in-Furness
Tim Bolton, Hull
Kevin Booth, Barrow-in-Furness
David Boulton, Bradford

Peter Bowen, Newcastle
Gerald Bowyer, Oldham
B. M. Boyns, Barrow-in-Furness
Graham Brannon, Barrow-in-Furness
Barry James Bray, Barrow-in-Furness
Marcus & Lynne Brocker, Dalton-in-Furness
George Brocklebank, Ulverston
Derek Brook, Barrow-in-Furness
Gordon Brown, Dalton-in-Furness
John Brown, Barrow-in-Furness
Ronald Brown, Leeds
W. Bullough, Wakefield
Myra Burley, Barrow-in-Furness
Bryan Burns, Barrow-in-Furness
John & Eileen Burns, Barrow-in-Furness
Robert Burns, Barrow-in-Furness
Jonathon Butcher, Altrincham
Keith Butcher, Ulverston
Richard Butcher, Altrincham
Frank Cairns, Millom
Anne Canavan, Barrow-in-Furness
James A. Capstick, Barrow-in-Furness
Paul Cargan, Barrow-in-Furness
Ronnie Carlisle, Barrow-in-Furness
Barry Carruthers, Barrow-in-Furness
Lee S. Carson, Ossett
Brian Carter, Barrow-in-Furness
Eric Carter, Workington
Eddie Casey, Barrow-in-Furness
Terry Casey, Bolton
Mike Castle, Barrow-in-Furness
S. M. Charnley, Barrow-in-Furness
Harry Chatfield, Barrow-in-Furness
Ian Chisnall, Barrow-in-Furness
Thomas Clancy, Barrow-in-Furness
Leslie Clark, Barrow-in-Furness
Tom Clarke, Barrow-in-Furness
Joan Cleasby, Barrow-in-Furness
Robert Clegg, Barrow-in-Furness
Tony Collins, Leeds
Jean Conway, Barrow-in-Furness
Algie Coombe, Barrow-in-Furness
Harold Cook, Barrow-in-Furness
Arthur Corless, Barrow-in-Furness
Ged Corner, Barrow-in-Furness
Jim Costley, Barrow-in-Furness
Mike Coutts, Telford
Rodney Cowen, Rothwell, Northants
John Craig, Barrow-in-Furness

Jack Bowen Crawford, Lowestoft
George Crayston, Barrow-in-Furness
Richard Creary, Dalton-in-Furness
George Cubiss, Barrow-in-Furness
Cubo, Barrow-in-Furness
Gerry Cummings, Barrow-in-Furness
Stan, Elsie & Janette Currie, Barrow-in-Furness
Dalton Book Club, Dalton-in-Furness
Alan Davies, Barrow-in-Furness
A. R. Davies, America
Colin Jamieson Davies, Barrow-in-Furness
Idwal G. Davies, Barrow-in-Furness
Jean Davies, Barrow-in-Furness
Roy, Brenda & Samantha Davies, Barrow-in-Furness
Winnie Davies, Dalton-in-Furness
Victor Daw, Barrow-in-Furness
Harry Dawson, Barrow-in-Furness
Bryan Dempster, Barrow-in-Furness
Mike Devereux, Barrow-in-Furness
John & Rose Devitt, Barrow-in-Furness
Bud Dickson, Barrow-in-Furness
Al Dinnen, Barrow-in-Furness
Jack Dinsdale, Slyne with Hest
Roger Ditchfield, Barrow-in-Furness
Alan Dixon, Barrow-in-Furness
Jeff Dixon, Barrow-in-Furness
Philip Dixon, Barrow-in-Furness
Bernard Docker, Barrow-in-Furness
Dave Donnan, Barrow-in-Furness
Jim Doughty, Barrow-in-Furness
George Downie, Hatch Beauchamp, Somerset
Jim Doyle, Barrow-in-Furness
Cheryl Draper, Barrow-in-Furness
T. M. Driver, Keighley
Dennis Ducie, Barrow-in-Furness
Mick Ducie, Barrow-in-Furness
Frank Duckworth, Barrow-in-Furness
Gordon Duff, Barrow-in-Furness
Richard Eccles, Carlisle
William Eddy, Ravenstown, near Grange-over-Sands
Connie Edge, Barrow-in-Furness
Matthew Edwards, Barrow-in-Furness
John Etty, Fleetwood
Barry Elliott, Harrogate
Brian Elliott, Barrow-in-Furness
John Ennis, Barrow-in-Furness
John Evans, Barrow-in-Furness
David W. Farish, Claremont, Perth, Australia
John Farish, Barrow-in-Furness
Mick Farish, Barrow-in-Furness
Malcolm Ferguson, Durham
John Fillingham, Barrow-in-Furness
Terry Fitzsimmons, Barrow-in-Furness
Stan Fleet, Dalton-in-Furness
Terry Ford, Barrow-in-Furness

Peta Forsyth, Bury St Edmunds
Phil Forsyth, Barrow-in-Furness
Brian Foster, Barrow-in-Furness
Brian Foxcroft, Ulverston
Stephen & Catherine Foxcroft, Ulverston
Bill Foxen, Barrow-in-Furness
George France, Barrow-in-Furness
William Friend, Barrow-in-Furness
Trevor Fry, Brisbane, Australia
Derek Fryer, Barrow-in-Furness
Jef Fullard, Barrow-in-Furness
Edna Furness, Barrow-in-Furness
Ray Gabriel, Barrow-in-Furness
Dennis Gallagher, Barrow-in-Furness
Fred Gallagher, Barrow-in-Furness
Eunice Gardner, Blackpool
Gordon & Betty Gardner, Barrow-in-Furness
James Gardner, Barrow-in-Furness
John Gardner, Barrow-in-Furness
Ray Gardner, Barrow-in-Furness
Peter Garner, Barrow-in-Furness
Robert Garnet, Barrow-in-Furness
Ian Garnett, Ulverston
D. Garratt, Ulverston
Robert E. Gate, Sowerby Bridge
Jeff Gibbon, Barrow-in-Furness
J. Gibson, Barrow-in-Furness
N. Gibson, Dalton-in-Furness
John Gill, Dalton-in-Furness
Andrew Gladwin, West Hampstead, London
Bob Glew, Barrow-in-Furness
Jim Goggin, Barrow-in-Furness
Nigel Goldsworthy, Barrow-in-Furness
David Goodwin, Barrow-in-Furness
Jef Graham, Barrow-in-Furness
Mick Graham, Levens Village
Ray Graham, Barrow-in-Furness
Doreen Grainger, Barrow-in-Furness
Jack Grainger, New Zealand
David Grant, Barrow-in-Furness
Norman Graveson, Clapham
Doreen Green, Barrow-in-Furness
Syd Greenhalgh, Dalton-in-Furness
Stephen Greer, Barrow-in-Furness
Martin Griffin, Rossendale
R. Griffiths, Barrow-in-Furness
Derek Grundill, Barrow-in-Furness
Alf Hadley, Barrow-in-Furness
Sylvia, Geoff, Mark & Scott Hall, Barrow-in-Furness
Tony Hall, Ulverston
John P. Halligan, Barrow-in-Furness
Stephen Hambly, Barrow-in-Furness
Arthur Hannah, Barrow-in-Furness
Lloyd Hannah, Barrow-in-Furness
Kevin Hanson, Warrington
E. P. Harrison, Garforth, Leeds
Wilf Hart, Barrow-in-Furness
Anthony Hartle, Barrow-in-Furness

Darren Hartle, Barrow-in-Furness
Julie Hartle, Barrow-in-Furness
Christine & Brian Hartlebury, Dalton-in-Furness
Frank Charles Hartlebury, Bolton
George William Hartlebury, Wallasey
Roger Harvatt, Hull
Jack Harvey, Barrow-in-Furness
Ron Hayhurst, Barrow-in-Furness
Bill Heavyside, Dalton-in-Furness
Stan Helliwell, Barrow-in-Furness
Bill Hemsworth, Furness Health Studio, Barrow-in-Furness
Brian & Val Henderson, Barrow-in-Furness
John Henry, Barrow-in-Furness
George Herrington, Barrow-in-Furness
Terry Heseltine, Barrow-in-Furness
James Hewitt, Barrow-in-Furness
Colin Hewson, Barrow-in-Furness
Ray Hewson, Barrow-in-Furness
Wilf & Martin Heywood, Barrow-in-Furness
Chris Hickson, Gloucester
John Hindmarch, Barrow-in-Furness
Harry Hingley, Barrow-in-Furness
Harold Hitchen, Barrow-in-Furness
Donald Hockaday, Barrow-in-Furness
Kevin, Anne, Claire and Ben Hockaday, Barrow-in-Furness
Mike Hodgson, Barrow-in-Furness
Geoph Holcroft, Barrow-in-Furness
Arthur Hollis, Barrow-in-Furness
Stephen Hollywell, Barrow-in-Furness
Bill Hool, Barrow-in-Furness
Alf Horne & family, Barrow-in-Furness
Edward Houghton, Warrington
Mr & Mrs J. Howard, Barrow-in-Furness
Ken Huddleston, Millom
Dave, Malcolm, Yvonne & Paul, Barrow-in-Furness
Mark Humphrey, Barrow-in-Furness
Derek Hurley, Barrow-in-Furness
M. D. Hurst, Christchurch, New Zealand
John Hutton MP, Barrow & Dalton
David Hyde, Barrow-in-Furness
Gordon Instance, Barrow-in-Furness
Con Irving, Carlisle
Brian Jackson, Halifax
D. Jackson, Ulverston
Keith Jackson, Barrow-in-Furness
Michael Jackson, Leeds
Phillip Jackson, Barrow-in-Furness
The Jackson Family, Barrow-in-Furness
Marie Jesson, Stourbridge
Wilf Jesson, Barrow-in-Furness
Raymond Joel, Barrow-in-Furness
C. F. Johnson, Barrow-in-Furness
Dot & Henry Johnson, Dalton-in-Furness
Des Johnston, Barrow-in-Furness
Noel Johnston, Barrow-in-Furness

Antony Jones (son of Joe Jones), Dalton-in-Furness
Melvyn Jones (son of Joe Jones), Dalton-in-Furness
Neill Jones, Millom
Robert Jones, Barrow-in-Furness
Walter Jones, Barrow-in-Furness
W. H. Jones, Barrow-in-Furness
Peter Jordan, Millom
G. Jumps, Hull
Mick Jury, Barrow-in-Furness
M. Keel, Silecroft
M. Kell, Silecroft
Ian A. Kellett, Barrow-in-Furness
Charles Kelly, Wolverhampton
G. & F. Kelly, Barrow-in-Furness
Ronnie Kendal, Barrow-in-Furness
Owen George Kendall, Barrow-in-Furness
Martin Kennedy, Barrow-in-Furness
Norman Kidson, Barrow-in-Furness
Harry Kissack, Windermere
William Kitto, Barrow-in-Furness
Mike Knott, Barrow-in-Furness
David Knowles, Barrow-in-Furness
Phil Kyte, Barrow-in-Furness
Derek Lancaster, Millom
Lancashire County Cricket Club, Old Trafford, Manchester
Albert Lavender, Barrow-in-Furness
William Benjamin Lawrence, Barrow-in-Furness
Clifford Lawton, Barrow-in-Furness
Clive & Rita Lazell, Barrow-in-Furness
Alice Leach, Barrow-in-Furness
Samuel Leach, Barrow-in-Furness
Mark Leech, Barrow-in-Furness
Vincent L. Leonard, Barrow-in-Furness
Hannah Lewis, Barrow-in-Furness
G. H. Lewthwaite, Whitehaven
M. W. Lind, Barrow-in-Furness
Tom Liney, Millom
Jimmy Linn, Barrow-in-Furness
Ron Linn, Barrow-in-Furness
James Little, Chorley
Arthur L. Livesey, Millom
Eric & Eileen Livesey, Barrow-in-Furness
Tommy Livesey, Barrow-in-Furness
Alan Lockett, Barrow-in-Furness
P. Loebell, Barrow-in-Furness
Malcolm Lonsdale, Dalton-in-Furness
Peter Loughran, Barrow-in-Furness
Dennis E. Lund, Barrow-in-Furness
D. G. B. Lyon, Barrow-in-Furness
Gordon Lysons, Barrow-in-Furness
Dennis Maguire, Erith, Kent
Kevin Mahony, Barrow-in-Furness
Dave Makin, Woodlesford, Leeds
John Malyj, Barrow-in-Furness

Alan J. Mark, Leeds
Terrence William Marshall, Baycliff
D. A. Martin, Barrow-in-Furness
Eric Mason, Barrow-in-Furness
Christopher Malcolm Massey, Barrow-in-Furness
George Anthony Matthews, Barrow-in-Furness
Paddy McAteer, Barrow-in-Furness
Terry & Betty McBride, Barrow-in-Furness
Stan McCarthy, Barrow-in-Furness
Steven McCarthy, Barrow-in-Furness
Chris McGrady, Barrow-in-Furness
James McGrady, Barrow-in-Furness
Danny McKeating, Satterthwaite, Ulverston
David McKenna, Barrow-in-Furness
Gerald McLoughlin, Wigan
Jack McMinn, Barrow-in-Furness
Claire & Sarah McPoland, Barrow-in-Furness
Trevor McQuillan, Barrow-in Furness
Chris McVeigh, Aspull, Near Wigan
John McVeigh, Barrow-in-Furness
Malcolm McVeigh, Barrow-in-Furness
Sam & Mary Mellen, Millom
Phil Melling, Swansea
John S. Michelbach, Pilling, Blackpool
Dawn Middleton, Barrow-in-Furness
Francis Millican, Askam-in-Furness
Alan Milligan, Arrad Foot
Alan Milmine, Barrow-in-Furness
Tommy Milmine, Barrow-in-Furness
W. T. Moffat, Barrow-in-Furness
Peter A. Moir, Rickmansworth
Geoffrey Moorhouse, Hawes
John Morgan, Askam-in-Furness
Stan & Les Morgan, Barrow-in-Furness
Mr Morris, Barrow-in-Furness
L. Morrow, Barrow-in-Furness
Ray Moser, Barrow-in-Furness
Steve Moss, Barrow-in-Furness
John Mowat, Barrow-in-Furness
Mr Murray, Barrow-in-Furness
John Myers, Barrow-in-Furness
Brian Neatis, Dalton-in-Furness
Steve Neep, Barrow-in-Furness
Bill Nelson, Cleator Moor
John Nelson, Barrow-in-Furness
S. Nicholson, Barrow-in-Furness
Clive Nixon, Barrow-in-Furness
Anthony Norman, Barrow-in-Furness
W. Norman, Fareham
Alan Norris, Barrow-in-Furness
Terence Nuttall, Altrincham
Kit & Eddie O'Hara, Barrow-in-Furness
Brendan O'Kane, Barrow-in-Furness
Mike O'Kane, Barrow-in-Furness
David Olliver, Barrow-in-Furness
Ken O'Neill, Barrow-in-Furness
Ralph Osten, Barrow-in-Furness

Bill Oxley, Barrow-in-Furness
Ged Oxley, Barrow-in-Furness
D. Palferman, Ulverston
D. J. Palferman, Ulverston
Derek Palmer, Barrow-in-Furness
Fred Palmer, Barrow-in-Furness
Jim Park, Barrow-in-Furness
John E. Park, Barrow-in-Furness
Reg Parker, Grange-over-Sands
Ernie Parkinson, Ulverston
Ken Parnell, Barrow-in-Furness
J. F. Patterson, Barrow-in-Furness
Kenneth Pearson, Barrow-in-Furness
Phil Pearson, Barrow-in-Furness
Allan Pedley, Barrow-in-Furness
Norman Pedley, Barrow-in-Furness
Alan Pemberton, Barrow-in-Furness
Keith Pemberton, Millom
Wilf Penzer, Barrow-in-Furness
Peter Phizacklea, Dalton-in-Furness
Jack Richard Pickerill, Barrow-in-Furness
John Plumbley, Auckland, New Zealand
Eric W. Pontefract, Huddersfield
Colin Poole, Millom
John Poole, Barrow-in-Furness
Dave Postlethwaite, Barrow-in-Furness
James Postlethwaite, Barrow-in-Furness
Jim Price, Barrow-in-Furness
Bill & Eunice Procter, Dalton-in-Furness
Kevin Proctor, Barrow-in-Furness
David Prosser, Nelson
Eric Purdham, Wigan
Freda Queen, Barrow-in-Furness
Eric Quinn, Barrow-in-Furness
Paul Quinn, Barrow-in-Furness
Colin Quirk, Barrow-in-Furness
Mr & Mrs J. E. Quirk, Marton, near Ulverston
John Ratcliffe, Barrow-in-Furness
Keith Rawlinson, Barrow-in-Furness
Dave Reid, Barrow-in-Furness
J. Richards, Gleaston, Near Ulverston
Ronnie Richards, Barrow-in-Furness
Jack Richardson, Barrow-in-Furness
James Ritson, Barrow-in-Furness
Michael Robinson, Barrow-in-Furness'
Will Robson, Barrow-in-Furness
W. Roper, Barrow-in-Furness
Greg Rose, Barrow-in-Furness
Alex Ross, Barrow-in-Furness
Howard W. Routledge, Bath
Iain "Blocker" Rowland, Soho, London
Bernard Rowlin, Hull
A. A. Royle, Barrow-in-Furness
Ernie Royle, Barrow-in-Furness
The Rugby Football League Archive
A & T Ruscillo, Barrow-in-Furness
Mike Rushton, Barrow-in-Furness
Tom Rushton, Barrow-in-Furness

Norah & Syd Samuels, Barrow-in-Furness
Peter Sanderson, Barrow-in-Furness
Vera Sargent, Barrow-in-Furness
Alex Service, St Helens
Roger Shackleton, Hebden Bridge
Phillip Sharp, Barrow-in-Furness
Graham Shaw, Barrow-in-Furness
Roger Shaw, Barrow-in-Furness
Thelma Shaw, Basrrow-in-Furness
J. Shepherd, Allestree, Derby
Chuck Shields, Barrow-in-Furness
Howard Shimmin, Millom
Harry Silver, Barrow-in-Furness
Michael James Ritchie Slee, Ulverston
Harry Smith, Barrow-in-Furness
Thomas William Snaith, Barrow-in-Furness
Gary Soulsby, Barrow-in-Furness
Dr J. Spears, Lindal-in-Furness
George Derek Spencer, Barrow-in-Furness
John Spiller, Barrow-in-Furness
Peter Stables, Nottingham
William Richard Stables, Barrow-in-Furness
Alan Stainton, Barrow-in-Furness
Cliff Stainton, Barrow-in-Furness
Andrew W. Stalker, Barrow-in-Furness
Adge Steel, Barrow-in-Furness
Brian Steel, Barrow-in-Furness
Brian Steele, Dalton-in-Furness
John Stevens, Barrow-in-Furness
Bill Strickland, Barrow-in-Furness
Laurence Arthur Swarbrick, Peterborough
Harry Swindlehurst, Barrow-in-Furness
John Michael Sykes, Barrow-in-Furness
Terry Tate & Family, Barrow-in-Furness
Alfred Taylor, Barrow-in-Furness
Brian Taylor, Poulton-le-Fylde
David Taylor, Barrow-in-Furness
Michael Taylor, Barrow-in-Furness
Rob Taylor, Barrow-in-Furness
George Richard Thackeray, Barrow-in-Furness
Arnie Thomas, Barrow-in-Furness
Garry Thompson, Dalton-in-Furness
Tom Thorburn, Barrow-in-Furness
Martin Todd, Barrow-in-Furness
Mr Fred Tomlinson, Dalton-in-Furness
John Tomlinson, Dalton-in-Furness
Ian Tongue, Barrow-in-Furness
Graham Troth, Barrow-in-Furness
Alan Troughton, Barrow-in-Furness
Frank Tucker, Barrow-in-Furness
Ron Turner, Hull
Eddie Tweedie, Barrow-in-Furness
Roy Twiname, Dalton-in-Furness
Tom Twiname, Dalton-in-Furness
Ron Wade, Barrow-in-Furness
Bryan Wadsworth, Barrow-in-Furness
Jack Waite, Barrow-in-Furness
Alf Wakefield, Dalton-in-Furness
Phoebe Walker, Barrow-in-Furness
Lil & Jack Waller, Haverigg, Millom
Mark Walling, Barrow-in-Furness
Ian Walmsley, Barrow-in-Furness
Len Walmsley, Barrow-in-Furness
Ernie Wassell, Barrow-in-Furness
Alan Waterhouse, Royton
Derek Watson, Dalton-in-Furness
Ian Watson, Scunthorpe
Alan Weir, Barrow-in-Furness
Eric Welch, Barrow-in-Furness
John West, Barrow-in-Furness
Buster White, Barrow-in-Furness
Paul White, Barrow-in-Furness
E. Whiteside, Ulverston
Terence Whittall, Barrow-in-Furness
Andrew Whitworth, Mascalles, near Ulverston
Steven Whitworth, Barrow-in-Furness
Tony Wickwar, Barrow-in-Furness
A. J. Wilkes, Barrow-in-Furness
Jill Wilkie, Lanchester, Co. Durham
Brian Williams, Keighley
Graham Williams, Leeds
Ian Williams, Colchester
Innes & Eileen Williams, Barrow-in-Furness
Kenneth Wilson, Barrow-in-Furness
William Stanley Wilson, Barrow-in-Furness
Harold Wilson-Mayor, Barrow-in-Furness
John N. Winnard, Chorley
Frank Winward, South Woodford, London
David Wood, Barrow-in-Furness
Greig, Alyson & Nicola Jane Wood, Barrow-in-Furness
John Bryan Woodend, Barrow-in-Furness
Anthony Woods, St. Helens
John Worth, Barrow-in-Furness
J. G. Wren, Newby Bridge, Ulverston
Don Yates, Failsworth, Manchester
Percy Yates, Askam-in-Furness
C. J. Yendole, Bideford
George Yorke, Barrow-in-Furness